Clean and Competitive?

EARTHSCAN
Earthscan Publications Ltd, London

Clean and Competitive?

Motivating Environmental Performance in Industry

Rupert Howes

Jim Skea

Bob Whelan

Earthscan Publications Ltd, London

First published in the UK in 1997
by Earthscan Publications Ltd

Copyright © Rupert Howes, Jim Skea and Bob Whelan, 1997

A catalogue record for this book is available from the British Library

ISBN 1 85383 490 4 paperback
ISBN 1 85383 491 2 hardback

Typeset and page design by Oxprint Design Ltd.
Printed and bound by Biddles Ltd, Guildford and Kings Lynn

Cover design by Andrew Corbett

For a full list of publications
Earthscan Publications Ltd
120 Pentonville Road
London N1 9JN
Tel: +44 (0)171 278 0433
Fax: +44 (0)171 278 1142
email: earthinfo@earthscan.co.uk
http://www.earthscan.co.uk

Earthscan is an editorially independent subsidiary of Kogan Page Limited and
publishes in association with WWF-UK and the International Institute for
Environment and Development.

Contents

List of Abbreviations

ACBE	Advisory Comittee on Business and the Environment (UK)
ACRIB	Air Conditioning and Referigeration Industry Board
ARCFCP	Alliance for Responsible CFC Policy
AoSIS	Association of Small Island States
AQS	air quality standards
BAT	best available technology/techniques
BATNEEC	best available techniques not entailing excessive cost
BCF	British Chemical Federation
BDI	Federation of German Industries
BPEO	best practicable environmental option
BRMA	British Rubber Manufacturers Association
CARE Vision 2000	Comprehensive Approach to the Recycling of Electronics
CBI	Confederation of British Industry
CCGT	combined-cycle gas turbine
CCl_4	carbon tetrachloride
CEC	Commission of European Communities
CECED	EC Trade Association for Domestic Electrical-Appliance Manufacturers
CEED	Centre for Economic and Environment Development (UK)
CEFIC	European Chemical Industry Council
CEGB	Central Electricity Generating Board (UK)
CEM	continuous emissions monitoring
CERCLA	Comprehensive Environmental Response, Compensation and Liability Act 1980 (US)
CEST	Centre for the Exploitation of Science and Technology
CFC	chlorofluorocarbon
CH_2Cl_2	methylene chloride
CH_3Br	methyl bromide
CH_3CCl_3	methyl chloroform
CH_4	methane
CHP	combined heat and power
CIA	Chemical Industries Association
CO	carbon monoxide

CO_2	carbon dioxide
COD	chemical oxygen demand
COP	Conference of the Parties
CRI	chemicals release inventory
DoE	Department of the Environment (UK) (to June 1997)
DETR	Department of the Environment, Transport and the Regions (UK) (from June 1997)
DTI	Department of Trade and Industry (UK)
DWI	Drinking Water Inspectorate
EA	Environment Agency (UK)
EA 1995	Environment Act 1995 (UK)
EC	European Community
EEE	electrical and electronic equipment
EIC	Environmental Industries Commission
EMAS	environmental management and audit scheme
EMERG	Electronic Manufacturers Equipment Recycling Group
EMS	environmental management system
ENDS	Environmental Data Services
EOL	end-of-life
EPA	Environmental Protection Agency (US)
EPA 1990	Environmental Protection Act 1990 (UK)
EPAQS	Expert Panel of Air Quality Standards
EPSRC	Engineering and Physical Sciences Research Council
ESRC	Economic and Social Research Council
EST	Energy Savings Trust
EU	European Union
FCIG	Film Coating Industry Group
FGD	flue-gas desulphurization
FoE	Friends of the Earth
GHG	greenhouse gas
GWP	global warming potential
HCFC	hydrochlorofluorocarbon
HCl	hydrochloric acid
HFC	hydrofluorocarbon
HMIP	Her Majesty's Inspectorate for Pollution
HMSO	Her Majesty's Stationery Office
HSE	Health and Safety Executive
ICER	Industry Consortium for Electrical and Electronic Waste Recycling
IChemE	Institution of Chemical Engineers
IFIEC	International Federation of Industrial Energy Consumers
IPC	integrated pollution control

IPCC	Intergovernmental Panel of Climate Change
IPPC	integrated pollution prevention and control
JUSCANZ	Japan/US/Canada/Australia and New Zealand Alliance
LAAPC	local authority air pollution control
LCC	large carbon canister
LCP	large combustion plants
LRTAP	long-range transboundary air pollution
LTA	long-term agreement
LWMI	Leicestershire Waste Minimization Initiative
MAF	minimum acceptable flow
MAFF	Ministry of Agriculture, Fisheries and Food (UK)
MEP	Member of the European Parliament
N_2O	nitrous oxide
NETCEN	National Environment Technology Centre
NGO	non-governmental organization
NO_x	nitrogen oxides
NRA	National Rivers Authority
O_3	ozone
OECD	Organization for Economic Cooperation and Development
OFWAT	Office of Water Service
PAN	peroxyacetyl nitrate
PC	personal computer
PIA	Petrol Industry Association
PO	photochemical oxidant
PPP	polluter-pays principle
PRA	Petrol Retailers Association (UK)
PREST	Policy Research in Engineering, Science and Technology
PRISMA	Project Industrial Successes with Waste Prevention (The Netherlands)
PRG	Producer Responsibility Group
REC	regional electricity company
RCEP	Royal Commision on Environmental Pollution
RSA	Royal Society for the Encouragement of Arts, Manufacture and Commerce
SAGTA	Soil and Groundwater Technology Association
SAVE Programme	Specific Action for Vigorous Energy Efficiency
SCEEMAS	Small Company Environmental Energy Management Assistance Scheme
SCP	small combustion plant
SEC	US Securities and Exchange Commission
SME	small- to medium-sized enterprise
SO_2	sulphur dioxide

SORG	Stratospheric Ozone Review Group (UK)
SPRU	Science Policy Research Unit
SWQO	statutory water quality objectives
TEAP	Technical and Economic Assessment Panel (UN)
UN	United Nations
UNCED	United Nations Conference on Environment and Development
UNECE	United Nations Economic Commission for Europe
UNEP	United Nations Environment Programme
UNFCCC	United Nations Framework Convention on Climate Change
UNICE	Union of Industrial and Employers' Confederations of Europe
USEPA	United States Environmental Protection Agency
UV	ultraviolet
UV-B	biological-active ultraviolet
UWWD	EU Urban Waste Water Directive
VAT	value added tax
VOC	volatile organic compound
WBCSD	World Business Council for Sustainable Development
WHO	World Health Organization
WMO	World Meteorological Organization
WRA	Waste Regulatory Authorities
WSA	Water Services Association
WSC	water service company
WSL	Warren Spring Laboratory

Units of Measurement

Gt   gigatonne
1 GtC (1 gigatonne of carbon) = 1 billion (1000 million (10^9)) tonnes of carbon

GW   gigawatt (1 billion watts)

kt   thousand tonnes

kWh   kilowatt hour

MtC   million tonnes of carbon

MW   megawatt

ppbv   parts per billion by volume

ppmv   parts per million by volume

Tg   terngrammes
1 Tg = 1 million million grammes = 1 million tonnes

tWh   ternwatt hour
1 tWh = 1 billion kWh

List of Illustrations

Figures

Tables

Boxes

Preface

This book has been produced as a result of a collaboration between the Centre for the Exploitation of Science and Technology (CEST) and the Science Policy Research Unit (SPRU). Both organizations have devoted considerable resources to environmental problems during the 1990s. CEST aims to identify emerging global issues which could give rise to significant commercial and technological opportunities. Working with industry, academia and government policy-makers, CEST analyses opportunities and stimulates companies to exploit them. All CEST projects are participatory and designed to help companies identify new opportunities earlier, and hence reduce the lead-time for them to realize a commercial gain. CEST's perspective is global but with a particular focus on the UK and Europe. CEST is funded mainly by industry with additional funding from the UK Government.

SPRU is an academic research organization which was established at Sussex University in 1966. It carries out world-class research and teaching on policy issues relating to scientific research and technical change, and disseminates its results to a wide audience. Its work is international in scope. The work for this project was carried out by SPRU's Environment and Technology Programme. The Programme's principal research areas include technological change and the environment, specifically in the energy industry; integrated environmental management, particularly at the firm level (for example life-cycle assessment); environmental indicators; science and regulation; and the development of environmental policy. The Programme's work on industry and the environment has been partly supported through an Economic and Social Research Council (ESRC)/British Gas Fellowship on Clean Technology and Industry under the ESRC's Global Environmental Change Programme. Other relevant SPRU work was supported by DGXII of the European Commission under the Framework III Socio-Economic Environmental Research Programme. Production of this book was generously supported by a grant from CEST.

We are grateful to Alasdair Maclean (Yorkshire Water), Keith Mason (the United States Environmental Protection Agency), Dorothy Mackenzie (Dragon International Consulting Limited), David Cope (UK Centre for Economic and Environmental Development – UK CEED), Ian Miles (PREST) and Mike Arnold (British Gas) for reading an earlier draft of the book and providing challenging insights and comments. This book has been greatly improved through their input. Our thanks also go to

Kath Kidd and Hilary Ougham at the Science Policy Research Unit for their patience and care as they helped us to prepare the final manuscript.

We gratefully acknowledge the reviewers and those bodies which supported the work. The views expressed are, however, those of the authors alone.

CHAPTER 1
The Business–Environment Debate

The environment has become one of the key challenges facing the business sector during the 1990s. Almost all major companies now take a strategic view of environmental issues, though the subject receives notably less attention in smaller companies. For larger companies at least, the operation of an internal environmental management system, the collection of environmental performance data and anticipating the needs and sensitivities of customers, suppliers and local communities has become part and parcel of everyday activity.[1] In part, this reflects changing attitudes among employees. Like other citizens, they have become more aware of environmental issues. Through this route, a broader shift in social attitudes is beginning to permeate companies. But attitude change, even among key individuals, is not enough to explain why companies operating under severe commercial pressures devote such a high level of resources – human and financial – to addressing environmental questions.

One of the most pervasive concepts underlying the business–environment debate of the 1990s has been that of the environmental/economic 'win–win' – the idea that certain measures can bring benefits in terms of both environmental and economic performance. The concept has been applied in relation to technological choice (clean technology), business environmental strategies and regulatory policies at the national level, as well as to tax reform. In the latter context, the shifting of the tax burden from labour to natural resources is characterized as bringing about a 'double dividend' through employment gains and reductions in environmental burdens. 'Having it all' has been a dominant theme of the 1990s.

We argue in this book that even the pursuit of win–win outcomes is insufficient to explain the level of resources being devoted to environmental issues by companies. Although opportunities to reap higher profits from cleaner products and processes undoubtedly exist, such investments often divert resources away from more profitable pursuits. Such outcomes are also not as readily available to all companies or as widespread as many believe. To ignore them would be foolish, but to rely on measures which business would regard as 'win–win' to deliver necessary environmental improvements would be simply naïve. Remaining competitive and delivering value for shareholders still remains the central goal of the complex commercial organizations within which concerned individuals work.

The theme of reconciling wealth creation with environmental sustainability is at the heart of this book. This theme can be addressed on several scales. International efforts to promote sustainable development have accelerated in the last decade. The

UN Commission on Sustainable Development's 1987 report (the Brundtland Report) set in motion preparations for the 1992 UN Conference on Environment and Development (UNCED) – more commonly known as the Rio Earth Summit – which in turn established more concrete initiatives: the Framework Convention on Climate Change, the Biodiversity Convention and Agenda 21. Over the same period, however, the world's economy has become more tightly integrated as trade barriers have fallen and capital has become more mobile. Developing countries are expanding economic activity in order to meet the growing aspirations of their populations. This growth sets competitive challenges in the industrialized world. Both countries and companies face intensifying pressures to reduce costs and remain competitive. At the grandest level, therefore, sustainability and the globalization of the world economy place competing demands on companies and countries.

This book is concerned with the reconciliation of wealth creation and sustainability on a more modest scale. The focus is on sectors, companies and specific environmental issues at the UK and European levels. However, the global context is vital. Nationally, companies must set their environmental strategies within the framework of wider developments, including the growth of environmental policy-making at the international level, the globalization of the world economy and the enhanced competitive pressures which these bring.

Why Industry Has Developed Environmental Strategies

Why have so many companies – multinational and smaller – invested effort in environmental management? The history of environmental affairs over the last 25 years goes a long way towards explaining this. UNCED in Rio de Janeiro in 1992 marked a high point in public concern about environmental issues. But there are lessons to be learned from previous waves of interest. The 1972 Stockholm Conference on the Human Environment marked a similar level of concern about environmental issues and a wave of government regulation which put business on the defensive. These vigorous public policy actions did not survive the oil-price-induced recession of 1973.

Renewed public interest in environmental issues in the 1980s was associated with a significant expansion of environmental regulation through the increasingly ambitious Action Programmes of the European Community. Persistent public concern coupled with a high level of regulatory activity has helped to create a sense of inevitability in the business community that the environment is a major and enduring issue. By the mid 1980s, the mismatch between what the public expected of business and how it actually behaved was beginning to have implications for profitability. Corporate practices were poorly adapted to the wider social environment in which businesses had to operate. Mismatches were revealed through:

- reactive approaches to regulation, leading to costly and inadequately planned compliance investments;
- lack of influence over the content and form of regulations which led to unnecessarily high compliance costs;

- difficulties in securing authorizations for new plants and processes because of public *and* local community concerns; and
- direct consumer reaction to the performance of individual firms.

The growth of green consumerism which rewards strong environmental performance has been less vigorous than originally anticipated but consumers are evidently prepared to punish what is seen as poor environmental performance through product boycotts. This highlights the fact that many company strategies are motivated by fear of environmental failure rather than the anticipation of environmental success.

Business has been making strong efforts to redress this situation, collectively and at the level of the individual company. The traditional approach to environmental management was to challenge new regulatory initiatives aggressively. The new softer approach involves modifying company behaviour in response to wider social demands, though influencing public opinion and the development of public policy remains an important element of business strategy.

Companies are striving towards what has become known as the 'compliance plus' approach to environmental management. This involves anticipating new regulations and adopting practices and innovation strategies which will place them ahead of evolving requirements. In the long term, this should help to reduce the cost of high standards of environmental performance and can promote competitiveness at the company level. It will reduce potential conflicts with community stakeholders, helping to remove barriers to business expansion. It will also reduce the risk of unacceptable environmental behaviour which will trigger consumer responses.

These observations apply in general to larger companies. There are huge differences between the environmental behaviour of different segments of industry. The multinationals are at the opposite end of the spectrum from small- to-medium-sized enterprises (SMEs) which struggle to remain in business, cannot command the managerial resources required to put environmental management systems in place and have enormous difficulties even complying with regulation. An important group of middle ranking companies – traditionally operating nationally but increasingly participating in export markets – occupy an intermediate position. These companies are large enough to bring managerial attention to bear on environmental issues but lack the overall level of resources available to the multinationals. Many middle ranking companies have consciously adopted environmental management procedures. In general, the sense of threat concerning environmental issues is more tangible in these companies which lack the corporate affairs capacity of the multinationals.

Environmental strategies also vary from one large company to another. IBM is not in the same business as ICI. Environmental management is inevitably tied to the nature of the business in which a particular company operates.

The Paradox of Proactive Environmental Strategy

One of the most striking observations to come from putting this book together is that any assessment of industry's performance depends very much on the starting point. Sitting inside a major company looking outwards, an affirmative view of corporate environmental behaviour is now typical and, in many respects, justified. A considerable amount of time will have been spent in formulating environmental strategy. An internal environmental management system – though less often an externally verified one – which engages staff throughout the organization will be in place. A dedicated environment unit, reporting to the Board, will coordinate activities and arrange for audits of company activities. Some companies are publishing environmental reports containing quantitative performance indicators. When these activities are combined with target setting for waste and emissions, impressive environmental improvements can be achieved.

Sitting outside the company and looking in from a public policy perspective, the picture can be less attractive. On a range of issues from local air and water pollution through to acid rain and climate change, industry is seen by outsiders to be contributing to environmental damage and resisting policy measures which would lead to environmental improvements. The internal perspective, which emphasizes business processes, and the external perspective, which focuses more on environmental outcomes, conflict. But each has a basis in truth.

The contrast between internal and external views of environmental conduct is sharpest in the case of large multinational companies. Not only have they taken environmental management furthest, they are also most in the public eye during public policy debates and when accidents, such as the *Exxon Valdez* oil spill in Alaska, occur. Smaller firms can often remain invisible to the public; larger companies act as lightning rods for more general criticisms of industry.

Attempting to reconcile these internal and external perspectives yields useful insights. The external dimension of environmental strategy is vitally important. Proactive companies try to play a full role in the development of new public policy and help to shape its direction. This has been just as strong a feature of recent corporate practice as the development of internal environmental management systems. In Europe, for example, the greening of business has been accompanied by the rapid development of European trade associations and even individual company offices in Brussels. Representatives monitor policy developments and feed in industry views. Frustrated by the slow pace of policy development, European Commission officials have begun to welcome this input in principle, if not in detail. The participation of business along with other social partners is now enshrined in the EU's Fifth Environmental Action Programme.

Participation in regulatory affairs has positive and negative aspects from the business point of view. On the one hand, it leads, from the business perspective, to better regulation. On the other hand, it can create a wider impression that business is frustrating environmental initiatives and undermines the benefits of a more active approach inside the company.

The Role of Regulation and Other Policy Instruments

The importance of the regulatory dimension – which we take to encompass both traditional approaches and new policy instruments – is so striking that it merits a broader discussion.[2] Regulatory policy is changing as rapidly as business behaviour and mirrors it in many respects. A spirit of regulatory reform is abroad, with a growing interest in new processes for negotiating regulations and alternatives to traditional instruments, such as voluntary agreements and market-based instruments.

There are divergent views about the role of regulation in stimulating changed corporate behaviour. At one extreme, some in business would argue that regulation has become almost irrelevant because environmental practices will improve through self-motivation and market drivers without any need for public policy. For certain progressive companies, this might be the case, especially when account is taken of the fact that, by the mid 1990s, the rate of development of new environmental regulations has begun to slow. The alternative view is that regulation is the *only* factor which will induce companies to alter their behaviour. This book takes a more pragmatic line. Most of the case study evidence presented suggests that regulation is still one of the most important factors leading to changes in practice. Small companies especially appear to change their behaviour only when required. But the non-regulatory factors, as discussed in Chapter 2, are still important.

For simplicity, industry can be seen as having two broad links to the outside world with respect to environmental issues. The first link is with the general public – acknowledging, however, the inadequacy of the phrase 'general public' in describing the diversity of roles which social groups and citizens assume – as voters, supporters of pressure groups, consumers of products and neighbours to production plants. The second link is with public bodies – institutions deriving their legitimacy from the democratic process. These bodies include political institutions, government departments, environmental regulators (increasingly with agency status) and local authorities. While these bodies in theory act in the public interest, their own relationship with citizens may be as complex and problematical as those of industry.

Several of the case studies in this book show industry in conflict with policy-makers as new environmental regulations are developed. This appears to sit uneasily with companies' public claims to have adopted a new proactive stance towards environmental issues. From the perspective of relations between industry and the general public, it creates a sense of disappointed expectations. Industry's view of regulation is ambiguous. Regulation in the abstract sense can bring benefits. It can serve the important role of legitimizing company behaviour in the eyes of the public. How many environmental strategies state that the company will "aim to comply with all applicable laws and regulations"? By reducing environmental performance to simple externally defined rules, the management task within companies approaches one of basic technical compliance. All companies carrying out the same activity are subject to the same rules, thus simplifying business life, maintaining a level playing field and reducing the number of dimensions on which business must compete. Level playing fields may not suit all companies, but in many sectors, especially those concerned with the production of intermediate products, these are attractive features.

It is when *specific* regulations come to be negotiated that conflicts between public bodies and industry emerge. The devil is very much in the detail. These debates are better understood if two basic premises are accepted. The first is the primacy of the profit motive in explaining underlying business behaviour. Environmental management in a company, however sophisticated, is not a goal in itself. The underlying objective is to create a more secure set of relationships with the general public and public institutions so as to allow companies and sectors to remain competitive. The chemical industry's Responsible Care Programme, which leans heavily on the concept of a 'licence to operate' in the eyes of society at large, exemplifies this approach.

The second premise is that regulatory authorities can and do propose policy instruments that are less than perfect. Flaws arise for a variety of reasons: lack of detailed technical knowledge on the part of the regulator; limited resources available for formulating policy; or the constraints of policy or legal precedents. Whatever the reason, it is not *necessarily* the case that regulatory debates are about public-spirited policy-makers being frustrated by industry opposing necessary environmental improvements. Environmental debates can take place because:

- the proposed policy may actually be counter-productive, adding to costs as well as failing to yield environmental benefits – a 'lose–lose' situation;
- the environmental goal may be valid, but the proposed instrument is inefficient in the sense that it imposes unnecessary costs;
- the proposed instrument may lead to changes in competitive conditions which disadvantage important sections of industry, or place industry in one jurisdiction at a disadvantage with respect to those in other countries or regions; or
- there is, in reality, an irreducible conflict between society's desire for higher standards of environmental quality and a company's or a sector's goal of adding to shareholder value.

The case studies presented in this book illustrate all of these dimensions. The evidence is that industry's active participation in such environmental debates does affect policy, either by modifying the form of regulations or, in some cases, by blocking them altogether. The rationale for industry's participation in such environmental debates is clear. Company participation succeeds to a greater or lesser degree in changing the direction of public policy.[3] Such participation can lead to public policy that is better as well as worse. Whether the influence is benign or not varies from one case to another and will almost certainly be open to debate between industry and environmental groups. Chapter 10 returns to the question of the role of industry in the policy-making process.

The Purpose of the Book

Two large questions set the background for this book. The first is whether the environmental footprints of current patterns of industrial activity are compatible with sustainable development. We take it as our premise that the answer to this question is 'no'. The second, more difficult question is whether industrial activity organized as it is, with its primary focus on profit and regulated by fallible political institutions, can ever be compatible with sustainable development. We do not pretend to supply the answer to that question. Some commentators have asserted that sustainable development is not compatible with current patterns of economic, social and political organization.[4] If that is so, the only answers are radical changes to the entire structure of society or the prospect of muddling through unsustainably – if that is not a contradiction in terms.

The goal of this book is more modest. We seek to understand what can be achieved in environmental terms within current patterns of organization. What can be expected from business in terms of reduced environmental impact? Have environmental challenges been as successfully absorbed and mastered by business as was hoped? What is the role of public policy in relation to business activity? Can technology succeed in squaring the environmental–economic circle and generate 'win–win' situations which promote sustainability?

The book addresses these questions by reviewing industry's response to seven environmental issues which have greatly concerned business during the 1990s and by assessing specific examples of different approaches to the management of environmental issues.[5] We return to the larger questions in the final chapter of the book.

The Structure of the Book

The remainder of this book falls into four parts. The first part of the book (Chapters 1 and 2) reviews evidence on how companies are managing environmental issues: is the environment regarded as a threat or an opportunity? What are the main drives for improved environmental performances: regulation, consumer pressure or investor pressure? What are companies doing in relation to the establishment of environmental management systems and environmental reporting? The second chapter also provides a commentary on recent business and environment literature, looking critically at various underlying hypotheses about business behaviour which have emerged. In particular, it considers the degree to which there may be 'win–win' opportunities for companies to improve environmental performance while improving their competitiveness or whether there must always be a trade-off between the environment and profitability.

The second part of the book reviews a set of seven key environmental problems faced by industry during the 1990s. The purpose of the review is to explore industry's broad response to these challenges and to identify common themes. The problems are grouped into three categories: global, national and regional/local. Chapter 3 deals with the two main global issues of stratospheric ozone depletion and global warming and climate change; transboundary and regional issues (air quality and transport, acid rain, and emissions of volatile organic compounds (VOCs)) are reviewed in Chapter 4 and two key local environmental issues – water quality and contaminated land – are considered in Chapter 5. Each of these chapters starts with a short summary section. An update and background on the particular environmental issue is provided, together with a brief overview of relevant legislation or proposed legislation. Industry's response is considered throughout the chapter. In addition, most sections also conclude by providing one or more brief accounts which focus on a particular example of 'industry's' response to the issue under consideration.

The third part of the book takes a more detailed look at four sets of approaches to environmental management, using specific case studies. Chapter 6 is concerned with what might be thought of as the traditional approach to dealing with industrial pollution – process regulation through formal, legally sanctioned authorization arrangements. It deals with the introduction of integrated pollution control (IPC) following the 1990 Environmental Protection Act. By way of contrast, the second case study (Chapter 7) examines an initiative built on a partnership between companies and public sector bodies. The Aire and Calder project demonstrated to companies the existence of cost-effective opportunities to improve environmental performance. This chapter considers the project's success in cutting costs and reducing environmental releases and assesses the degree to which companies can be encouraged to take up the 'win–win' opportunities which manifestly exist.

Chapter 8 considers attempts within the electrical and electronics sector to establish mechanisms for reducing and recycling post-consumer waste. This is a form of partnership, engaging companies which undertake diverse activities related to a single waste stream. The chapter considers the establishment and operation of the Industry Consortium for Electrical and Electronic Waste Recycling (ICER).

The final case study (Chapter 9) deals with economic instruments for dealing with environmental problems. In 1990, the UK government professed strong support for economic instruments, such as taxes and tradable emission permits, to deliver environmental policy goals.[6] In fact, other than the landfill tax, little progress has been made in developing economic instruments which would have a direct impact on the industrial sector. Chapter 9 reviews developments and assesses why progress has been so slow.

The final part of the book, Chapter 10, draws together the conclusions, revisiting the themes laid out in Chapter 2 and reappraising the conclusions in the light of the more detailed case study work. This final chapter considers whether industry has embarked on a new approach to environmental issues, the location and the extent of the often elusive 'win–win' environmental measure, the role of technology and the institutional arrangements which would contribute to future environmental progress.

CHAPTER 2
Managing the Environment

Introduction

Industry's approach to environmental issues has changed significantly over the last three decades. From initial positions of hostility and resistant adaptation to environmental legislation, individual firms are now adopting a far more positive and strategic approach. Many commentators and academics in business schools maintain that there has been a paradigm shift.[1] Business, or at least big business, no longer sees the environment as a threat but now embraces more stringent environmental challenges as an opportunity to enhance competitiveness and expand market share. Environment is good for business. Or is it?

The governance of environment affairs, both inside and outside companies, is clearly changing. Practice may actually be evolving more quickly than is an understanding of the changes which are underway. Assessing the literature on both business/environment and technology/environment, which has mushroomed during the 1990s, several notions are evident. At best, these can be regarded as hypotheses, amenable to testing. At worst, they are simply asserted as self-evident truths:

- Environmental challenges are growing ever more complex and larger in scale. Global issues such as climate change and loss of biodiversity must be addressed as well as local pollution problems. This expansion of the environmental agenda has been characterized as a transition from the easy politics of the environment (waste or pollution) and the hard politics (securing the productivity of the ecological base).[2]
- Corporate environmental management goes through several stages in which companies proceed from resistant adaptation to environmental standards, through compliance strategies and subsequently compliance-plus or even the sustainable enterprise.
- Clean technology can help to solve environmental problems by providing opportunities to reduce simultaneously environmental impacts and production costs. This basic idea has been around for some time and has, for example, been promoted through the UN Environment Programme (UNEP) Clean Production Programme.[3]
- Environmental regulation, far from damaging the competitiveness of firms, enhances it by stimulating innovation. Dynamic firms will gain 'first mover' advantages by anticipating changing social demands, searching out clean

technology opportunities and not wasting resources fighting regulatory developments.[4] These ideas are collectively known as the Porter hypothesis, originally set out in 1991.[5]

■ Alternatively, environmental regulation can destroy value in companies which have taken up win–win clean technology opportunities and which must then devote large proportions of their investment budgets to unproductive compliance projects. This revisionist view has been argued by Walley and Whitehead of McKinsey.[6]

These hypotheses are not always entirely compatible with each other; occasionally, as in the case of Porter versus Walley and Whitehead, they are in direct conflict. However, in each case, they are amenable to testing by calling on the growing body of evidence about industry's management of environmental issues. The detailed case studies in this book help to address these questions.

This chapter takes a more conceptual approach. It starts by assessing the nature of the environmental challenges which have faced business during the 1990s, assessing those which have had the largest practical impact. The chapter goes on to consider the four specific drivers which appear to stimulate changed business practice: regulation, consumer pressure, community stakeholders and investor pressure. The chapter finishes by addressing the role of technology in providing win–win solutions to environmental challenges and examines critically the extent of the elusive double dividend.

Environmental Challenges

By the beginning of the 1990s, a cumulative set of developments was beginning to create a sense of environmental crisis on a global scale. The discovery of the Antarctic ozone hole coupled with a convincing chemical account of the link between ozone depletion and chlorofluorocarbons (CFCs) led policy-makers into a remarkably rapid set of international negotiations. Climate change had emerged as an issue which might have even more far-reaching implications. And somewhat smaller-scale environmental disasters, such as the 1989 Alaskan oil spill, served to remind the world that environmental threats still existed on the ground as well as high in the atmosphere.

In this book, we argue that the future environmental agenda will not be purely global. The issues which have the most significant technological and economic consequences for industry will be manifested on different scales. Rising concern about the management of waste streams, for example, shows that local issues still have the capacity to make considerable demands on industry and call forth both technological and organizational innovation. Indeed, tangible local issues appear to activate public concern to a greater extent than larger-scale abstract problems such as climate change.

What global challenges – and the inevitable public and political response – have done is to alert business to the need to address environmental challenges in a more systematic and proactive manner. From a UK perspective, the challenges were particularly large because environmental policy during much of the 1980s had been relatively weak and undemanding. By the early 1990s, analysts and environmentally progressive companies began to share a new conventional wisdom which was reflected in a review of industrial opportunities arising from new environmental priorities conducted by CEST:[7]

- concern for the environment was a major and enduring issue for industry;
- the environment presented opportunities as well as problems, in that new markets for goods and services would emerge and environmental performance would contribute to competitive advantage;
- ever-tightening environmental regulations, often originating in more environmentally aware countries, would be a major driver of change;
- clean-up solutions to environmental problems would initially predominate but would increasingly be replaced by clean technology and waste minimization approaches; and
- UK firms were, in general, reactive and ill-informed about environmental issues.

CEST held further consultations with interested groups in order to understand better the future environmental agenda. It was recognized that predicting future developments was intrinsically difficult. The most appropriate goal would be greater preparedness arising from the collaborative exchange of views between those who would help to shape the agenda: government, industry, research organizations, higher education, environmental non-governmental organizations (NGOs) and environmental consultants. Building a strategic capacity to respond to emerging challenges would involve: obtaining better understanding of socio-economic factors and the effects of environmental problems on specific human populations (research); government coordination of the procurement and use of environmental data (information); and a better understanding of public perceptions of risk and improved environmental accounting (problem analysis).[8] There was also a need for clearer policy goals and direction, more UK leadership in the international arena, more use of economic and fiscal incentives, more consultative approaches to policy development, and the integration of environmental and other policy domains, for example in the energy sector. Recognizing the inherent difficulty of prediction, CEST formed a consensus around the following propositions:

- The environmental agenda in 2005 will look quite similar to that of the early 1990s: current issues will persist and become more mature.
- Air pollution problems, especially global climate change, would dominate the agenda.
- Future issues will have both natural environment and human health-related dimensions.
- The UK agenda will be dominated by industrial problems rather than resource depletion and associated ecosystem degradation.
- The environmental and energy agendas will become increasingly aligned.
- According to NGOs, the key issues will be energy policy, transport-related environmental problems, land use planning, climate change and sustainable development.

Many, but not all, of these predictions about the development of the environmental agenda during the 1990s have been confirmed by developments. The practical impacts of climate change policies, in particular, have so far been less pervasive than might have been expected in the highly heated political lead-in to the 1992 Rio Conference. The UN Framework Convention on Climate Change contained no specific quantitative commitments. Such commitments are being developed within the framework of the Berlin Mandate established at the first meeting of the Conference of the Parties in April 1995. The UK's carbon dioxide stabilization target for 2000 is likely to be met, but mainly through large-scale investment in clean gas-fired power stations which was motivated only in part on environmental grounds. The Berlin Mandate may lead to more demanding quantitative emission targets for the period 2005–2010. Decisions on targets and timetables are to be taken in December 1997 during the Third Conference of the Parties in Kyoto.

The pace of internationally led policy change has been slower than anticipated. As well as the relatively weak UN Framework Convention on Climate Change, the growing importance of the subsidiarity principle within the EU means that framework environmental measures, which leave more to the discretion of Member States, are growing in importance. The uniform standards-based approach, transferring higher standards from the EU green bloc (German, The Netherlands and Denmark) to other member states, may be receding in importance.

Air pollution has proved to be a key issue, but local rather than global-scale problems – especially those related to transport activity – have captured the political agenda. The human health dimension, which was not prominent in the environmental debates of the 1980s, has begun to play a significant role alongside natural environment-related concerns.

Energy issues, which are closely linked to the climate change problem, have become much less visible. Economic regulation of the energy sector is a major public policy concern, but this is now almost entirely divorced from debates about energy efficiency and greenhouse gas emission reduction. The abolition of the Department of Energy in 1992 and the splitting of its functions between the Department of the Environment (energy efficiency) and the Department of Trade and Industry (energy supply and economic regulation) has institutionalized this divorce of the energy and environmental policy domains. Furthermore, progress in developing economic and fiscal environmental policy instruments has been painfully slow. The failure of the proposed EU carbon and energy tax is the most striking symbol of this policy failure. In the UK, the single exception is the new landfill tax which will raise modest revenues and will affect incentives to landfill as opposed to incinerate or to avoid waste. The idea of using tradable emission permits (switchable emission quotas) to implement acid rain controls has been studied intensively but has not evolved into any formal policy proposal.

In 1991, CEST identified a potential market of £140 billion over the period 1991–2000 associated with 13 key environmental issues. Two of the problems – climate change and water quality – accounted for over half of this potential expenditure. The big five problems – climate, water quality, air quality, VOCs/odour and waste management – accounted for 70 per cent of the total. It is clear that by the year 2000, these sums of money will not have been spent in the way suggested. This gap between expectations and outcomes underlines the need for industry and others to prepare flexibly for ever-shifting challenges rather than attempting simply to predict the future. The Office of Science and Technology is continuing to address UK priorities through the Natural Resources and the Environment Panel convened under the Foresight Programme.

Chapters 3 to 5 examine environmental issues on three different scales. Seven of the 13 issues addressed by CEST are covered. Climate change and stratospheric ozone depletion are taken as examples of global issues which have been dealt with through international negotiations and agreements. The earlier ozone agreements have by now had very real impacts on technologies and industrial practice. However, the climate agreements are still far from having a major impact.

The local level issues considered in the book are contaminated land and water quality, both of which have had new and tangible impacts on industrial practice. Finally, a wide range of environmental problems fits somewhere between the local and global levels. In Chapter 4, we look at transport-related environmental problems, emissions of volatile organic compounds (VOCs) and acid rain. In each case, industry is struggling with real problems associated with changing techniques and practices in order to lower environmental impacts.

Environmental Drivers

Ultimately, the only reason why companies have begun to address environmental issues in a strategic way is because of social concern about impacts on human health and ecological systems. Broad social concerns are converted into specific pressures on companies through a few well-recognized mechanisms. The four principal drivers for improved environmental performance are regulation, customer preferences or demand, relations with local communities, and investor requirements.

As noted in Chapter 1, a range of studies has shown that regulation, and anticipation of regulation, still remains the most important driver influencing corporate environment-related decisions.[9] Regulatory issues are of particular importance to those companies carrying out extractive or basic processing activities high up the materials supply chain. Companies operating closer to final markets are more conscious of the concerns of final consumers, though early expectations about a growing market for green products have not been borne out in practice. Companies in several sectors, ranging from telecommunications to chemicals, are beginning to place greater emphasis on developing and maintaining an image of being good neighbours in local communities. Investor pressure on companies – from banks, other lending institutions and shareholders – although still limited, is set to increase as the degree of financial risk associated with environmental liabilities becomes clearer.

The relative importance of each driver in influencing company behaviour varies considerably depending on position in the materials supply chain and company size. There are important synergies between the various drivers. Regulation, for example, although often characterized as a burden to companies, can perform an important role in legitimizing corporate environmental behaviour in the eyes of the public. Equally, the legal and regulatory framework helps to define the environmental liabilities which influence investor behaviour. When an environmental problem is perceived to be urgent, as was undoubtedly the case with ozone depletion, public pressure drives regulation forward. Eco-labelling measures bridge the gap between consumer concern and the regulatory approach.

The Role of Regulatory Pressure

Regulatory pressures are of paramount importance for most companies. Of particular relevance for many high-impact industries such as metals, chemicals, paper and energy are the costs of obtaining (and maintaining) authorization under the UK's system of Integrated Pollution Control (IPC). The outcome of IPC authorizations and requirement to meet new plant standards and achievable release levels have potentially huge cost implications for those companies requiring process authorizations.[10] As discussed in Chapter 6, the average total cost associated with obtaining IPC authorization is somewhere in the region of £1.6 million.

Many affected companies have devoted substantial resources to preparing applications for authorization and debating authorization conditions with regulators. In all cases, companies are just as concerned about anticipated changes in regulation as they are about existing regulations that already affect them. Information about new regulations is picked up from corporate affairs departments or through trade associations. As discussed in Chapters 3–5, many companies and trade associations also devote a considerable amount of resources and effort into attempting to block or modify forthcoming rules (successes of this industrial lobbying activity include the virtual abandonment of the EU's carbon and energy tax, the UK's decision to postpone VOC controls on the coating industry and the EU's abandonment of several energy-efficiency measures for consumer electronics).

Regulations can also play a positive role for companies; compliance, for example, can serve, in a way similar to certification under the EU's Environmental Management and Audit Scheme (EMAS) or the UK's BS7750, to legitimize the companies' activities. An increasing but still modest number of companies have expressed an interest in or have obtained registration under these schemes (see below). The regulatory framework can also serve to empower environmental managers and enable them to secure funding for environmental projects and investments that may otherwise not have been made available.

Despite these more positive aspects, environmental regulation, in general, is still seen as a threat by industry. Regulations and standards inevitably require businesses to change the way that they carry out their activities; these changes are seen as imposing a net additional cost and hence having a negative impact on competitiveness. However, as discussed below, industry is not homogenous. Whilst some sectors and companies may lose, others stand to gain as regulations create new markets and opportunities.

Final Consumers and Industrial Customer Pressure

Companies manufacturing products for final consumption are acutely aware of consumer perceptions and what consumers want from their products. However, there are very few genuine green products and there is also a substantial gap between consumer attitudes and consumer behaviour. Consumers think green only when buying a limited range of products and are generally more concerned with functionality and cost rather than the environmental impacts associated with their consumption patterns and choices. Reflecting this, as well as the recognition of the loss of credibility associated with untenable advertising claims about green products in the past, companies now appear to be taking a lower public profile on environmental issues, making fewer green claims in advertising, while actively trying to improve environmental performance.

Of more importance, perhaps, is the company's overall environmental image which many companies now regard as an essential component of company branding. The fear of environmental failure is perhaps a more potent consideration in driving corporate environmental policy for many companies than is the prospect of expanding market share through green claims. This is graphically illustrated by Shell's experience over the disposal of the *Brent Spar* oil platform in 1995. Irrespective of the arguments for and against deep sea disposal and what exactly was or was not on the 14,500-tonne installation, Shell's failure to meet public expectations of corporate environmental responsibility resulted in a widespread and damaging consumer boycott of its petrol stations. This in turn ultimately led to a last minute, dramatic and financially expensive policy U-turn by the company when it announced, much to the dismay and anger of the UK Government, that it had abandoned its plans for deep sea disposal in favour of a land-based disposal option.

Pressures relating to environmental performances exerted by industrial customers on those operating further up the supply chain also appear to be of increasing importance. At this stage, however, environmental criteria for selecting suppliers remain weak and there is little attempt to audit supplier performance. Environmental factors are now addressed by purchasing departments but, in practice, questionnaires for suppliers serve mainly to heighten environmental sensitivities. Common questions relate to legislative compliance, the adoption of environmental management standards, such as BS7750, or the use of specific substances such as ozone depleters or brominated flame retardants.

Community Stakeholders

Community initiatives, projects and relationships in general are increasingly being reported on in both corporate annual reports and, when produced separately in company environmental reports. Companies across industrial sectors, from information technology and telecommunications to oil and gas and mining enterprises, are beginning to place greater emphasis on developing and maintaining an image of being good neighbours. There are general benefits to be derived from good community relationships, such as less managerial time spent dealing with public complaints and press enquiries. Good relationships can also smooth the way for new investments and process changes which require approval under planning law or pollution control regulation.

To what extent this impacts on corporate environmentally related decisions is uncertain. However, in a series of interviews conducted by SPRU, community stakeholders were mentioned on a number of occasions by companies operating high-impact sites. The issues generally related to very direct and local impact environmental problems such as particulate emissions and odour. Large-scale environmental problems such as climate change did not feature in company–community relations.

Investor Pressures: Environmental Liability

Investor pressure on companies – from banks and other lending institutions and shareholders – although limited at this time, is set to increase. The current situation partly reflects the reluctance of the financial institutions, in a competitive and international banking market, to press environmental conditions on customers. It also reflects the current lack of disclosure by companies of environmental information to investors in a usable form – despite the increased level and degree of corporate environmental reporting over recent years. Investors and other stakeholders, such as fund managers, analysts and shareholders, need deeper knowledge of businesses' environmental performance to help them to form more accurate judgements on the risk profile, worth and prospects of their investment decisions, according to the Government's Advisory Committee on Business and the Environment (ACBE). ACBE also maintains that the preparation of such information can be of benefit to businesses.

Existing requirements to disclose environmental information in the UK, under the Financial Services Act 1986, Stock Exchange rules and the Companies Act 1985 are essentially limited to the need to disclose material liabilities. These are non-specific and remain open to the usual interpretations of 'material' and what does or does not constitute 'a true and fair view' of a company's affairs. This contrasts with US Securities and Exchange Commission (SEC) rules, for example, which require companies to disclose the costs of complying with environmental laws and legal proceedings on environmental matters, and which include a discussion of uncertainties under the headings of management discussions and analysis.

The demand for and recognition by companies that they must disclose more detailed environmental information to investors is increasing. In situations where banks and financial institutions find themselves exposed and potentially liable to financial risk, for instance in relation to contaminated land, the demand for such information has already increased. Lenders' liability for contaminated land has become a highly sensitive and controversial issue within the financial services sector (see Chapter 5). The potential impact (financial cost) of such liability is well illustrated by reference to the US experience under the Superfund legislation. Not surprisingly, banks and financial institutions are beginning to set more stringent lending conditions in these and other situations where they may be exposed and potentially liable to financial risk.

Adding to the pressure for greater disclosure, ACBE has recently proposed a draft set of guidelines on good practice with regard to environmental reporting.[11] In preparing the code of practice, ACBE intends to draw on guidelines already under preparation by several UK and European professional accounting bodies covering the reporting of environmental liabilities, costs and assets in company accounts. The organization also believes that the operating and financial review section of company annual reports should summarize the environmental risks facing the business, the costs incurred and initiatives taken, and make appropriate links and references to the accounts section, covering capital and revenue expenditure, liabilities and provisions. An explanation of how the firm's environmental management system has affected its performance, its risk management policy and its compliance record should also be disclosed.

Although currently representing only a small percentage of total funds, the rapid growth and impressive performance of ethical investment trusts and pensions, often incorporating environmental as well as ethical considerations into their investment selection criteria, also suggests that investor pressure may become more significant in the future. The Co-operative Bank's high profile and successful advertising campaign to promote its position on ethical and environmentally sensitive banking also suggests that investor pressure may become a more important consideration in shaping corporate environmental strategies.

Business Environmental Strategies

The four sets of drivers discussed above have a clear impact on company strategies. According to Fischer and Schot, the response of firms to mounting environmental pressures can be categorized in two phases.[12] From the 1970s to somewhere in the mid-1980s, firms changed from fighting and resisting environmental legislation to adopting a more proactive and positive approach to the environment. During the first era environmental issues were seen as a threat to business. Investment in pollution abatement technology and clean-up costs to meet legislative compliance could only be achieved at the expense of competitiveness and profits. There was a clear trade-off between ecology and the economy. On the whole, this period was characterized by industry's lack of willingness to internalize environmental issues. Instead, business frequently responded to external pressures in a reactive and ad hoc manner rather than as part of a coherent strategy. Corporate environmental objectives that existed at that time often went no further than: "We will comply with all governmental laws and regulations"; companies generally met the minimum standards required to achieve legislative compliance but went no further.

A number of major environmental accidents during the mid-1980s, such as the leak of methyl isocyanide in 1984 at a Union Carbide plant in Bophal in India – which resulted in several hundred deaths – a chemical spill into the Rhine following a fire at a Sandoz plant in 1986 and the Chernobyl nuclear accident, also in 1986, served to intensify the demands for improved environmental performance and to encourage this shift. More recently various oil disasters such as the *Exxon Valdez* spill in Alaska in March 1989, the *Braer* spillage in 1995, and the *Sea Empress* spillage in 1996 have all served to keep corporate environmental accountability and responsibility in the media. Tougher and more outcome- or results-oriented environmental legislation (as opposed to technology-prescriptive regulations), together with increased public pressure and demand for improved environmental performance and accountability, forced industry to recognize that its current and past approach to environmental issues was no longer adequate. Sometime during the mid-1980s, industry, according to much of the post-1992 Rio Earth Summit business literature, shifted from a defensive position towards environmental issues to a more positive, proactive and, in some instances, offensive approach. Some authors suggest that businesses progress through various developmental stages in their approach and response to the environment. Stages or particular strategies include ignoring environmental issues completely; endeavouring to do no more than the bare minimum to comply with regulation – essentially a fire-fighting and crisis-management approach to environmental regulation – to a range of more sophisticated compliance-plus and proactive type strategies. Others suggest that businesses do not need to *progress* through these stages but instead choose their own strategy depending upon their own particular circumstances and priorities.[13] There are some specific features of the corporate response:

- Larger companies have not only become more aware of environmental issues but have also become more proactive. Most major companies now have formal environmental management systems and environmental auditing programmes and many produce environmental reports for public consumption.
- There has been a growing interest in externally certified environmental management systems. An increasing but still modest number of companies are also seeking registration under the UK's environmental management standard, BS7750 or the EU's Environmental Management and Audit Scheme (EMAS). By the spring of 1996, some 60 or so firms had obtained BS7750 certificates and eleven industrial sites had been registered under EMAS. A handful of firms have also been certified to the draft ISO 14001 standard on environmental management.[14] However, small businesses, although increasingly aware of environmental issues, have by and large not formalized internal management systems.
- A wide range of companies has been drawn into the environmental debate and not simply the traditional brown sectors – chemicals, energy and metals – which are threatened by tighter regulatory controls. Many firms involved in retailing or the manufacture of consumer products have been drawn in because of concern about customer reaction to their environmental performance.
- Companies operating close to consumers are also concerned about post-consumer waste, the introduction of producer-responsibility concepts and the development of waste-stream consortia.
- As potential markets expand, there is an increasing perception of common interests among suppliers of environmental goods and services. This industry has traditionally been fragmented. The Environmental Industries Commission (EIC), for example, now puts forward the argument that consistent development and application of environmental rules will bring both environmental and economic benefits in the form of a healthy UK supply sector.

■ The use of partnership approaches to dealing with environmental problems is growing. Partnerships can involve links between industry, regulators and environmental non-governmental organizations (NGOs) – or any subset of these groups. For industry, partnership approaches help to enhance the credibility and legitimacy of operations and practices.

Although these trends suggest an environmentally proactive industrial sector, other indicators point in a different direction. Many smaller companies remain less positive in their management of environmental issues. The take-up rate, for example, among companies invited to participate in waste minimization schemes is still low in spite of potential economic benefits. Larger companies with formal environmental management structures may still find it difficult to embed environmental awareness in everyday company activities.

Business itself is learning how to manage better the environmental policy process, influencing or sometimes slowing the development of new environmental rules which may have adverse economic impacts. The pay-off from lobbying activity is still seen to be high. Greater environmental awareness has contributed to a higher level of competence in managing the environmental policy process.

The Appeal of the Double Dividend

The Win–Win Scenario

The literature on business and the environment, as well as the more optimistic official documentation, is replete with references to the environmental and economic double dividend or win–win situation.[15] One goal of this book is to place these concepts in their proper perspective. Win–win is about enhancing resource productivity and hence economic competitiveness. By producing more from less, and from cleaner production processes, both shareholder value and the environment can benefit. According to Michael Porter in his influential articles in *Scientific American* and the *Harvard Business Review*, the perceived conflict between environmental protection and economic competitiveness is a false dichotomy. Instead of hindering competitiveness, strict and sensibly constructed environmental standards act as a catalyst to stimulate firms to innovate and re-engineer their technology. The static cost impacts of environmental regulation can be more than offset by important innovative productivity benefits. These can result, in many cases, in processes that not only pollute less but lower costs or improve quality.[16]

The appeal of the win–win rhetoric is obvious. We can essentially carry on business as usual by "producing the new products and technologies that foster economic progress without environmental destruction".[17] Those companies that are going to succeed and prosper will be those that develop a more proactive environmental strategy which seeks to develop a competitive advantage out of stricter environmental standards. Simple legislative compliance will no longer be sufficient.

There are numerous examples of win–win outcomes in support of Porter's argument. Many process investments that yield both economic and environmental benefits have been identified by SPRU: for example, combined-cycle gas turbine electricity-generating plants and the use of VOC reduction technology in paint shops are examples of process innovation resulting in both economic and environmental benefits. There are also many examples of win–win outcomes resulting from more traditional waste minimization and energy efficiency initiatives. As discussed in Chapter 7, the 11 companies participating in the Aire and Calder waste minimization initiative are now saving in excess of £3.3 million a year. Other waste minimization initiatives such as the Department of Trade and Industry's (DTI) Project Catalyst have also resulted in significant savings.

Technology and the Double Dividend

Technological innovation and the adoption of cleaner technologies which bring economic and environmental benefits are at the heart of the double dividend argument. The key distinction is between *clean* (or cleaner) technologies and *end-of-pipe* or *clean-up* technologies. The underlying assumption is that clean technologies, by preventing pollution at source, represent the best and most efficient approach to reducing the environmental impacts of industry. Clean technologies often represent an intrinsic process change which is cost-reducing and environmentally benign. In contrast, end-of-pipe technologies are deemed to be inefficient, wasteful and costly. Combined-cycle gas turbines, for example, are mooted as an example of cleaner technology whilst flue-gas desulphurization (FGD) or waste water treatment are cited as the epitome of wasteful and expensive end-of-pipe technologies.

The majority of existing environmental investments would probably fit more comfortably into the end-of-pipe category. However, in practice, the distinction between cleaner technologies and end-of-pipe represents an oversimplification. Companies make investment decisions for a variety of reasons, and the circumstances under which there is a realistic choice between clean or clean-up technology may be quite rare. For example, when regulatory demands are immediate or when basic processes are approaching their engineering limits, end-of-pipe technologies may represent the only feasible solution. Few companies consciously use the concept of clean technology to shape their resource and development strategies or their investment decisions. However, they almost certainly aspire towards more efficient process technologies, the adoption of which will generally confer environmental benefits.

It is more useful to approach technology adoption from the perspective of companies' decision-making structures, rather than according to the physical features of the technological options. Investment which brings environmental benefits can be characterized by the following broad classes:

- integral process change;
- product design;
- cost-saving investment; and
- compliance technology.

Integral Process Change and Product Design

Integral process change and product design are motivated primarily by strategic business considerations. Such investments are the key to the future profitability of any major company and a relatively long-term view (5 to 15 years if not longer) will be taken. Changes to production processes can be incremental or radical and, although usually motivated for non-environmental reasons, can have implications for environmental performance. On the whole innovation has tended to reduce the environmental impact of production processes, partly because of the economic incentives to reduce raw material use, energy consumption and the generation of waste. Not surprisingly, integral process changes of this kind are often seen as examples of cleaner technology.

Cost-saving investments

Cost-saving investments are usually taken at the discretion of plant management and are subject to shorter-term project appraisal techniques. Cost-saving investments can be aimed at cutting labour costs as well as the cost of raw materials and waste disposal. Environmental investments usually take the form of changes in operating practice or incremental adaptations to existing plant which lead to waste reduction or improved efficiency in energy use. Such investments can usually be justified in economic terms and often have very short pay-back periods. Waste minimization initiatives (which are discussed in Chapter 7) essentially focus on cost-reduction investments. Similarly, many clean technology and cleaner production programmes run by public or international agencies are, in practice, focused on cost-saving investments of this sort which yield environmental benefits.

The profitability of cost-saving investments is closely related to the costs of raw materials, energy and landfill costs. Legislation (for example, the imposition of landfill taxes) or anticipation of legislation (for example, proposals for an EU carbon and energy tax) can therefore act as a stimulus to undertake such investments on a preventive basis. SPRU, for instance, found examples of companies which had relaxed the pay-back criteria used for energy-efficiency investments as a precautionary move in view of the proposed carbon and energy tax. As discussed in Chapter 7, the first round of measures adopted under pollution prevention programmes are, in general, highly cost-effective. However, diminishing returns in further investments can serve to inhibit companies from going beyond simply picking the low-hanging fruit.

Compliance investments

Compliance investments are regarded by industry as mandatory responses to government regulations. They often, but not always, entail investments in pollution abatement equipment, corresponding to the end-of-pipe technology definition. The economic and competitiveness impacts of such investments are generally negative and, as a consequence, they tend to be resisted by the industries or companies concerned (see Chapter 6). However, they also present major opportunities for suppliers of pollution abatement equipment.

Taking this perspective, the distinction between end-of-pipe and clean technology, which are abstract categories, becomes almost meaningless. A company may, however, decide to bring environmental criteria into the design of new process technology. This may not have an immediate effect on environmental performance. But the cumulative consequence of decisions to invest in new plant will then result, in the longer term, in a reduced need for compliance investment made simply to meet regulatory or wider social demands. Such a strategy may take some time to pay off – and end-of-pipe investments linked to existing process plant may be unavoidable – but in the longer term it could generate the elusive economic and ecological win–win. In the real world, what is more important than choosing an end-of-pipe or clean technology is a refocusing of strategy at a higher level in such a way as to build environmental criteria into decision-making and the technology development processes.

The Limitations of the Double Dividend Argument

The simplified win–win and double dividend argument can create unrealistic expectations. Businesses are not homogenous and although impressive examples of cost-saving environmental investments can be found, they are not widespread and they do not necessarily represent the norm for individual companies. In many instances the substantial savings realized from waste minimization initiatives or programmes aimed at improving resource productivity and reducing pollution are insignificant when placed next to a company's overall level of environmental spending and investment. From a survey of over 100 academic and government studies, Stavins concluded that "not a single empirical analysis lends convincing support" to the view that environmental regulation stimulates innovation and competitiveness.[18]

Companies make environmental investments for a number of reasons. These include legislative compliance, to take advantage of and realize potential cost savings, and strategic reasons. It is not always easy to identify the degree to which environmental factors play a role in environmental investments. For example, as discussed in Chapter 6, few investments which lead to reduced environmental releases are undertaken solely for regulatory reasons. Capital investments may be undertaken to replace obsolete plant, to expand capacity or to reduce unit production costs. It is therefore often difficult to quantify the environmental component of any investment decision.

Cost pressures are seen as a key issue in relation to environmental management within industry. Unless compelled to do so, companies will not undertake investments on environmental grounds alone. The cost savings associated with waste reduction and reductions in the use of raw materials and energy are often the major motivation. However, wider environmental concerns and the prospect of enhanced legislation (particularly with regard to priority waste streams and producer responsibility) have served as a stimulus to search for both changes in practice and modest process investments which reduce operating costs. Without the initial regulatory stimulus, many of these opportunities would not have been identified.

At the national level it may be possible to foster a more competitive environment industry through stricter regulatory controls. To that extent, a double dividend may be possible. But, at the level of the individual company, stricter environmental standards will create winners and losers. This is borne out by many of the examples discussed in Chapters 3 to 5. Far from embracing environmental legislation, many companies have adopted a positively hostile approach to attempts to enhance regulatory standards. Companies in heavily polluting industries, perhaps locked into out-dated technology, face extinction from higher standards, not enhanced profits. In contrast, the companies most likely to embrace higher standards are those in environmental consultancy or in the pollution abatement industry. Tougher and properly enforced standards are likely to mean more customers and hence increased profits.

This point is illustrated by the Environmental Industries Commission (EIC)'s severe criticism of the UK Government's decision to postpone controls on emissions of volatile organic compounds (VOC) from the coatings industry, following intense lobbying by those industries that were going to be affected (see Chapter 4). The ten sectors concerned had been due to upgrade to new plant standards between April 1996 and April 1997. However, the Government's decision pushed back these deadlines by 9 to 27 months. According to the EIC, the postponement has resulted in a significant loss of orders for suppliers of VOC-abatement equipment and is also likely to damage industry's overseas competitiveness. The European VOC-abatement market is growing at 15 per cent per year and expected to reach £660 million by 1997. Since environmental regulation was intended to force industry to internalize those costs previously inflicted on the rest of society, it is unrealistic to expect all environmentally related investment to provide a pay-back or positive rate of return.

Conclusions

Some sectors of industry, notably those which provide environmental goods and services, have benefited from higher levels of environmental concern. Some companies have been able to gain competitive advantage by anticipating higher environmental standards more quickly than their competitors. Industry has certainly developed a more sophisticated approach to environmental issues and there are examples of double dividend outcomes where substantial economic savings have been made. However, these are not as widespread as might be expected following a cursory look at the 1990s business literature. Savings achieved through waste minimization, energy-efficiency measures and resource-efficiency improvements often appear small in relation to a company's overall level of environmental spending.

As major companies in all sectors have sought to incorporate environmental considerations into their operations, there is little evidence to suggest that smaller companies, although aware of environmental challenges, have moved beyond meeting minimum legislative requirements. Environmental concern has created clear winners and losers in industry. While some corporate environmental policies are compatible with commercial self-interest, others have been driven by the fear of environmental liability and failure, with the level of environmental investments outweighing any immediate private gain.

Substantial efforts by industry over the last ten years or so have reduced significantly the rate at which industrial activities contribute to overall environmental degradation. However, sustainable industrial production encompasses more than simply producing more from less, and reducing environmental loadings is very different from reversing the decline in environmental quality. There is still a long way to go.

CHAPTER 3

Global Environmental Issues: Ozone Depletion and Climate Change

Introduction

The three following chapters address seven environmental issues which range in scale from the global to the local. Chapter 3 deals with the two main global issues of stratospheric ozone depletion and climate change. Transboundary and regional issues (air quality and transport, acid rain, and emissions of volatile organic compounds – VOCs) are reviewed in Chapter 4 and two key local environmental issues, water quality and contaminated land, are considered in Chapter 5. Each of the reviews starts with a short summary section. An update and background on the particular environmental issue is provided, together with a brief overview of relevant legislation or proposed legislation. Industry's response is considered throughout the reviews. In addition, most sections also conclude by providing one or more brief accounts which focus on a particular example of industry's response to the issue under consideration.

Some common threads run through all of the analyses. A major theme, when looking at industry's performance from the point of view of regulatory negotiation, is one of industrial opposition, at least initially, and resistance to confront or address most of the issues under consideration. The reviews provide more examples of trade-offs than win–win outcomes. However, this is not always the case and in some instances certain sectors or individual companies have benefited from more rigorous and stricter environmental standards. Voluntary action on the part of industry is rare and where it has occurred, for example in The Netherlands and Germany, it has often been in response to government prompting or as a means to delay or prevent the implementation of legislation. This is illustrated by the recent initiative by the Federation of German Industries to cut CO_2 emissions by 20 per cent by 2005. In return, the German Government has promised to postpone certain regulatory measures to combat climate change.

Legislation still appears to be the main driver or motivator for industry to take environmental action. Proposed legislation and existing environmental standards and regulations are generally, but again not always, resisted by industry. Opposition is usually based on concern over the likely impact such legislation is having or may have on profitability, international competitiveness and employment.

With regard to the issues reviewed in Chapters 3 to 5, negotiation by industry has often served to delay legislation and in some instances has resulted in policy initiatives being abandoned. For example, work on a series of directives to impose energy efficiency standards for appliances under the EU's SAVE Programme was abandoned in the spring of 1995 following intensive industrial opposition. The preparation of a national inventory of potentially contaminated land in the UK, regarded by many as a necessary first step in any comprehensive strategy aimed at dealing with the problem, has also been dropped following strong opposition from a broad range of business interests. Opposition by industry to the proposed European carbon and energy tax, despite the relatively modest level at which the tax was to be set and exemptions for energy-intensive industries, has delayed and effectively thwarted the EU's hopes to introduce the tax across all of Europe as part of an overall climate strategy.

The following reviews provide other examples. Stricter VOC emission controls are resisted by industry on the grounds of their impact on competitiveness and the costs of investing in abatement technology. Car manufacturers continue to fail to deliver realistic and achievable improvements in vehicle fuel efficiency which could help to improve air quality. Lack of scientific evidence and uncertainty are also used to justify pursuing a 'business as usual' approach to some environmental issues. Sixteen years passed between the United Nations 1972 Conference on the Human Environment, which first highlighted the link between UK sulphur emissions and acid damage, and the UK entering into any international commitments aimed at addressing the issue. The UK's Central Electricity Generating Board (CEGB) argued that the 'excessive costs' of investing in flue-gas desulphurization (FGD) could not be justified because of the uncertainty surrounding the issue. Similarly, in the climate debate, lack of scientific certainty is often used to justify restricting measures aimed at reducing anthropogenic emissions of greenhouse gases and favouring those that can be taken on a 'no regrets' basis: in other words, to those measures that would be economical and cost-effective irrespective of whether predictions of global climate change actually materialize.

The review of industry's response to the seven environmental issues may present a more gloomy and pessimistic impression than is actually warranted. Some companies have undoubtedly benefited from tougher environmental standards. More stringent and enforced environmental standards can be used by companies to keep out 'cowboy' operators and to provide a competitive edge over existing competitors. However, in general, the companies benefiting from environmental legislation tend to be the ones selling environmental goods and services: suppliers of pollution abatement equipment, environmental lawyers and contaminated land consultants. Forecast expenditure to deal with water quality and contaminated land clean-up alone runs into billions of pounds and, over the last 20 or so years, environmental consultancy has become a £400 million per year industry employing 12,000 people.

The reviews do not provide any clear examples of the win–win outcomes discussed in Chapter 2. That is not to say that they do not exist. They do. For example, the development of water-based paints as an alternative to solvent-based paints, to reduce VOC emissions, has become a highly profitable activity amongst manufacturers and a factor in a recent take-over bid. These examples would appear to be rare. Although limited, the reviews do indicate that business is not adopting the proactive stance that some authors suggest would be in their best interest.

Stratospheric Ozone Depletion

Summary

The ozone layer is a very thin layer of ozone (O_3) molecules in the stratosphere which effectively acts as a shield, protecting the earth's surface from excessive levels of ultraviolet (UV) radiation. It is now recognized that various man-made chemicals, principally chlorofluorocarbons (CFCs) and halons, are depleting this protective layer and exposing the earth to dangerous levels of radiation. Increased levels of UV radiation could have detrimental effects on human health, agricultural production systems, fisheries and natural ecosystems.

It is important to distinguish between stratospheric and tropospheric ozone. While the former performs an essential role in maintaining the health of living organisms and ecosystems, tropospheric ozone, formed principally by the action of sunlight on emissions of VOCs and oxides of nitrogen (mainly from road transport), is a major air pollutant and source of poor air quality (see Chapter 4).[1]

The idea that CFCs could destroy the earth's ozone layer was first suggested in the early 1970s. Mounting evidence from further scientific studies and the discovery of the ozone hole in 1985 eventually led to the signing of the Montreal Protocol on Substances that Deplete the Ozone Layer in September 1987. The Treaty was hailed as the most significant international environmental agreement to date. Reflecting the magnitude of the potential consequences of continued ozone destruction, the Treaty requires the complete phase-out of many ozone-depleting substances between 1996 and 2030. With implications for billions of dollars of investment worldwide and hundreds of thousands of jobs, the initial reaction of the chemical industry to the potential loss of this valuable part of their business was hostile. Lack of scientific certainty was effectively used to delay and weaken measures intended to control ozone-depleting substances. Subsequently, major producers adopted a more proactive approach to CFC regulation. This change in approach provides an example of how, in some instances, tighter regulation can have differential impacts on companies operating within the same sector. Producers' strategies with regard to the main CFC replacements, hydrochlorofluorocarbons (HCFCs) – which are also ozone-depleting substances – and hydrofluorocarbons (HFCs), varied according to their own particular circumstances.

Under the Montreal Protocol, producers are allowed to supply ozone-depleting substances for various 'essential uses' beyond the phase-out deadlines. Pressure from producers may persuade governments to seek wide definitions of 'essential' uses. Of particular concern is the employment of HCFCs, the use of which is being widely promoted in both the developed and developing world by the former CFC producers. There is also concern over the use of HFCs. Although these chemicals do not destroy the ozone layer, they are powerful global-warming gases. HFC-23 has a global-warming potential (GWP) 9500 times greater than CO_2 and persists in the atmosphere for 390 years.

Over the last decade the evidence of ozone depletion has moved in a consistently more pessimistic direction. In 1994 the Department of the Environment's Stratospheric Ozone Review Group (SORG) reported that ozone depletion over Europe reached record lows, with levels 25 per cent below normal, in 1991–93. In September 1995 the World Meteorological Organization (WMO) reported that an ozone hole the size of Europe had been detected over Antarctica, and European scientists reported that ozone loss during the winter of 1995 was the largest ever measured – with losses of up to 50 per cent below levels in previous years being detected. As this trend continues the demand for tighter controls and more rapid phase-outs of ozone-depleting chemicals is likely to increase.

The Issue: What Are CFCs and Other Ozone-Depleting Substances and What Are They Used For?

The pollutants most associated with ozone depletion are chlorofluorocarbons (CFCs) and halons.[2] Invented in the 1930s, mainly by Du Pont, the use of the CFC family of chemicals (defined by the combination of chlorine, fluorine and carbon in their molecules) expanded dramatically in the post-war years. By 1987 production had grown steadily from insignificant levels to nearly 400,000 tonnes per year (CFC-11) and about 425,000 tonnes per year (CFC-12). One of their principal attractions, some-what ironically, was their chemical stability: they did not degrade. In addition, the chemicals were non-flammable and non-carcinogenic. The gases have been – and for some sectors, still are – widely used in industry, principally as aerosol propellants, heat transfer agents for refrigeration and air conditioning, for cleaning electronic components, and in the manufacture of foam insulation. The chemicals are also used in fire-fighting equipment.

The Science

Ozone, an unstable form of oxygen composed of three, rather than two, atoms of oxygen, has been characterized as the single most important chemically active trace gas in the earth's atmosphere. This significance is due to the vitally important role the gas plays in the upper atmosphere. Stratospheric ozone, effectively a very thin layer of ozone molecules in the upper atmosphere, absorbs a proportion of the biological-active ultraviolet (UV-B) radiation that would otherwise reach the earth's surface. A 1 per cent loss of ozone is thought to increase the amount of high-energy UV-B radiation at the earth's surface by nearly 2 per cent. Increased exposure to UV-B radiation has been linked to diseases such as skin cancer, cataracts and immunological deficiencies. Increased UV radiation is also thought to affect crop growth. Implications for world agricultural production at a time of increasing demand could be significant. There is also concern about the potential impact on the productivity of fisheries, via possible disruption of the aquatic food chain caused by radiation damage to phytoplankton and other organisms living or reproducing near the ocean surface.[3] There may also be other, as yet unknown, impacts on the ecosystem and food chain.

In the mid-1970s, research into the effects of possible chemical emissions from rockets indicated that chlorine released into the stratosphere could unleash a complicated chemical process that would continually destroy ozone for several decades. A single chlorine atom, through a catalytic chain reaction, could eliminate tens of thousands of ozone molecules.[4] Subsequent research revealed that CFCs, depending upon their individual structure, could remain intact for many decades to several centuries. Migrating slowly up to the stratosphere, CFCs would eventually be broken down by solar radiation and in the process release large quantities of chlorine.[5] Because of their long lifetimes, as much as 90 per cent of all CFCs ever emitted may still be in the atmosphere.

What's Happening to the Ozone Layer?

Ozone depletion became front-page world headlines following the discovery of the Antarctic ozone hole in 1985 by British scientists. Their findings suggested that spring ozone levels over the Antarctic were reduced by 50 per cent or more. The 'ozone hole' had been discovered. More recently, in 1994, the DoE's Stratospheric Ozone Review Group (SORG) reported that ozone depletion over Europe reached record lows, with levels around 25 per cent lower than normal, over the winters of 1991–92 and 1992–93.

SORG maintains that even if CFCs are phased out by 1996, ozone levels will continue to fall until about 2005 and will only then begin to recover slowly. SORG concluded that "until the amounts of chlorine and bromine in the stratosphere have been stabilized, the downward trend in ozone will continue". Back-of-the-envelope calculations suggest that total depletion of the ozone layer over the UK could reach 20 to 30 per cent.

Legislation: The Montreal Protocol

The Montreal Protocol was adopted in 1987 and has been revised three times: in 1990 in London, in 1992 in Copenhagen and most recently in Vienna, in December 1995. Both the London and Copenhagen meetings brought forward the phase-out dates for the major ozone depleters, such as CFCs and halons, as scientific evidence pointed to a more severe threat to the ozone layer than had previously been expected. The Vienna meeting was less successful. Although controls on ozone depleters in industrialized countries were tightened, albeit modestly, the conference failed to persuade developing countries to accept substantial controls on HCFCs and methyl bromide. The meeting had been intended to mark the phase-out of CFCs in industrialized countries and to begin the process of phasing out ozone-depleters in developing countries.

At the Copenhagen meeting the following agreements were reached:

- CFCs: The phase-out date was brought forward from January 2000 to January 1996, with a 75 per cent reduction, based on 1986 levels, by January 1994. Under EC deadlines, CFC production was to be cut to 15 per cent of the 1986 level by January 1994 and phased out completely by January 1995.
- *Carbon tetrachloride:* Phase out by January 1996, with an 85 per cent reduction, based on 1989 levels, by January 1995. The original phase-out deadline was 2000.
- *Halons:* Phase out by January 1996. Again, the original phase-out date was 2000.

- *Methyl chloroform:* Phase out by January 1996, with a 50 per cent reduction on 1989 levels by January 1994. The previous phase-out deadline was January 2005.
- *HCFCs:* Consumption of these chemicals was to be capped in January 1996 at a level amounting to the sum of their consumption in 1989 plus 3.1 per cent of the level of consumption of CFCs in 1989. The chemicals are to phased out by 99.5 per cent by 2020, with consumption of up to 0.5 per cent allowed to service existing equipment until a complete phase-out by 2030.
- *Methyl bromide:* Consumption is to be frozen at 1991 levels by 1995.

The main changes agreed for industrialized countries at the Vienna meeting included lowering the cap on the consumption levels of HCFCs to 2.8 per cent, from the 3.1 per cent agreed in 1992 (with no amendment to the phase-out date) and an agreement to phase out the use of methyl bromide completely by 2010. However, the US pushed through substantial exemption clauses for the use of methyl bromide in quarantine and preshipment purposes and 'critical agricultural uses', which will be decided by the United Nations Environmental Programme's Technical and Economic Assessment Panel (TEAP).[6]

Under the Protocol, production of substances may continue beyond the stipulated deadlines if a particular use is considered essential and there is no suitable alternative. Of particular concern and controversy is the use of the CFC substitute, HCFCs. The chemicals are being promoted by former CFC producers as temporary replacements for CFCs. However, SORG have stated that if HCFCs are used at the full level permitted by the protocol, the time for which chlorine loading is above the 1990 level could be prolonged by up to eight years.

The controls on HCFCs agreed at Copenhagen will allow HCFC consumption to increase globally from about 220,000 tonnes in 1989 to anywhere between 600,000 and 800,000 tonnes in 1996. According to Friends of the Earth (FoE), by the time they are phased out in 2030, more than 11 million tonnes of the substances may have been consumed.[7] The controversy surrounding the use of HCFCs was heightened in 1994 when TEAP reported back on their assessment of the nominations for the 'essential use' of CFCs. The TEAP concluded that HCFCs are needed as CFC substitutes in most refrigeration and air conditioning applications, manufacture of insulated foams, selected solvent uses, and fire-protection applications where space constraints exist. These conclusions were particularly criticized by the Scandinavian and German officials at the meeting.

Developing nations are also against further controls and tightening of deadlines for phasing out HCFCs because of fears that they will not recoup investments already made in HCFC technology, notably in refrigerator manufacture. After considerable negotiation in Vienna, an agreement was reluctantly reached to freeze consumption of HCFCs in 2016 based on 2015 levels and to phase them out completely by 2040. The deadline for the phase-out of CFCs for developing countries remains at 2014, despite attempts to bring forward the ten-year grace period to 2006. This move was effectively blocked by India (now a major exporter of CFCs to the developing world).

Developing nations also lobbied against tighter controls on the use of methyl bromide, a soil fumigant and pesticide used in warehouses before and after shipment of export crops. Worldwide consumption of methyl bromide, in the order of 700,000 tonnes a year, is increasing at the rate of about 7 per cent per year. Because of its relatively short tropospheric lifetime, reduced consumption would give a rapid reduction in the amount of bromine being carried into the stratosphere. For this reason, many now regard the chemical as the key to ozone recovery.

Under the 1992 revisions, the use of the chemical by industrialized countries was to be frozen at 1991 levels by 1995. The US had originally pressed for a complete ban by 2000. Despite exemptions for its use in quarantine and preshipment applications, developing nations argued that the freeze and strict interpretations of what actually constitutes 'quarantine' and 'preshipment applications' could restrict their export trade. Many industrialized countries insist that produce is treated as a condition of import. The final agreement reached in Vienna was for developing countries to freeze consumption in 2002 against a baseline averaged over three years from 1995–98.

EC Draft Regulation on Ozone-Depleting Substances

The European Union, a signatory of the Montreal Protocol, is also developing its own domestic policy and legislation aimed at controlling ozone-depleting substances. A draft regulation lays down tighter phase-out timetables than those under the Montreal Protocol, as well as controls on illegal imports, and will introduce new measures to deter leaks and venting of ozone depleters. In relation to HCFCs, Ministers have agreed to lower the cap on production to their production level in 1989 plus 2 per cent of CFC production in 1989, and to phase HCFCs out by 2015, 15 years ahead of the phase-out date agreed in Copenhagen. In response, the food and refrigeration industries have argued that 2015 is too soon because of the 20- to 30-year lifetime of refrigeration equipment.

Industry's Response

Industry's initial reaction to measures aimed at curbing the use of CFCs was perhaps predictably hostile. Global sales of CFCs and investment and research into CFC technology ran into billions of dollars. Restrictions on CFC production also had implications for hundreds of thousands of jobs in related sectors.

The remainder of this section reviews the response of Du Pont and ICI, two major CFC producers, to national and international initiatives aimed at controlling and limiting the use of CFCs. The discussion largely follows H Landis Gabel's chapter on 'Environmental Management as a Competitive Strategy' in *Principles of Environmental and Resource Economics: A Guide for Students and Decision-Makers*.[8] The review is presented to illustrate the complexity of the interactions between firms and regulators and the fact that environmental regulation, in certain circumstances, can serve to strengthen an individual firm's competitive position. As discussed below, the proactive stance taken by Du Pont, for whatever reason, set an industrial precedent and undoubtedly facilitated moves to bring forward the phase-out dates for CFCs. The strategies discussed below were anticipatory and involved thinking several steps ahead of the regulator and competitors.

Box 3.1 concludes the section with a brief account of the process that led to the signing of voluntary agreements on the use of HFCs by various producer and user sectors within the refrigeration and air conditioning industries. The box provides a useful lead into the review of climate change, the second of the global environmental issues dealt with in this chapter. HFCs, as previously noted, are powerful greenhouse gases and are therefore subject to control under the United Nations Framework Convention on Climate Change (UNFCCC). It also provides an account of how overseas manufacturers have attempted to bypass completely both CFC substitutes, HCFCs and HFCs, by using propane and butane refrigerants.

Du Pont

In response to the initial studies of the early 1970s which hypothesized that escaped CFCs could destroy the ozone layer, the US EPA banned the non-essential use of CFCs in 1978 – in effect, the use of CFCs in aerosols. The ban halved US demand for CFCs and since the US market represented about half of the world market, the ban served to effectively cut world demand by a quarter. In response, the US chemical company Du Pont, the world's largest producer, established the Alliance for Responsible CFC Policy (ARCFCP) with the stated aim of preventing, or at least mitigating, any further regulatory threat to the CFC business. However, following the discovery of the ozone hole, Du Pont argued for a proactive, international regulatory policy to restrict CFC production: "it would be prudent to limit worldwide emissions of CFCs while science continues to work to provide better guidance to policy-makers".

There are several possible explanations for this apparent change of policy. The unilateral decision to ban non-essential CFC use in the US clearly benefited Du Pont's overseas competitors. Japan and Europe continued to use CFCs in aerosols. The promotion of an internationally agreed initiative would help to create a level playing field. The 1978 ban also resulted in an industry price war as capital-intensive producers fought to maintain market share in an industry dominated by fixed costs. This proved collectively disastrous for producers. CFCs were substitutes for few other chemicals and the share of CFCs in the cost of their end products is negligible. Consequently there was no corresponding increase in market demand in response to falling prices. CFC production had become something of a 'cash trap' by the early 1980s, at best earning low returns. Another theory suggests that Du Pont may have been ahead of its competitors in developing CFC replacements and would therefore profit from a forced conversion. Or, perhaps, the company recognized the damage being caused by its products and was making a self-sacrificing ethically motivated decision?

Following the signing of the Montreal Protocol, Du Pont was faced with three options. It could, as it had earlier promised, exit the CFC business unilaterally and promptly.[9] It could ignore the promise and work to meet the commitments under the Montreal Protocol. Or it could lead an industry-wide initiative to accelerate the reductions. In the end the company announced in March 1988 that it would unilaterally phase out CFC production over a ten-year period.

Why did Du Pont take this strategy? Gabel argues that Du Pont's shift from resisting to abetting a forced reduction in CFC production was in fact extremely enlightened and clearly in the company's best interest. In contrast to measures aimed at reducing demand, supply restrictions – implemented through a system of tradable permits – were likely to force up CFC prices and enable producers to make 'economic rents' or excess profits. In 1987 ARCFCP forecast that quantity controls on CFC-11 would push its price up 400 per cent. The EPA predicted that producer profits attributable to its quota policy would be between $1.8 and $7.2 billion. Consequently, a voluntary ten-year phase-out provided years of continued production, the prospects of high profits and plenty of time to introduce replacements.

In the end the EPA did opt for a system of tradable permits. However, the US Government taxed CFCs to reduce quota rent and demand fell along with supply. Although demand was price-inelastic, users were facing more than potential price rises: they were facing the eventual disappearance of CFCs at any price. Anticipation of this significant market change forced users to explore other options and, in some cases, develop alternative processes not requiring the use of CFCs.[10]

Following Du Pont's announcement that it would phase out CFC production, most of the major producers followed suit in the period March to December 1988. Du Pont also confirmed its commitment to produce HCFCs and HFCs as CFC substitutes, reflecting research and development and related patents dating back to the 1970s. According to Landis Gabel, Du Pont's strategy was to push users rapidly into employing already available HCFCs. Once users had invested in this conversion they would be locked into the chemicals and would therefore be allies in any future regulatory battle. To support this, Du Pont was in favour of CFC recovery and destruction, rather than recycling, and maintained high CFC prices to encourage an earlier switch to HCFCs. This is in sharp contrast to ICI's strategy.

ICI

Six months after Du Pont's decision to phase out CFCs, ICI announced that it would phase out its CFC production by 1995. Unlike Du Pont, ICI decided not to invest in HCFC production but, instead, to opt for HFCs as CFC replacements. CFC factories were closed, ICI gave its production quota to Akzo, another CFC producer, and multi-million pound HFC production facilities were opened in the early 1990s. ICI encouraged prospective customers to bypass 'transitional' HCFCs and actively promoted the use of its KLEA range of HFCs as 'ozone benign alternative' refrigerants to both CFCs and HCFCs. To support this strategy ICI maintained a relatively low price for CFCs through their phase-out period in order to delay as long as possible user demands for the first available alternative: HCFCs. The company also encouraged the recycling of CFCs, thereby prolonging the effective lifetime of CFC vintage equipment. According to Gabel, it was also in ICI's interest to create an atmosphere of doubt, fear and uncertainty over the future availability of HCFCs to discourage investment. Perhaps with this in mind, the company argued in 1990 to limit HCFC production immediately. With the current agreement under the Montreal Protocol to phase out HCFCs by 2030, including a European agreement to phase them out by 2015 and a firm commitment not to legislate specifically to control HFC production, ICI may have backed the best strategy.

The Use of Environmental Regulation as a Competitive Tool

The cases illustrated above suggest that environmental regulation can be used as competitive tool. Stricter and more ambitious legislation can give an individual company within a sector an edge over competitors. Not only did Du Pont's actions pave the way for enhanced profits, they also pre-empted further and possibly more severe controls by the regulators. In addition, they gave the company a 'first mover' advantage. As discussed above, Du Pont had research and patents for CFC replacements dating back to the 1970s. By acting first, the company sought to maintain its advantage. An initial position of unified industrial opposition to controls on CFC production gave way as individual producers pursued alternative strategies depending upon their own particular circumstances. While Du Pont argued for the unrestricted use of both HCFCs and HFCs until sometime between 2030 and 2050, ICI successfully argued that HCFC production should be limited immediately, irrespective of any contemplated mandatory phase-out. As detailed above, the 1992 Copenhagen amendments to the Montreal Protocol require HCFC production to be capped in 1996 and to be completely phased out by 2030 (the Vienna meeting has not substantially altered this position). The European decision to phase out HCFCs by 2015, 15 years ahead of the Montreal deadline, also suggests that there may be a potential for creating competitive advantage by playing one compound off against another in 'the corridors of the regulatory authorities', as well as in the market place. It seems likely that the Montreal Protocol may be brought into line with the most restrictive country in future negotiations.

Box 3.1 Voluntary agreements on the control of HFCs

In the run-up to the first Conference of the Parties to the United Nations Framework Convention on Climate Change (UNFCCC) (discussed in the following sections) the Air Conditioning and Refrigeration Industry Board (ACRIB) – representing nine trade associations – issued a position paper urging the Government to argue against any tighter controls than those already agreed upon. The signatories represented both producers – ICI, Du Pont, Elf Atochem and Rhone-Poulenc – and users, including ACRIB, the British Aerosol Manufacturers Association, the British Refrigeration Association, and the Cold Storage and Distribution Federation. The industry maintained that further controls would harm UK competitiveness in international markets and threaten investment in environmental improvements.

Following heavy investment in HFCs as substitutes for ozone-depleting chemicals, the UK refrigeration and air conditioning industry in particular expressed deep concern at the prospect of any further controls.[11] However, recognizing that their commitment under the UN Convention on Climate Change to stabilize greenhouse gas emissions at their 1990 levels by 2000 applied to hydrofluorocarbons (HFCs), the UK Government announced in early 1994 that it planned to control the use of these gases through voluntary agreements agreed with industry. HFC producers and their customers hoped that HFCs would be regarded as part of a 'basket' of greenhouse gases, allowing trade-offs between increasing their use while decreasing the use of other gases.

For a year and a half the refrigeration and air conditioning sector, the largest potential user, refused to even enter into talks with Government on the basis that such negotiations would be a precursor to legislation. However, despite considerable resistance and industry-instigated delays, a number of voluntary agreements were reached at the end of 1995. These included agreements with the aerosol, foam and fire-fighting equipment industries. ACRIB felt unable to sign an agreement on behalf of the refrigeration and air conditioning industries, so a much weaker 'declaration of intent' was eventually agreed. The terms of the declaration include a commitment by the Government that it has no intention of banning the production or use of HFCs in order to meet its commitments under the UNFCCC up to 2000. In return, industry has stated that it intends to contribute to the climate change strategy by encouraging various practices aimed at reducing leakages and inappropriate use of HFCs amongst its members. The voluntary agreements are also scant on firm commitments and contain several qualifying statements such as: "the use of HCFCs may have to increase if pressures on the (aerosol) industry to reduce emissions of VOCs intensify."

Other countries have attempted to completely by-pass both CFC substitutes, such as HCFCs, and HFCs. Major German refrigerator manufacturers have been converting the majority of their domestic ranges to run on propane and butane refrigerants. Companies such as Bosch-Siemens and Lieherr have effectively sought to develop an environmental edge for their products and market them on this basis. In contrast, Hotpoint has opted to design refrigerators that use a blend of HCFCs and HFC-134a as refrigerants. The company has stated that without the consumer support for CFC- and HFC-free products, UK firms are unlikely to move quickly down the propane and butane route without legislation.[12]

Climate Change

Summary

Human activities are substantially increasing the atmospheric concentrations of several greenhouse gases (GHGs). By adding to the natural greenhouse effect, anthropogenic emissions of these gases, principally carbon dioxide (CO_2) from the combustion of fossil fuels and the destruction of forests, methane (CH_4) from agriculture and nitrous oxide (N_2O) from agriculture and industry, are increasing global mean surface temperatures. The Intergovernmental Panel on Climate Change (IPCC), set up by the World Meteorological Organization (WMO) and the United Nations Environment Programme (UNEP) in 1988 to examine and report back on the issue of global warming, estimates that global mean surface temperatures will increase by some 1 to 3.5°C by the year 2100 compared to 1990. This rate of warming will probably be greater than any seen in the last 10,000 years (see Box 3.3). This enhanced greenhouse effect, or global warming, is expected to alter atmospheric and ocean temperatures and associated circulation and weather patterns.[13] The severity and frequency of extreme weather events are expected to increase, precipitation patterns are forecast to change and sea level is anticipated to increase by some 15 to 95 centimetres by the end of the next century.[14]

Despite the uncertainty surrounding climate change, particularly with regard to the timing, magnitude and regional patterns of climate change impacts, the implications of global climate change are severe. Economic activity, particularly agriculture, could be profoundly affected. By 1990 a series of international conferences issued urgent calls for a global treaty to address the problem. This resulted in the adoption of the United Nations Framework Convention on Climate Change (UNFCCC), adopted at the 1992 Rio Earth Summit. The ultimate objective of the Convention is the "stabilization of greenhouse gas concentrations in the atmosphere at a level that would prevent dangerous anthropogenic interference with the climate system." Most Annex I Parties (OECD and countries in transition), including the European Union, have interpreted the wording of the Convention as a commitment to return their GHG emissions to their 1990 levels by 2000. However, as it stands, the Climate Convention includes no internationally binding obligations to reduce anthropogenic emissions of GHGs to any specific level in any set year. It is also generally accepted that present commitments to reduce GHG emissions will be inadequate to meet the Convention's ultimate objective.

The first Conference of the Parties (COP-1) to the Climate Convention, held in Berlin in March 1995, failed to make any commitment to reduce GHG emissions beyond 2000 – despite concluding that the present commitments of developed countries to reduce their GHG emissions to 1990 levels by the year 2000 were inadequate.[15] Instead, an agreement was reached, generally referred to as the Berlin Mandate, to make a decision by 1997 on how to achieve emission reductions beyond 2000. This was in spite of demands from the Association of Small Island States (AoSIS), which called for OECD countries to cut emissions by at least 20 per cent, and advice from the scientific working group of the IPCC. The second Conference of the

Parties (COP-2), held in Geneva in July 1996, reaffirmed that stronger commitments were needed but again deferred any decisions on what those commitments might be. It is now hoped that a protocol, or other legal instrument, detailing specific and timetabled emission reductions for developed countries beyond 2000 will be adopted at the third Conference of the Parties (COP-3) in Kyoto, Japan, in December 1997. Recognizing the inadequacy of current commitments, the EU has set a goal to reduce its total emissions of a basket of greenhouse gases by 15 per cent by the year 2010, compared to emission levels in 1990. This is the negotiating position the EU intends to adopt at Kyoto. At a meeting of EU Environment Ministers in March 1997, negotiations have so far secured the agreement of Member States for an overall 10 per cent reduction. The additional 5 per cent reduction required to attain the 15 per cent target reduction in global EU emissions will be negotiated after Kyoto.

The UK ratified the Climate Convention in December 1993 and pledged to return greenhouse gas emissions to their 1990 level by 2000. Despite the failure of several of the Government's initiatives intended to reduce UK CO_2 emissions by 10 million tonnes of carbon (MtC) – the estimated required reduction to achieve stabilization – by 2000, such as VAT on domestic fuel, the Energy Saving Trust and the Making a Corporate Commitment Campaign, the latest official UK energy projections indicate that the UK will be able to meet this commitment comfortably. Emissions of CO_2 are now forecast to be some 6 to 14 MtC (4 to 8 per cent) below their 1990 level by 2000. These revised predictions are based on anticipated reductions in the carbon intensity of electricity supply and assume that the revised expectations of savings from measures under the climate plan are also realized. The commitment is more likely to be met by accident rather than design.

The predicted fall in CO_2 emissions, largely a result of the UK's dash for gas and levels of economic activity, prompted the Secretary for the Environment to advocate that Annex I Parties to the Convention should agree to cut emissions of all greenhouse gases to between 5 to 10 per cent below 1990 levels by 2010. Subsequently, the UK has stated its commitment to reduce its emissions by the full 10 per cent by 2010, and following the General Election of May 1997, the UK's new Labour Government has pledged to reduce UK CO_2 emissions by 20 per cent by 2010. Other countries have made more ambitious commitments. Germany, for example, intends to reduce its 1990 CO_2 emissions by 25 per cent by 2010.

In the late 1980s and the early part of this decade, global warming and the prospects of catastrophic global climate change dominated the environment debate. The issue received extensive media coverage and political attention and was forecast to be the largest area for environmental spending in the decade to the year 2000. Some reports suggested that the UK alone would spend in excess of £45 billion by the turn of the century on measures directed at mitigating and dealing with global warming.[16] This is a sum greater than the estimated total spending on the environmental issues of water quality and waste management combined. By 1996 the priority attached to global warming seemed to decline. Although there is still a great deal of public concern over the issue, industry seems largely unaffected. To date, the predicted expenditure on environmental goods and services has also not been made.

The Issue: What Is Global Warming?

The Science: The Natural Greenhouse Effect and Radiative Forcing

The ultimate energy source for all weather and climate is radiation from the sun (called solar or short-wave radiation). About one third of incoming solar radiation is reflected back into space and the rest absorbed by the earth. This energy is then redistributed by the atmosphere and ocean and reradiated to space at longer (thermal, terrestrial or infrared) wavelengths. Various naturally occurring greenhouse gases in the atmosphere, principally water vapour, CO_2, methane, ozone, and nitrous oxide, trap a proportion of the outgoing radiation. This reabsorption of energy occurs because the gases are relatively transparent to the incoming short-wave radiation but absorb the long-wave (infrared) radiation re-emitted from the earth, effectively acting as a blanket by keeping a portion of the heat in (hence greenhouse gases). Because of this asymmetry, the earth, its atmosphere and its oceans are some 33°C warmer than they would be in the absence of such gases – that is, the natural greenhouse effect maintains the conditions necessary to support life.

As detailed in Table 3.1, human activities, principally the combustion of fossil fuels and the destruction of forests, are substantially increasing atmospheric concentrations of greenhouse gases. Consequently, anthropogenic emissions enhance the natural greenhouse effect, resulting in an additional warming of the earth's surface, or 'global warming'.[17]

Table 3.1 Principal greenhouse gases, sources and atmospheric concentrations

Greenhouse gas	Principal sources	Pre-industrial atmospheric concentrations	Current atmospheric concentrations and rate of annual increase	Direct percentage contribution of the gases to radiative warming[18]
CO_2	Fossil fuel burning (c.77%); deforestation (c.23%)	280 ppmv	356 ppmv (0.5%)	64%
CH_4	Rice paddies, enteric fermentation, gas leakage	800 ppbv	1720 ppbv (0.9%)	19%
N_2O	Biomass burning, fertilizer use, fossil fuel combusion	280 ppbv	310 ppbv (0.8%)	6%

Source: adapted from IPCC 1994 and IPCC 1995[19]

The Effects of Enhanced Global Warming: Changing the Earth's Climate

The enhanced greenhouse effect is expected to alter atmospheric and oceanic temperatures, and associated circulation and weather patterns. Increases in global mean temperature at the earth's surface are not expected to be felt uniformly over the globe. Surface air is expected to warm faster over land than over oceans; the warming is predicted to be 50 to 100 per cent greater than the global mean in high northern latitudes in winter. It will be less than the global mean in regions of sea-ice in summer. Altered rainfall patterns together with sea level rises could have a profound effect on economic activity and agricultural production for particular locations.[20] Precipitation is predicted to increase on average in mid- to high-latitude continents in winter. Another possible consequence of climate change could be a shift in large-scale weather patterns such as depression tracks, which could substantially alter the extremes and variability of regional weather patterns. Climate change may also increase the frequency and intensity of severe storms.

Box 3.2 The scale of the problem: principal sources of anthropogenic greenhouse gas emissions

Carbon Dioxide

The two main sources of CO_2 are fossil fuel combustion and deforestation. Cement production is a further important source. According to the IPCC's 1994 report, annual average anthropogenic emissions of CO_2 between 1980 and 1989 amounted to about 7.1 GtC (gigatonnes of carbon).[21] Seventy-seven per cent of these emissions resulted from the combustion of fossil fuels and cement manufacture. After allowing for uptake by the oceans, Northern forest regrowth and other terrestrial sinks (eg CO_2 fertilization), anthropogenic emissions are estimated to have added some three GtC annually to the atmosphere. Although emission estimates have varied, these figures help to illustrate the magnitude of anthropogenic emissions. Anthropogenic emissions are, however, very small in comparison to natural sources and sinks of CO_2 which account for 97 per cent or more of all sources and sinks.[22]

Methane

Total annual global emissions of methane amount to some 535 Tg of CH_4 (535 million tonnes) annually.[23] Anthropogenic sources, principally from agriculture (rice paddy cultivation, animal husbandry), biomass burning, landfills and fossil fuel production and combustion, account for about 70 per cent of this total. Of this, agriculture accounts for about two-thirds. The main natural sources are emissions from wetlands, termites and from the ocean. Annually, some 40 million tonnes (Tg) of methane are added to the atmosphere.

Nitrous Oxide

Nitrous oxide is an important long-lived greenhouse gas. The principal anthropogenic sources include emissions from cultivated soils, biomass burning, stationary combustion and from the production of adipic and nitric acid. There is a great deal of uncertainty surrounding the various sources and sinks of nitrous oxide. The IPCC Scientific Committee reported in its 1992 assessment that "the sum of all known anthropogenic and natural sources of N_2O is still barely sufficient to balance the calculated atmospheric sink or to explain the observed increase in the atmospheric abundance of N_2O." The atmospheric load of N_2O is calculated to be growing by about 3 to 4.5 TgN annually.[24]

Box 3.3 The IPCC's conclusions

The Intergovernmental Panel on Climate Change (IPCC), set up by the World Meteorological Organization (WMO) and the United Nations Environment Programme (UNEP) in 1988 to examine and report back on the issue of global warming, estimates that:

- Global mean surface temperatures will increase by some 1 to 3.5°C by the year 2100 compared to 1990 with a 'best estimate' of 2°C (taking into account both the effects of greenhouse gases and aerosols). In all cases the average rate of warming would probably be greater than any seen in the past 10,000 years.
- Average sea levels will rise as a result of the thermal expansion of the oceans and the melting of glaciers and ice sheets by between 0.15 and 0.95 metres by the year 2100 with a 'best estimate' (taking into account both the effects of greenhouse gases and aerosols) of 50 centimetres. Because of the thermal inertia of the oceans, sea level is anticipated to continue to rise for several centuries thereafter, even if concentrations of greenhouse gases are stabilized by that time.

These estimates are based on the IPCC's mid-range emission scenario, which shows global CO_2 emissions rising threefold by 2100 (to around 20 Gt of carbon per year). This would give a CO_2 concentration of over 700 ppmv by 2100 with further increases thereafter. Even if CO_2 emissions were maintained at near current (1994) levels, they would still lead to a nearly constant rate of increase in atmospheric concentrations for at least two centuries, reaching about 500 ppmv (approaching twice the pre-industrial concentration of 280 ppmv) by the end of the twenty-first century.

In order to stabilize atmospheric concentrations of CO_2, CH_4 and N_2O at current levels, substantial reductions in anthropogenic emissions would be required. Returning emissions to their 1990 levels would not be sufficient. The IPCC has estimated that stabilization of CO_2, CH_4 and N_2O concentrations at today's levels would require a 50 to 70 per cent, 8 per cent and more than 50 per cent reduction in anthropogenic emissions respectively. Immediate cuts would be required because the atmospheric concentrations of long-lived gases adjust only slowly to changes in emissions.[25]

Legislation: The United Nations Framework Convention on Climate Change

During the 1980s, the scientific community increasingly recognized that in the absence of any attempt to reduce anthropogenic-enhanced global warming, the earth was heading for an increase in global average temperatures unprecedented in human history. Mounting scientific evidence about the possibility of global climate change led to heightened public concern, fuelled by somewhat sensationalist and alarmist media coverage of the issue, and demands for action. By 1990, a series of international conferences had issued urgent calls for a global treaty to address the problem, culminating in the adoption of the United Nations Framework Convention on Climate Change (UNFCCC).

Despite the great uncertainty surrounding the likely impacts of global warming, particularly with regard to the timing, magnitude and regional patterns of climate change, concern over the potentially disastrous consequences of continued increases in anthropogenic emissions of GHGs resulted in over 155 countries signing the UNFCCC at the 1992 United Nations Conference on Environment and Development. The Treaty entered into force on 21 March 1994.

International Obligations: Commitments Under the UNFCCC

The ultimate objective of the Climate Convention is "the stabilization of greenhouse gas concentrations in the atmosphere at a level that would prevent dangerous anthropogenic interference with the climate system" (Article 2). The Article goes on to state that "such a level should be achieved within a timeframe sufficient to allow ecosystems to adapt naturally to climate change, to ensure that food production is not threatened and to enable economic development to proceed in a sustainable manner" (UNFCCC, Article 2). Signatories or Parties to the Convention are required to adopt measures to limit anthropogenic emissions of all greenhouse gases not controlled by the Montreal Protocol. Parties are specifically required to promote, cooperate and apply practices and processes that control, reduce or prevent anthropogenic emissions of GHGs in all relevant sectors.

Reflecting the intrinsic difficulties involved in international treaty negotiations, the Climate Convention (as it stands) contains no internationally binding obligations to reduce anthropogenic emissions of GHGs to any specific level in any set year. Despite this, most Parties, including the European Commission, interpreted the wording of the Convention as a commitment to return their GHG emissions to their 1990 levels by 2000. However, few Annex I countries are actually expected to realize this aim. Based on current trends and emission projections, most will be unable to return their CO_2 emission to 1990 levels by the year 2000 without implementing additional policy measures.

In March 1997, the EU set a target to reduce total EU emissions of a basket of greenhouse gases by 15 per cent by the year 2010 compared to emissions in 1990 (see below). Although unable to reach an agreement on how this 15 per cent reduction is to be achieved (current negotiations have only secured the commitment by Member States for an overall 10 per cent reduction), the EU intends to adopt the 15 per cent target reduction as the EU's negotiating position in Kyoto this December, at the third Conference of the Parties.

The UK's Climate Strategy

The UK ratified the Climate Convention in December 1993. Under the Treaty, the UK's Climate Programme "sets out measures aimed at returning emissions of each of the main greenhouse gases to 1990 levels by 2000."[26] Since CO_2 emissions account for over 87 per cent of the UK's anthropogenic emissions of greenhouse gases, based on direct global warming potentials, the following review concentrates on the UK's strategy for reducing CO_2 emissions. Table 3.2 details 1990 baseline emissions for each of the three main greenhouse gases, including 1992 forecast emissions for the year 2000 (CO_2 emissions are per *Energy Paper 59*; see p. 45).

Despite substantial reductions in the forecast emissions of methane and nitrous oxide, the UK – unlike the Netherlands or Germany – did not adopt more ambitious reduction targets for these gases but simply stuck to the position of returning emission levels to 1990 levels by 2000. The programme did not state the UK's position beyond 2000. However, following downward revisions to forecast UK energy demand, the Secretary of State for the Environment subsequently advocated that all Annex I Parties should agree to cut emissions of all GHGs to between 5 and 10 per cent below 1990 levels by 2010. The UK has since adopted a target to reduce its emissions of CO_2, CH_4 and N_2O by 10 per cent by 2010, compared to emission levels in 1990. The UK reaffirmed this commitment at the March 1997 meeting of EU Environment Ministers despite calls from the Presidency for the UK to cut its emissions by 20 per cent in order to help the EU achieve its overall goal of a 15 per cent reduction in total EU emissions by 2010.*

Table 3.2 UK Greenhouse Gas Emission Inventory and
Forecast Emissions (million tonnes)

Greenhouse gas	1990 Emissions	Forecast emissions 2000	Percentage change 2000 emissions to to 1990 emissions	Relative direct contribution to global warming 1990 emissions[27]
CO_2	158	158	0%	87.3%
CH_4	5	4.4	(12%)	8.1%
N_2O	0.11	0.03	(73%)	4.4%

Source: adapted from *Climate Change: The UK Programme*, HMSO, 1994
Note: bracketed figures denote negative values

The UK's programme "is based on a partnership approach" and seeks "to achieve savings as cost effectively as possible."[28] The strategy places a strong emphasis on voluntary measures, particularly in the domestic and business sectors, and the provision of information. Where "instruments" are used to "stimulate improvements in energy efficiency", the programme states that "the Government is adopting a presumption in favour of economic instruments rather than regulation." Figure 3.1 summarizes the UK's original CO_2 emission reduction strategy as detailed in the 1994 Climate Change Programme. As discussed below, many of these anticipated savings had to be substantially revised downwards in 1995. These revisions are also shown in Figure 3.1.

* Following the May 1997 election, the UK's new Labour Government has confirmed its commitment to reducing UK CO_2 emissions by 20 per cent by 2010.

Sector	Expected reduction in MtC emissions by 2000[1]	Revised expected reduction in MtC emissions by 2000[2]
Energy consumption in the home ■ VAT on domestic fuel ■ new Energy Savings Trust ■ energy efficiency advice and information ■ eco-labelling ■ EC SAVE Programme (standards for household appliances) ■ revision of building regulations to strengthen energy efficiency	4	1.4
Energy consumption by business ■ energy efficiency and information including Making a Corporate Commitment, Best Practice Programme, Regional Energy Efficiency Offices, Energy Management Assistance Scheme ■ Energy Savings Trust schemes for small businesses ■ Energy Design Advice Scheme ■ possible EC SAVE Scheme (standards for office machinery) ■ revision of building regulations to strengthen energy efficiency	2.5	1.9
Energy consumption in the public sector ■ targets for central and local government and public sector bodies	1	0.8
Transport ■ increases in road fuel duties and commitment to real increases of at least 5% on average in future budgets	2.5	3
Renewables	–	0.4
Total	10	7.5

Source: [1]adapted from *Climate Change: The UK Programme*, HMSO, 1994
[2]*Climate Change: The UK Programme – Progress Report on Carbon Dioxide Emissions*, DoE[31] 1995.

Figure 3.1 Development of the UK CO_2 Abatement Strategy Savings

Specific measures aimed at reducing industrial emissions of CO_2 are largely absent in the UK's climate strategy. Instead, the programme has two main elements to reduce CO_2 emissions from the business sector: the Making a Corporate Commitment Campaign and "provision of information and advice" to companies on how to improve energy efficiency. Overall savings of 2.5 million tonnes of carbon (MtC) from the business sector were anticipated.

In 1995 these savings were revised down to 0.9 MtC, or just 12 per cent of total anticipated savings. Much of the savings were due to come from the Energy Efficiency Office's Best Practice Programme and the Energy Management Assistance Scheme. However, uptake of this scheme has proved disappointing and the expected CO_2 savings were cut several times before the scheme was eventually absorbed into a wider project: the Small Company Environmental Energy Management Assistance Scheme (SCEEMAS), which promotes environmental management systems. Despite the Government's continued confidence in the Making a Corporate Commitment Campaign, it seems likely that this part of the strategy will also be unable to deliver the anticipated savings originally hoped for.

Launched in 1991, the campaign sought to get the UK's top 2000 businesses to commit themselves to setting energy savings targets and to report their performance publicly. To date, awareness of the campaign remains low and from a comprehensive survey carried out by March Consulting, covering 700 of the 1850 or so signatories, it appears that only 70 per cent of the companies involved in the campaign have an energy policy and only 75 per cent have set performance improvement targets.

The UK's strategy placed a strong emphasis on reducing energy consumption in the domestic sector. Forty per cent of the 10 MtC targeted reduction in CO_2 emissions would be realized from measures aimed at reducing energy consumption in the home. However, in the Government's 1995 *Progress Report on the Climate Strategy*, savings from the residential sector have now been revised down from 4 MtC to 1.4 MtC.[29] The main reason for this substantial reduction is due to revisions in the anticipated savings from the work of the Energy Saving Trust (EST) and the Government's failure to raise VAT on domestic fuel and power to the full rate of 17.5 per cent.

The EST's work in overseeing financial incentives, loan options and customer advice on energy efficiency measures had been expected to result in savings of 2.5 MtC – a quarter of the overall targeted reduction. To achieve this the EST was expected to oversee a dramatic increase in energy efficiency investments to £400 million in 1998, the funding coming from levies on gas and electricity consumers. However, the decision by the electricity regulator to limit spending on energy efficiency by the regional electricity companies (RECs) to £100 million over four years, and the gas regulator's decision to block a levy on gas bills because it was akin to a tax, has left the EST cash-starved. As a result, the Trust now expects to save just 0.3 MtC by 2000. The extension of VAT at 17.5 per cent to domestic fuel and power was expected to save 1.5 MtC. Now fixed at 8 per cent, savings resulting from the imposition of VAT on domestic fuel and power are only anticipated to be in the order of 0.4 MtC. Even this may be an overestimate given recent actions by the gas and electricity regulators to reduce domestic energy prices.[30] Following the July 1997 mini-Budget in which the new Labour Government reduced VAT on domestic fuel and power to 5 per cent, it seems likely that this estimate will have to be revised downwards.

Other measures are also in doubt. A targeted expansion of combined heat and power

(CHP) capacity from four gigawatts (GW) to five GW by 2000 was anticipated to result in savings of one MtC. However, uncertainties over the operation of the liberalized electricity and gas markets has cast doubts over achieving this target. By mid-1995, the UK's CHP capacity was approximately 3.4 GW, spread across some 1200 sites.[32] Despite this, the revised figures still anticipate 1 MtC of savings from this source.

The commitment to increase road fuel duty by 5 per cent per annum to 1999 was expected to reduce CO_2 emissions by 2.5 MtC. However, the long-awaited Royal Commission on Environmental Pollution's report on transport and the environment disagreed with the Government's estimation and suggested that a 5 per cent increase would bring CO_2 savings of only 1.4 MtC by 2000 – over 1 million tonnes short of the Government's expectations. The report called for fuel duty to be raised by 9 per cent per year until 2005 (see Chapter 4). Despite this, the Government's revised figure for CO_2 savings from transport has actually been increased to 3 MtC.

Revised Energy Projections

Despite the shortfall in anticipated CO_2 emission savings from the UK strategy, it seems likely, according to figures detailed in *Energy Paper 65* (EP65), that the UK will comfortably meet its international commitment to return CO_2 emissions to their 1990 level by 2000.[33] According to modelling work carried out by the Department of Trade and Industry (DTI), the UK's CO_2 emissions are now expected to fall by between 6 and 13 MtC from the 1990 level by 2000.[34] EP65 has six scenarios for economic growth and energy prices. Under its central growth low-price scenario forecast CO_2 emissions in 2000 are 150 MtC, 8 MtC below 1990 levels.

Official projections for CO_2 emissions have tended to fluctuate. The DTI's current estimates for reduced emissions are based on several key assumptions, many of which are open to debate. In the short term, the main factors include the expectation that gas-fired power will continue to squeeze coal out of the market and that the contribution from existing nuclear power stations will increase.[35] In the longer term, reduced emissions are anticipated due to a substantial fall in forecast energy demand. The revised forecasts also assume that the Climate Change Strategy will still deliver reduced CO_2 emissions in the order of 8 MtC.

Table 3.3 illustrates the extent to which forecast CO_2 emissions fluctuate. The table details forecast emissions from *Energy Paper 58* (1989), *Energy Paper 59* (1992) and *Energy Paper 65* (1995). The figures disclosed are based on the DTI's central growth low-price emission scenario.

Table 3.3: Forecast UK CO_2 emissions

Energy Paper	1990	1995	2000	2005	2020
EP 58 (1989)	167	188	202	211	233
EP 59 (1992)	160	159	170	183	221
EP 65 (1995)	158	–	150	162	184

Source: *Energy Papers* 59 and 65 (DTI) and *Energy Paper 58* (Department of Energy)

Latest International Developments

Despite demands to make firm commitments to cut GHG emissions after 2000, the first Conference of the Parties (COP-1) to the UN Climate Convention, held in Berlin in March 1995, only managed to achieve a somewhat vague agreement to make a decision by 1997 on what action may be required to achieve emission reductions beyond 2000. Uncertainties in the science were seized upon and effectively used by the fossil fuel industry, oil-producing states and the JUSCANZ alliance (made up of Japan, the US and Canada, Australia and New Zealand) to delay the debate on further commitments and thwart demands from the Association of Small Island States (AoSIS), among others, for firmer commitments. AoSIS called for a 20 per cent reduction in OECD emission levels by 2005 (some Pacific atolls may face land losses of 80 per cent or more, based on the IPCC's mid-range emission projections); Germany reiterated its commitment to reduce CO_2 emissions by 25 per cent by 2005; and despite no unilateral commitment, the UK urged all developed nations to reduce all GHGs by between 5 and 10 per cent by 2010.

By the second Conference of the Parties (COP-2), held in Geneva in July 1996, attitudes began to change. Ministers from over 100 countries endorsed the 1995 *IPCC Second Assessment Report* "as currently the most comprehensive and authoritative assessment of the science of climate change, its impacts and response options now available." They also stated that the Report "should provide the scientific basis for urgently strengthening action to limit and reduce emissions of greenhouse gases."[36] The US also adopted a more positive approach to the negotiations, acknowledging that the science now called "us to take urgent action" and endorsing the need for binding targets.[37]

In March 1997 the EU adopted a target to reduce total EU emisisons of the principal greenhouse gases by 15 per cent by the year 2010 compared to emisison levels in 1990. The current agreement allows for some Member States to increase their emissions; for example, Greece will be allowed to increase emissions by 30 per cent over the period, while other countries, such as Germany, aim to reduce their emissions substantially. Negotiations have so far secured the commitment of Member States only to an overall 10 per cent reduction in EU emissions. Despite this, the EU has adopted the 15 per cent target as its negotiating position for the third Conference of the Parties (COP-3), to be held in Kyoto this December. Although many obstacles remain, it is now hoped that a protocol, or other legal instrument, detailing specific and timetabled emission reductions for developed countries beyond 2000 will be reached and adopted at this meeting.

Industry's Response

In the late 1980s, science predicted that global climate change would become the dominant environmental issue facing industry. In the decade to 2000, some forecasts suggested that spending on measures aimed at dealing with climate change could exceed £45 billion in the UK alone. Despite these predictions, industry seems largely unaffected by the issue, and the predicted expenditure on environmental goods and services has not been made to date. However, anticipation of policy measures aimed at dealing with climate change, such as a carbon/energy tax, may have affected corporate investment decisions.

Industry has not adopted a unified position on climate change. Some parts of US industry maintain that in the absence of conclusive evidence any action is unwarranted. In contrast, perhaps reflecting greater European public concern and awareness over the issue, European industry has tended to adopt a more neutral, diplomatic position. Although opposed to the implementation of taxes and other measures that could impact on competitiveness, industry within Europe does advocate action that can be taken on a 'no regrets basis'. The global oil industry, not surprisingly, is sceptical of claims that the world is on the brink of a catastrophic increase in global temperatures and is therefore not in favour of action.

The remainder of this section focuses on one policy area – energy efficiency standards for electrical appliances – where industrial opposition has been particularly effective in delaying and weakening proposed legislation. A detailed review of industry's response to the European Commission's proposals for a carbon/energy tax is provided in Chapter 9. Box 3.4 concludes this section with a review of voluntary agreements between industry and government in Germany and The Netherlands and contrasts the apparent success of these initiatives with the failure to implement similar schemes in the UK.

The Abandonment and Resurrection of Energy Efficiency Standards for Applicances

Several years after its first appearance, EC Energy Ministers finally agreed at the end of 1995 to a common position on a draft Directive on energy efficiency standards for refrigerators. The common position, formally adopted by the Council of Ministers in March 1996, called for a 15 per cent improvement in efficiency standards over three years – a considerably weaker target than both the European Commission and Parliament had proposed. In addition, the acceptance of last-minute amendments to allow more lenient targets for appliances made for hotter countries (Southern Europe) could substantially reduce the effectiveness of the weakened Directive even further. The Directive was finally approved on July 25 1996.

The slow progress, delays and compromise associated with this Directive provide a good example of how effective industrial opposition, stonewalling and lobbying can be at weakening proposed legislation. At one point, in March 1995, the EC announced that they had actually stopped work on this and other directives aimed at imposing minimum energy efficiency standards for appliances, following intense lobbying and protracted negotiations with manufacturers. These measures formed a major part of the EC's policy to promote energy efficiency and to reduce CO_2 emissions under the SAVE Programme (Specific Action for Vigorous Energy Efficiency).

The original proposal from the Commission called on manufacturers to achieve a minimum 10 per cent improvement in the energy efficiency of refrigerators by 2000. Members of the European Parliament (MEPs) derided this as "astonishingly unambitious" and voted for an amendment to achieve a minimum 20 per cent improvement within two years of the Directive being adopted, with a second target of 40 per cent improvement within five years. The European Parliament's Committee on Research, Technological Development and Energy pointed out that refrigerators had almost reached the Commission's proposal to increase minimum energy efficiency by 10 per cent compared to 1992 – hence more ambitious targets were required. Industry's initial response was to offer to cease production in the sector containing the 10 per cent least energy-efficient appliances, which would have given an effective average improvement of about 2 per cent.[38] The approved Directive now requires a 15 per cent improvement in the energy efficiency of refrigerators by September 1999.[39]

The Commission's attention to the issue of efficiency standards was prompted by Dutch plans in 1992 to introduce unilaterally measures requiring a 15 per cent reduction in the average energy consumption of appliances on the market within ten months of their introduction. The Commission's response was to order the Dutch to suspend their regulations because of their potential to obstruct free trade, and agreed instead to propose EC-wide mandatory standards within a year. According to the Commission, if their original proposal (based on a 10 per cent improvement) took effect in 2000, energy consumption in domestic refrigeration would be reduced by 40 terrawatt hours (tWh) per year. This is equivalent to the current electricity consumption of Portugal and Ireland. The savings would avoid the emission of 17 million tonnes per year of CO_2.

One of the reasons for the slow progress of the Directive was due to the Commission discussing the possibility of voluntary agreements – in place of legislation – with the European Trade Association for Domestic Electrical-Appliance Manufacturers (CECED). An offer for a voluntary agreement was made in 1993 but no satisfactory answer was received.[40] Industry's 'offer' was apparently even lower than the original 10 per cent improvement proposed by the Commission. In contrast, measures introduced in the US in 1993 required a 25 to 30 per cent improvement in energy consumption by refrigerators. These have now been met with only a 1 per cent reported increase in the cost to consumers.[41] At the time of implementing the measures, only 7 of 2114 models on the market reached the standards.

The last-minute amendment agreed by Ministers allows derogation from the targets for refrigerators manufactured for warmer countries such as Spain, Portugal, Italy and Greece on the grounds that the hotter weather requires more powerful appliances. However, this amendment could open up a loophole for any manufacturer to claim an exemption on the basis that it is producing for these countries – even if the same models and appliances are sold in Northern Europe. According to Environmental Data Services (ENDS), the Commission has privately admitted that this Spanish amendment will make the Directive unworkable.[42] As it stands, the regulation will probably do little more than enforce the underlying rate of improvement in energy standards of refrigerators in the industry.

The saga of energy efficiency standards for refrigerators is far from over. With equal weighting in deciding the outcome of Directives with the Council, Parliament could have decided to reject the amendment and push for a proposed 20 per cent improvement target within two years. This narrative illustrates that lobbying and lack of cooperation by manufacturers has effectively stalled EC initiatives aimed at improving energy efficiency for electrical appliances by several years. It has allowed producers to carry on business as usual, despite US evidence which suggests that substantially more ambitious improvements could have been achieved in a considerably shorter timeframe and with little if any impact on competitiveness.

Box 3.4 Voluntary agreements: German and Dutch experience

Voluntary agreements between industry and government form a major part of The Netherland's climate strategy, which aims to reduce the country's emissions of CO_2 by 3 to 5 per cent by 2000 compared to emissions in 1990. Agreements take the form of a covenant or long-term agreement (LTA). The LTA is effectively a contract in which signatories commit themselves to the obligations of the agreement. The intention is to draw up agreements with 31 sectors accounting for 90 per cent of industrial energy consumption. So far 22 sectors have signed up. Most are aiming for energy efficiency improvements of around 20 per cent by 2000. By the end of 1993 an average 8 per cent improvement in energy efficiency was achieved by the first 12 sectors signing up to agreements.

Following the Dutch example, similar agreements have been made in Germany. Under an initiative by the Federation of German Industries (BDI), 15 sectors of German industry have signed an agreement with the Government to cut emissions of CO_2 by 20 per cent by 2005. The sectors account for about two thirds of industrial energy consumption. Targets vary and each sector has offered its own package of measures. The chemical industry has promised a 20 per cent production-related reduction based on 1987 energy consumption levels by 2000 in Western Germany alone. This is expected to reduce its CO_2 emissions from 79 to 45 million tonnes. Gas and water utilities have combined to offer CO_2 emissions by 30 to 40 million tonnes per year by 2005 for households and small consumers. They intend to do this by increasing the use of modern gas technology, and investing in energy-efficient appliances, district heating schemes and fuel cells. In return, the Government has promised to postpone certain regulatory measures to combat climate change.

Attempts to initiate voluntary agreements between industry and government have failed in the UK. Three years ago the Government's Advisory Committee on Business and the Environment (ACBE) attempted to encourage the six major industrial sources of CO_2 – iron and steel, chemicals, food, drink, tobacco and minerals – to set voluntary energy-saving targets. However, this initiative failed from lack of interest. The Confederation of British Industry (CBI) was sceptical about the effectiveness of such measures. Purely voluntary measures may also suffer from the 'free rider' problem and place the spotlight unfairly on large firms.

Conclusions

This chapter has reviewed industry's response to two major global environmental issues: ozone depletion and climate change (see also Chapter 9 for industry's response to the EU's proposals for an carbon/energy tax). In both cases industry, at least initially, refused to confront or address the issues. The response to proposed policy measures was hostile and the lack of scientific certainty was successfully used to delay, weaken and in some instances thwart the implementation of specific policy measures. Industry's response to the proposed use of economic instruments was as hostile as it was to the implementation of more traditional regulatory controls. Industrial opposition to confront the issues also inhibited the development of voluntary agreements and initiatives between government and industry. Voluntary action by industry – action taken without the threat of regulatory controls in the absence of such action – has also been limited.

The contrast between how industry subsequently responded, and how industry has been affected by the above issues, is explained by the nature of the problems themselves and also by the degree of importance attributed to them by government as translated into a political will to take real action. There are relatively few ozone-depleting chemicals. Substitute chemicals are readily available for most ozone-depleting substances and emission sources are known. In contrast, anthropogenic emissions of the principal GHGs result from virtually all human activities. There are numerous sources, including point sources non-point and diffuse sources – such as GHG emissions from the agricultural sector. Hence control of emissions poses a considerably harder challenge to both industry and policy-makers. Whilst the death knell has now been sounded for the CFC industry – CFCs and HCFCs will be completely phased out throughout the world by 2040 – industry still remains largely unaffected by policy measures aimed at addressing global climate change.

Mounting scientific evidence that CFCs could destroy the earth's ozone layer, and recognition of the potentially dire consequences of further stratospheric ozone loss, forced governments to take action. Following the signing of the Montreal Protocol in 1987, industry was left with little room for manoeuvre and was forced to work within an ever-tightening legislative framework. Timetabled and detailed targets were set and brought forward as the uncertainties surrounding the issue were resolved. Although industry still resisted moves to tighten phase-out dates, the opportunity to significantly weaken controls had gone.

It has proved more difficult to negotiate binding protocols under the United Nations Framework Convention on Climate Change. As it stands, the Convention contains no internationally binding targets or timetable for reducing greenhouse gas emissions. The practical difficulties of attempting to control anthropogenic emissions of GHGs have inhibited policy intervention. Instead, the UK Government, among others, has relied upon a partnership approach with industry in its strategy to return its GHG emissions to their 1990 levels by the year 2000 – a target recognized as inadequate to meet the Climate Convention's ultimate objective. A unified political will at the international level to make cuts in anthropogenic emissions has been absent, and those countries which are forecast to return their emissions to their 1990 levels by 2000 are more likely to do so by accident rather than by design.

Following the publication of the IPCC's Second Assessment Report and the second Conference of the Parties (COP-2) to the Climate Convention in July 1996, there now appears to be more acceptance amongst signatories to the Convention of the need to reduce GHG emissions. It is hoped that a protocol detailing specific and timetabled emission reductions for developed nations will be adopted at the third Conference of the Parties in December 1997. However, many obstacles remain to be resolved. Several countries are still opposed to the idea of a protocol and there is no mechanism currently in place to agree and vote on such a measure. Agreement on reduction targets and implementing a timetable is also likely to be fraught with difficulties, delays and compromise.

Because of the concern over jobs, profitability and international competitiveness, global environmental problems require globally negotiated and enforced intervention. Without adequate incentives, either in the form of regulation, the threat of regulation (in the absence of adequate voluntary initiatives), or the implementation of economic instruments, industry will not, and cannot really be expected to, internalize and adequately address such global environmental challenges. Even in situations where the possibility of the so-called double dividend or win–win outcome exists – outcomes which generate profits and reduce environmental impacts – industry appears to be reluctant to take action without some form of encouragement or incentive from government. Given that world energy demand is forecast to double sometime during the next century, voluntary initiatives by industry – in isolation – will be able to do little more than slow down the rate of increased anthropogenic emissions.

CHAPTER 4
National Environmental Issues

Acid Rain

Summary

Acid rain and its ecological consequences first received widespread attention in Scandinavia in the late 1960s and early 1970s. Decreases in fish stocks and the acidification of lakes and streams were linked to acid emissions, principally sulphur and nitrogen oxides, from power generation, industrial activity and the transport sector.[1] In the 1980s extensive forest damage, notably in West Germany, added momentum to the debate and demand for policy action.

The major policy initiatives in Europe aimed at reducing sulphur and nitrogen oxide emissions include the 1979 United Nations Economic Commission for Europe (UNECE) Geneva Convention on Long-Range Transboundary Air Pollution (LRTAP) and the 1988 European Union Directive on Large Combustion Plants (LCP). To date three protocols have been negotiated and attached to the Geneva Convention: the 1985 Helsinki Protocol, the 1988 Sofia Protocol and a second Sulphur Protocol in 1994. Under the Helsinki Protocol signatories were required to reduce their sulphur emissions by 30 per cent between 1980 and 1993. Although the UK did not sign the Protocol, emissions did fall by about 30 per cent over the required period (from 4.9 million tonnes to 3.2 million tonnes). The Sofia Protocol committed signatories to freeze NO_x emissions at 1987 levels by 1994.

Over the period 1970–93, UK sulphur dioxide emissions decreased by 50 per cent, from over 6.4 million tonnes per annum to just under 3.2 million tonnes. Over the same period NO_x emissions increased modestly from 2.32 million tonnes in 1970 to 2.35 million tonnes in 1993, with annual emissions peaking in the late 1980s and early 1990s at just over 2.7 million tonnes. Under the UNECE Sulphur Protocol the UK is committed to reducing sulphur emissions from all sources by 50 per cent by the year 2000 compared to emissions in 1980. After considerable negotiation the UK has also agreed to a 70 per cent reduction by 2005 and a 80 per cent target reduction by 2010, both compared to emissions in 1980. The current EU Directive on emissions from Large Combustion Plants commits the UK to cut sulphur emissions from all LCPs by 60 per cent by the year 2003 compared to emission levels in 1980. The Directive also sets emission limits for new plant and 40 per cent reduction targets for NO_x and particulate matter.

This section is principally concerned with sulphur emissions and focuses on those emissions arising from the energy sector. Nitrogen oxide emissions from transport, the single largest source of emissions, are reviewed later in the chapter under air quality and transport.

The Issue: UK Emissions and Trends

What is acid rain?

In the strictest sense, acid rain means precisely what the term implies – rain which is more acidic than normal.[2] However, the term has come to be used to describe both the wet and dry deposition of all air pollution which derives from potentially acid-forming substances.[3] Wet deposition covers acid rain, snow and hail, as well as scavenging by surface features (hills, trees) from mist and low cloud. Dry deposition is the direct fallout and absorption by buildings, soils and crops.[4]

Sources and scale of emissions

The principal pollutants responsible for the formation of acid rain are sulphur dioxide and nitrogen oxides released from power generation, industrial activity and transport. In 1993 UK emissions of sulphur dioxide totalled 3188 thousand tonnes (kt).[5] Of these 66 per cent were from power stations (by UNECE source category). By fuel type, coal accounted for 72 per cent of total emissions. In the same year UK emissions of NO_x totalled 2347 kt, of which 52 per cent were accounted for by road transport and 24 per cent by power stations. By fuel type, emissions from the combustion of petroleum accounted for 62% of total NO_x emissions and coal for 25 per cent.[6]

Acid Rain Damage

The two classes of damage attributed to acid rain that have provided the greatest spur to political action have been, first, to lakes and, second, streams, particularly in Scandinavia, and to forests, most predominantly in West Germany. Acidification of lakes and streams reduces fish stocks and other aquatic life, results in the loss of nutrients and also leads to the accumulation of toxic metals. In severe cases acid damage has resulted in the complete loss of all aquatic life and the appearance of 'dead lakes'. In combination with other pollutants, acid rain is also responsible for widespread forest dieback across much of Europe. Other types of damage attributable to acid rain affect crops and vegetation and human health (mainly aggravating respiratory problems). The economic cost of acid damage to masonry, paint and other building materials is also recognized.

Legislation

Sulphur emissions are subject to several, often overlapping, EU and UNECE measures. They could arguably be regarded as overregulated, and the complexity of the present situation and uncertainty about future requirements is certainly daunting. The most relevant pieces of legislation include the EU's Large Combustion Plants (LCP) directive, one of three daughter directives resulting from the 1984 Framework Directive on emissions from industrial plant, and the second Sulphur Protocol under the UNECE/Geneva Convention on Long Range Transboundary Air Pollution (LRTAP). Both pieces of legislation were subject to considerable debate and resistance, notably by the UK. The LCP Directive took five years to negotiate an acceptable compromise, during which time the original requirements were significantly scaled down. Similarly, the final text of the Sulphur Protocol, signed in Oslo in June 1994, was considerably weaker and less ambitious than the original proposal discussed in 1993.

The Large Combustion Plant (LCP) Directive

The LCP Directive was proposed in 1983 in order to reduce emissions of SO_2, NO_x and particulate matter. The Directive contains emission limits for new plants and overall national emission targets. The regulatory process associated with the Directive was particularly drawn out. From the initial Commission proposal that each Member State should reduce its SO_2 emissions from pre-1987 combustion plant by 60 per cent by 1995, a significantly modified version was only approved in late 1988. Under the Directive the UK now has until 2003 to achieve an overall 60 per cent reduction in SO_2 emissions, eight years longer than under the original proposal.[7] The revised Directive also set interim sulphur emission reduction targets for the UK of 20 per cent by 1993 and 40 per cent by 1998 (targets for individual countries varied). The UK is also required to cut NO_x emissions by 30 per cent by 1998 compared to emissions in 1980.

Publicly, strong UK opposition to the proposal in the mid-1980s was justified on the grounds of a lack of direct scientific evidence to link the UK's SO_2 emissions with acid rain damage. Other factors underlying the UK Government's position centred on the likely impacts of the Directive on the proposed privatization of the electricity-generating industry.

The Second Sulphur Protocol

In June 1994, the UK agreed to the second Sulphur Protocol under the UNECE Geneva Convention on Long Range Transboundary Air Pollution. Unlike the EU LCP Directive, the Protocol commits the UK to reducing sulphur emissions from all sources. Emission reduction targets are 50 per cent by the year 2000, 70 per cent by 2005 and 80 per cent by 2010 from emission levels in 1980.[8] Consequently, together with further legislative measures currently being considered (see below), pressure on industry to reduce sulphur emissions is set to increase.

The Current Situation and Future Developments

The EU is currently considering revising the LCP Directive. One proposal under review is to replace the 1988 Directive with a daughter directive under the new Integrated Pollution Prevention and Control (IPPC) Directive. This could result in extending EC emission limits to existing plants, and may broaden the controls to include gas turbines or clean coal technologies in an assessment of 'best available technologies' (BAT).[9]

The Commission is also considering implementing a directive on the sulphur content of liquid fuels. Although a 1976 directive set a ceiling on the sulphur content of gas oil-diesel and lighter oils used for domestic and industrial heating, heavy fuels, responsible for over 80 per cent of the SO_2 emissions from the combustion of oil products, have so far escaped regulation.[10] Current national plans to reduce emissions of SO_2 under the LCP Directive – by fitting flue-gas desulphurization (FGD) and switching to low-sulphur fuels – will mainly cut emissions from coal combustion. Consequently, without control measures, the proportion of emissions from the petroleum sector are set to increase. Similarly, emissions from small combustion plants (SCPs) are accounting for an increasing proportion of total emissions; without regulation, SCPs could provide a natural market for 'dirty' high-sulphur fuels.

Industry's Response

Compared to other EU member states, particularly Germany, the UK Government and energy sector's response to international and later domestic demands to reduce the environmental impacts of energy generation have been far from proactive. Sixteen years passed between the 1972 Stockholm Conference on the Human Environment, which first highlighted the problem of acid rain, and the UK entering into any international commitments aimed at addressing the issue.

The early response from the state-owned Central Electricity Generating Board (CEGB) was one of scepticism about the link between UK sulphur emissions and acid damage. Due to this scientific uncertainty, the CEGB argued that the excessive costs of FGD could not be justified. After the 1973 oil crisis, the CEGB also subscribed to the general view which emerged within the UK energy establishment that the SO_2 problem would vanish during the 1990s and beyond as traditional coal-fired power stations were replaced by nuclear reactors and clean-coal technology fired stations.[11] Although the UK signed the 1979 Geneva Convention on LRTAP, it fought against the inclusion of any specific commitments to stabilize or reduce emissions. The UK also failed to sign the subsequent Helsinki Protocol to the Convention requiring countries to reduce their SO_2 emissions by 30 per cent.

Opposition to acid emission controls was also voiced by the Confederation of British Industry, representing a wide range of industrial interests. The CBI argued that it would be "premature and unwise to make costly legislative demands" (CBI, 1984). However, by the mid-1980s the UK was under increasing international pressure to take some action. The Scandinavian countries were pressing for emission reductions in the Helsinki Protocol and the EU had issued the initial proposal for the LCP Directive. In addition, the UK had been branded as the 'dirty man' of Europe by environmental NGOs and an international Stop Acid Rain Campaign was active over this period.

By 1986 attitudes began to change and the CEGB put forward a proposal to retrofit FGD at two UK power stations. The programme required 6000 megawatts (MW) of generating capacity to be fitted with FGD by 1997, ten years after the decision had been made. This contrasted with Germany's ambitious 37,000 MW FGD programme which cut German SO_2 emissions by 80 per cent and was completed in just five years.

To meet the LCP Directive, the Government later increased this pledge to cover 12,000 MW of generating capacity. However, following privatization and the UK's 'dash for gas', this commitment was scaled down in 1990 to 8000 MW.

To date only 6000 MW of FGD capacity are operating: 4000 MW at National Power's Drax facility (the UK's largest power station) and 2000 MW at PowerGen's Ratcliffe on Soar plant. PowerGen does not intend to deliver its previous commitment to fit FGD at the 2000 MW Ferrybridge plant in south Yorkshire.

With UK emissions currently some 18 per cent below the ceiling, well ahead of the LCP Directive requirements, PowerGen's argument that the investment is no longer necessary may be plausible. However, reductions in emissions have largely been achieved because of the loss of market share by the two large generators to Nuclear Electric and from the increased use of gas-fired combined-cycle gas turbines (CCGTs).

In terms of cost, the retrofit programmes at Drax and Ratcliffe cost in the region of £680 million and £280 million respectively. According to National Power, the UK power industry has committed £5 billion to projects committed to producing 'clean' electricity. The company also suggests that this total may rise to £8 billion by the turn of the century. However, the bulk of this expenditure relates to investment in CCGT stations. Of National Power's stated £2 billion investment programme to meet the requirements of Integrated Pollution Control (IPC), under the EPA 1990 and the EU LCP Directive, over half is accounted for by four new CCGT stations. Consequently, considering the excess capacity in the UK power-generating industry, it seems likely that these investment decisions have more to do with competition in the energy market and strategies aimed at maintaining market share than a commitment to the environment.

Air Quality and Road Transport

Summary

In recent years the negative health, environmental and economic impacts of poor urban air quality have rarely been away from the headlines. The increased incidence of childhood asthma and widely reported breaches of World Health Organization (WHO), EU and national air quality guidelines have fuelled the debate further. The problem essentially comes down to the virtual explosion in the number of vehicles on the roads and the distances they travel. There are now over 22 million vehicles in the UK travelling in excess of 340 billion kilometres annually. These vehicles are the main source of several common air pollutants. In 1990 road transport accounted for 46 per cent of black smoke, 51 per cent of nitrogen oxide emissions, 90 per cent of carbon monoxide emissions and 41 per cent of volatile organic compound (VOC) emissions.[12] Emissions of carbon dioxide from road transport were in the order of 20 million tonnes of carbon – 21 per cent of total UK emissions.

With the Department of Transport predicting an increase in the number of vehicles of between 88 per cent and 143 per cent between 1988 and 2025, transport policy and measures aimed at tackling poor urban air quality are likely to be key policy areas in the coming decades. However, several million motorists and a well-funded and sophisticated road lobby make transport policy one of the most politically charged issues facing the Government. Despite the UK's creeping transport paralysis, the country still lacks a comprehensive transport strategy. Measures currently being considered to improve air quality may also be inadequate. Proposals for an air quality strategy, issued by the Department of the Environment in early 1995, are unlikely to be sufficient to meet national and internationally recommended air quality standards (AQS). Although the EU has proposed a more ambitious Framework Directive on air quality, various aspects of the proposals, particularly legally binding AQS, are being resisted by the UK.

In its long-awaited report on transport and the environment, the Royal Commission on Environment and Pollution (RCEP) outlined eight key objectives in the autumn of 1994, which it regards as essential to provide a solid basis for a sustainable transport policy.[13] These include the achievement of air quality that will prevent damage to human health; the encouragement and promotion of environmentally less-damaging modes of transport; and an aim to reduce carbon dioxide emissions from transport. To achieve these objectives, the RCEP has called for a doubling of petrol prices in real terms by 2005, substantial increases in fuel efficiency of new vehicles, halving of expenditure on trunk roads, new controls on transport-related land use, greater support for public transport, and targets to cut CO_2 emissions from transport. The report met with a hostile response from the road lobby and scepticism from the Government in terms of the implications for jobs, the economy and individuals. Many believe, however, that unless the fundamental issue of the number of cars and the distances they travel is addressed, no amount of tinkering at the edges will deliver a truly sustainable transport system with consequent improvements in urban air quality.

The Issue: The Economic, Environmental and Health Impacts of Road Transport

"We are not anti-car or anti-lorry. But the growth in traffic which has been forecast cannot be accommodated in a sustainable transport policy"

Sir John Houghton, Chairman of the Royal Commission on Environmental Pollution, summarizing the main conclusion of the eighteenth Report, *Transport and the Environment*.

As long ago as 1971 the RCEP warned that it would be dangerously complacent to ignore the environmental implications of the increasing number of motor vehicles and commercial flights. Little heed was taken of these warnings. Road traffic has doubled since 1970 and the distance travelled by passengers on international flights from the UK has increased almost threefold.

The sources, total emissions and the relative contribution to total emissions accounted for by road transport of six common air pollutants are detailed in Table 4.1. In brief, the major environmental and health impacts associated with these pollutants are as follows. Sulphur and nitrogen oxides contribute to acid rain; nitrogen oxides and volatile organic chemicals are the precursors of tropospheric ozone or smog which is toxic to humans and can damage vegetation (see volatile organic compounds, below); particulate matter (smoke) and carbon monoxide adversely affect human health; and carbon dioxide emissions are the major source of human enhanced global warming. Table 4.2 details the contribution to road transport emissions from passenger cars alone (1990).

In recent years a growing body of research has emerged that strengthens the link between adverse health effects and exposure to these air pollutants. In 1994 *New Scientist* reported the findings of a US EPA epidemiologist which suggested that airborne particulate matter levels in England and Wales may account for 10,000 deaths annually. Several studies in the UK have shown associations between respiratory diseases and SO_2 and smoke at levels well below current EC guide values. The sharp increase in asthma since the late 1970s has also been linked to rising emissions from vehicles. Between 1979 and 1990 recorded asthma cases in Britain increased by 136 per cent and now up to one in ten children in the UK are estimated to suffer from asthma. Other vehicle emissions may also be causing harm. According to doctors from London's University College Hospital, benzene emissions from vehicles may cause 3000 deaths from leukaemia in the UK each year.

In addition to the 'substantial costs' of low-level air pollution in terms of health services, a recent DoE discussion paper on improving air quality also acknowledged the economic costs of air pollution in terms of impediments to economic efficiency, the cleaning of buildings and the environment, and damage to the international perception of British cities as attractive places to live and do business. In their report, the RCEP put the external costs of air pollution, climate change, noise and accidents at between £9 and £17 billion. However, this estimate specifically excluded 'unquantifiable' environmental costs such as loss of land, habitat destruction and visual intrusion. It also excluded the costs of congestion – estimated by the Confederation of British Industry (CBI) to be in the region of £15 billion per year.

Another estimate, by David Pearce, former advisor to the Department of the Environment, suggests that the external costs of road transport, not including road costs, are as high as £25.7 billion (compared with road tax revenues of £14.7 billion).[14]

Table 4.1 Sources of principal air pollutants in the UK (1990)

Source	% of Total Emissions					
	Sulphur dioxide	Black smoke	Nitrogen oxides	Carbon monoxide	Carbon dioxide	Volatile organic compounds
Road Transport	2	46	51	90	19	41
Electricity Supply Industry	72	6	28	1	34	–
Other Industry	19	14	9	4	26	52
Domestic	3	33	2	4	14	2
Other	7	1	9	–	7	4
Total (kT)	3774	453	2719	6659	160	2396

Source: *The UK Environmental Foresight Project: Road Transport and the Environment, The Future Agenda in the UK*, HMSO, 1993

Table 4.2 Passenger car contribution to total UK road transport emissions (1990)

Pollutant	% from Passenger Cars
Carbon monoxide	93
Volatile organic compounds	61
Nitrogen oxides	57
Particulates	6
Sulphur dioxide	39
Carbon dioxide	69

Legislation

EU Policy

In 1994 the EC proposed a new framework Directive on air quality assessment and management. The objective of the Directive would be to put pressure on Member States to achieve continuous improvements in air-quality and to move closer towards harmonization of national air quality measurement programmes. The Commission also set itself the ambitious objective of drafting legislation setting air quality standards (AQS) for as many as 14 air pollutants by 1999.[15]

Currently, there are four existing air quality directives. These deal with suspended particulate matter (smoke), SO_2, NO_x and ozone. Lead concentrations are also covered by a 1982 Directive (82/884). The main motivation for the air quality directives is the impact of pollution on human health. Except for ozone, the directives establish limit-values or air quality standards, and monitoring requirements. Under the NO_x legislation (85/203), both binding limit-values and a non-binding guide value were established. Recent measurements in the UK demonstrated that limit-values were being broken in some urban areas while up to one third of the country exceeded the guide value. The UK has also been criticized by the EC for the small number of monitoring sites in operation, just seven for NO_x compared to Germany's 200. Under the Ozone Directive, although no limit values have been established, monitoring requirements and 'alert thresholds' based on WHO guidelines have been introduced.

Box 4.1 Objectives for a sustainable transport strategy –
the RCEP's Eighteenth Report: *Transport and the Environment*

In its report, the RCEP outlined eight key objectives which it regards as essential to
provide a solid basis for a sustainable transport policy. In pursuing these objectives
the Commission has called upon the Government to set clear and, wherever
possible, quantified targets. The objectives are as follows:

- to ensure that an effective transport policy at all levels of Government is
  integrated with land-use policy and gives priority to minimizing the need for
  transport and increasing the proportion of trips made by less-damaging modes;
- to achieve standards of air quality that will prevent damage to human health and
  the environment;
- to improve the quality of life, particularly in towns and cities, by reducing the
  dominance of cars and lorries and providing alternative access;
- to increase the proportion of personal travel and freight transport by
  environmentally less-damaging modes and to make the best use of existing
  infrastructure;
- to halt any loss of land to transport infrastructure in areas of conservation,
  cultural, scenic or amenity value unless the use of that land has been shown to be
  the best practical environmental option;
- to reduce CO_2 emissions from transport;
- to reduce substantially the demands which transport infrastructure and the vehicle
  industry place on non-renewable materials;
- to reduce noise from transport.

Among over 100 recommendations – many involving quantified targets and specific
measures, the Commission has called for a 40 per cent increase in the average fuel-
efficiency of new cars sold in the UK between 1990 and 2005 (with smaller improvements of 20 per cent for light goods vehicles and 10 per cent for heavy duty
vehicles). The Commission has also called on the Government to make a commitment to return CO_2 emissions from surface transport to 80 per cent of their 1990
level by 2020. CO_2 emissions from transport currently account for 21 per cent of
total UK emissions but are forecast to rise from 47 million tonnes (of carbon) in
1990 to 60 million tonnes by 2020. Other measures include raising fuel duty in order
to double the price of fuel, in real terms, by 2005, graduating road tax steeply to
favour cars with greater fuel-efficiencies and abolishing any remaining taxation
perks for company cars.

   In reviewing evidence from the British Roads Federation and the Department of
Transport, the Commission concluded that the extension of the road network
merely "leads to an increase in the total amount of traffic". Concerned over the
impact of the £21 billion roads programme (which has subsequently, but not substantially, been reduced) on landscape and national and international commitments
to protect species and habitats, the Commission called for planned expenditure on
motorways and trunk roads to be halved. This would release in the order of £1.5 billion per year which the Commission believes should be spent on improving public
transport.

   Ultimately, the achievement of a sustainable transport policy will require a re-
think on our approach to the car and the car culture. The Commission recognize
that patterns of settlement, employment and consumption must change to achieve
this goal.

Source: *Transport and the Environment*, Eighteenth Report, HMSO, and *ENDS Report 237*.

Current UK Policy

In January 1995 the DoE issued proposals for an air quality strategy. Under the 'strategic framework', local authorities would be required to identify and draw up plans to tackle areas of poor air quality (the Environment Act 1995 requires local authorities to conduct regular air quality reviews from April 1997). If standards set by Government are not met, authorities will have to declare *air quality management areas* and implement remedial management plans. The strategy's cornerstone will be a series of national air quality standards for nine key pollutants. Alert thresholds will be set where air quality is "so poor that an immediate response would be justified to prevent serious damage" and long-term guideline figures will also be set, subject to consideration to the costs and benefits of further abatement, at a level where the pollutant has been rendered harmless to health and the environment.

The effectiveness of the strategy is very dependent upon the adoption of meaningful targets and timescales. Although it seems likely that the DoE's Expert Panel on Air Quality Standards' (EPAQS) recommendation of AQS for benzene, 1,3-butadiene and carbon monoxide are likely to met by the year 2000 from existing policy, this is not the case for other pollutants, notably ozone. The Government has been criticized for rejecting the 50 parts per billion (ppbv) ozone standard, as an eight-hour average, recommended by the EPAQS. This standard is widely exceeded across the UK on up to 80 days each year. To achieve compliance with this level, EPAQS have estimated that emissions of VOCs and NO_x would need to be cut by 75 to 90 per cent. Under existing international commitments the UK must reduce emissions of both pollutants by only 30 per cent, from their peak values in the 1980s, by the end of the century.

In February 1996 the Department of the Environment (DoE) announced that 14 trial areas, covering 80 councils, were selected to test new guidance and procedures before April 1997. The selected areas include large conurbations, industrial areas, coal-burning areas, small towns and rural areas.[16] However, proposals for the DoE's overall strategy have now been delayed until the summer of 1996. They had originally been promised by the end of 1995.

A major difference between the UK scheme and the EC's proposal is that the European Commission wants to introduce legally binding AQS. Friends of the Earth (FoE), a UK environmental NGO, have criticized the UK's proposals as avoiding legally binding AQSs or failing to crack down on polluting factories or unnecessary car use during severe pollution episodes. There is also uncertainty over what powers will be made available to local authorities to prevent both long-term and exceedances and acute episodes – and in what circumstances they will be used. Local authorities have until 1997 to draw up their air quality plans.

Industry's Response: The Impacts of Legislation

Initially European car manufacturers were hostile to policy initiatives aimed at introducing strict, US-style vehicle-emission control standards. Opposition and resistance resulted in over ten years of delay between the first negotiations back in 1983 to introduce such measures and their eventual implementation in 1993. Before

1993, EC standards were voluntary – member states were not required to adopt them, and, in general, the standards were not particularly high. Regulation had remained largely in the hands of industry, with standards negotiated inside the Committee of European Community Automobile Makers.

From the US experience of the 1970s it was well known that emission abatement would involve major compliance costs to industry. This was particularly so for producers, such as the UK, of smaller, lower-value cars and hence for a sector of the European vehicle market for which competition was particularly fierce. Central to the debate was the technology choice for the car engine of the 1990s. This had considerable commercial implications and led to fierce rivalry between European manufacturers.

The choice of technology was between three-way auto catalysts or lean-burn engines. The auto catalyst effectively 'cleans' vehicle exhaust gases, turning carbon monoxide, nitrogen oxides and hydrocarbons into water vapour, nitrogen and carbon dioxide. In contrast, lean-burn engines concentrate on improving vehicle fuel-efficiency by reducing the richness of the fuel-air mix in the engine. Improved fuel-efficiency and reduced carbon dioxide emissions are achieved at the expense of somewhat lower emission reductions. Both the US and Japan had opted for auto catalysts, partly because lean-burn engines were unable to meet tough US NO_x emission standards. US legislation was primarily aimed at dealing with urban-air quality and smog and hence at reducing NO_x and hydrocarbon and VOC emissions – precursors of photochemical smog.

UK competitiveness was threatened by stringent emission standards. Consequently, the UK adopted a strategy of resistance and delay. In terms of technology, the preferred option was the use of lean-burn engines. Significant research and development had been committed to developing these engines and it was recognized that the require-ment to fit auto catalysts would be particularly damaging to the already ailing UK car industry in the run-up to privatization.[17] The European Commission had argued that catalytic conversion would increase the price of small cars by 13 per cent. In contrast, West German producers moved from an initial position of resisting strict and manda-tory standards, at least unilaterally, to favouring their implementation. This change in attitudes was for two reasons. German industry stood to gain from such standards. Producing larger, more expensive cars for the top end of the market, producers could more easily absorb the costs of auto catalysts than their UK and other European competitors. Consequently, stricter standards offered a competitive advantage. In addition, political and public demands to deal with acid rain made such a strategy more acceptable if not inevitable. Forest die-back, or *Waldsterben*, had become a major issue and the political system was sufficiently activated to demand technological change from a successful export-oriented industry. The German electronics industry and automotive spare parts industry also stood to gain from the adoption of auto catalytic converters.

The conflict over standards and technology choice was not restricted to the UK and Germany. It divided Europe. Major battles also took place between the two US producers: General Motors and Ford. While General Motors had adopted auto catalysts, the *winning technology* in the US, to meet emission requirements, Ford had favoured the use of lean-burn engines. Having lost the debate in the US, Ford endeavoured to ensure that Europe would become a market for lean-burn engines. However, by 1990 Norway, Sweden, Austria and Switzerland required all new cars to be fitted with catalytic converters. In West Germany 98.2 per cent of cars were fitted with auto catalysts compared to only 3.9 per cent in the UK.[18] Although European legislation never actually prescribed a specific technology, the final agreement to introduce mandatory emission standards from 1993 effectively made three-way catalysts on new petrol engine cars compulsory. The UK had backed the wrong technology.

Box 4.2 Catalytic converters: how do they work?

Catalytic converters effectively 'clean' exhaust gases by passing them through a tightly packed, honeycombed ceramic or steel block coated with a microscopically thin layer of platinum and rhodium. These metals act as catalysts, initiating the chemical reactions that 'clean' the gases but take no part in the reaction themselves. The catalyst is housed in a metal case, similar in size and shape to the exhaust silencer, and is sited close to the engine so it can heat up as quickly as possible after ignition to the 200°C to 250°C temperature required to trigger the cleaning reaction. The reactions convert carbon monoxide, hydrocarbons and nitrogen oxides into carbon dioxide, water vapour and nitrogen.

Volatile Organic Compounds

Summary

Volatile Organic Compound (VOC) emissions result from the use of hydrocarbons in almost every aspect of the production, use and disposal of commercial, domestic and personal products. Significant emissions also result from their production and consumption as fuel. Anthropogenic VOC emissions are currently estimated to be in the order of 10 million tonnes per year in Europe. UK emissions total some 2.4 million tonnes. The major pollution issue surrounding VOC emissions concerns their role in the formation of photochemical oxidants, particularly tropospheric ozone, which are toxic to humans, damage ecosystems and exacerbate the problem of acid rain. Over the past 100 years the pre-industrial near ground-level background concentrations of ozone have doubled from 10 to 15 parts per billion (ppbv) per annum to approximately 30 ppbv per annum over the UK. VOC emissions are also associated with global and more localized pollution issues.

Pressure to cut UK VOC emissions is increasing. However, a lack of awareness and a generally hostile response from industry to the various emission reduction proposals currently being considered could reduce the ability of UK industry to capitalize on the increased market – both within the UK and overseas – for pollution abatement and environmental technologies aimed at reducing VOC emissions. This market could be worth in the region of £12 billion. Recent legislative pressures include the UNECE

Protocol on VOC emissions and proposed EC Directives on the use of solvents, petrol distribution and vehicle refuelling. The DoE is now pushing for an ozone strategy for Europe within the UNECE framework.

The emergence of VOC emissions as one of the major environmental issues of the mid 1990s, together with the magnitude of the market for VOC abatement technology, was not generally anticipated. Despite the uncertainties, evidence suggests that the scale of the problem is so large and poorly understood that the current approaches to solving it may be insufficient. The DoE has conceded that without further policy developments, health-based guidelines for ozone will continue to be exceeded into the foreseeable future. Consequently, it seems likely that legislative controls and regulation of VOC emissions will become more severe in the medium to long term.

The Issue: Sources and Scale of UK VOC Emissions

VOCs are any organic compounds, other than methane, that are capable of producing photochemical oxidants (POs) as a result of reactions with oxides of nitrogen (NO_x) in the presence of sunlight.[19] VOCs themselves are not photochemical oxidants. However, this working definition reflects the importance attached to the role they play in producing POs such as ozone, hydrogen peroxide and peroxyacetyl nitrate (PAN).

Major VOC sources include emissions resulting from the use of solvents (for example, paint, printing, metal cleaning, personal products), mobile sources (for example motor vehicles, aircraft), petrol evaporation, the chemical industry and from stationary combustion (for example, power stations, waste incineration and agriculture). In 1993 total UK VOC emissions amounted to 2418 thousand tonnes (kt) of which approximately 39 per cent originated from mobile sources. Table 4.3 details these emissions by UNECE source category.

Table **4.3** 1993 UK VOC emissions by UNECE source category

By UNECE source category	1993 Emissions (1000 tonnes)	Percentage of total in 1993
Power stations	10	–
Domestic	35	1
Non-combustion processes	417	17
Other	5	–
Extraction & distribution of fossil fuels	237	10
Solvent use	674	28
Road transport	913	38
Other transport	25	1
Waste treatment and disposal	22	1
Forests	80	3
Total	2,418	100

Source: *Digest of Environmental Statistics No.17*, DoE, 1995

VOCs can contribute to local, regional (transboundary) and global air pollution. At the local level VOC emissions could be a contributory factor to the so-called sick building syndrome. Other examples of VOC pollution at the local level include odour pollution from the chemical industry, abattoirs, foundries and agriculture. Although rarely hazardous to health, these sources of pollution can have a considerable effect on the quality of life.

At the global level, VOCs contribute to the destruction and depletion of stratospheric ozone. CFCs and HCFCs are also greenhouse gases, contributing to human-enhanced global warming. However, it is their role in producing photo-chemical oxidants which is the most important pollution issue relating to VOCs. Photochemical oxidants are toxic to humans, damage vegetation and exacerbate the problem of acid rain. Estimates indicate that the government's own Expert Panel on Air Quality Standards' (EPAQS) recommended 50 ppbv air quality standard (as a rolling eight-hour mean) for ozone, and health-based guidelines issued by the World Health Organization, are exceeded across much of the UK on 20 to 60 days per year.[20] Low-level ozone concentrations are rising by 1 to 2 per cent per year in the UK and could be causing significant economic losses through decreased agricultural yields, as well as damaging human health and sensitive ecosystems.[21] In the US it has been esti-mated that ozone damage reduces agricultural output by 5 per cent.

Legislative Pressure

As a signatory of the United Nations Economic Commission for Europe (UNECE) Protocol to reduce VOC emissions, the UK is committed to reducing VOC emissions by 30 per cent by 1999 from a 1988 baseline. Further pressure on industry to reduce VOC emissions will come from proposed EC Directives on solvent use, petrol distribution and vehicle refuelling. Emissions of VOCs are also controlled under the Environmental Protection Act 1990.

As shown in Table 4.4, the UK would appear to be on target to meet the required UNECE 30 per cent reduction. However, due to the complexities of the chemical reactions involved in the formation of photochemical oxidants and the uncertainties surrounding the precise importance of the other main ozone precursor – oxides of nitrogen – it seems likely that a 30 per cent reduction in VOC emissions will be insufficient to meet the EPAQS's recommended health standard for ozone. The DoE has conceded that "without further policy developments", the health-based guidelines for ozone "will continue to be exceeded for the foreseeable future."[22] To attain the 50 ppbv ozone air-quality standard would require VOC emissions to be cut by as much as 75 to 85 per cent or current NO_x emissions to be cut by 95 per cent – or some compromise between the two.

Table 4. 4 Projected UK VOC emissions ('000 tonnes)

Year	1988	1993	1997	1998	1999
Stationary sources	1,606	1,426	1,233	1,089	1,048
Mobile sources	988	920	642	588	540
Total	2,594	2,347	1,875	1,676	1,588
% Reduction from 1988		9.5	27.7	35.3	38.8

Source: *ENDS Report 238*, Nov 1994

Current Issues and Industry's Response

The remainder of this section reviews the response of industry to EU measures aimed at reducing VOC emissions from the petrol chain and stationary sources. The impression gained from these two particular examples is one of industry resistance justified on the basis of cost and implications for competitiveness. Persistent and unified lobbying by industry on the issue of VOC emissions from solvents has now resulted in a delay to tighter emission standards under the EPA 1990 for many industrial sectors. In contrast, proposed measures to reduce VOC emissions from vehicle refuelling seem to have set the oil and car industries against each other. Each side is lobbying and endeavouring to prove with claims and counter-claims that the other should bear the costs of VOC abatement. As demonstrated by the different approaches and strategies adopted by the major CFC producers (discussed in Chapter 3), industry does not always adopt a unified or joint position on environmental legislation.

The Petrol Chain: an Illustrative Study

Within the EU, petrol vapour emissions account for 15 per cent of anthropogenic VOC emissions. The sources concerned are losses from cars (10 per cent), storage terminals and distribution operations (3 per cent), and car refuelling (2 per cent). The first of three EU Directives aimed at controlling emissions from these sources was passed in 1991. The Directive requires all new cars to be fitted with small carbon canisters, from January 1993, to capture petrol vapours from the fuel tank and other evaporative loses within the engine. It will take at least ten years to install them across the car fleet as old cars are replaced by new.

The second Directive, referred to as Stage I , will require control of VOC emissions from petrol storage terminals and distribution operations, including unloading at service stations. Although now close to adoption, the proposed measures were fiercely contested by the UK's Petrol Retailers Association (PRA) and the Petrol Industry Association (PIA). The PRA believed that the compliance cost of fitting vapour recovery systems could force some of their members out of business. Similarly, the third element of the EU's strategy, referred to as Stage II, will extend the controls to vehicle refuelling. The proposed Directive will require the phasing-in of vapour recovery equipment at petrol stations, along with standardized filler nozzles and vehicle fuel-tank necks to minimize VOC losses. These measures are also being fiercely contested.

The oil companies argue that it would be cheaper and more cost-effective to recover VOCs emitted during refuelling by fitting large carbon canisters (LCCs) to cars. After a protracted battle in the courts, this was the route eventually taken in the US. Under US legislation, 40 per cent of cars will have to be fitted with LCCs by 1998, rising to 100 per cent in 2000. However, the oil companies were also required to fit vapour recovery units at petrol stations where levels of ozone were classified as serious to extreme, mainly in big cities.[23]

Within the UK the DoE has come down strongly against LCCs. A recent DoE-commissioned report concluded that VOC abatement using Stage II equipment would cost between £355 and £369 per tonne of VOC not emitted, while fitting new vehicles with LCCs would cost £2723 per tonne of VOC not emitted. The Petroleum Industry Association (PIA) is taking issue with the findings of this report, disputing both cost estimates and discount rates used, and points to the US decision to opt for LCCs. In contrast, Germany introduced measures in 1993 requiring the retrofitting of Stage II equipment to all service stations selling more than one million litres of petrol annually over a phased period. Other countries such as Sweden and Austria have also opted to fit petrol pump controls. Other objections to the LCC route are the length of time it would take to achieve reduced VOC emissions. Tackling pumps would enable a size-able portion of refuelling emissions to be cut within a few years, while enlarged canisters would take at least a decade to permeate the fleet.

Solvents

VOCs emissions from solvent use amounted to 674,000 in 1993, 28 per cent of total UK emissions and the second largest single source after vehicle emissions. Industrial emissions, which account for about 68 per cent of these emissions, are subject to control under Part B of the EPA 1990 – processes subject to local authority air pollution control (LAAPC). Of the 9786 process authorizations issued by local authorities by March 1994, 2614 are concerned directly with the control of VOC emissions.

Industrial groups have argued that the costs of existing and proposed measures to control VOC emissions outweigh the environmental benefits. Such claims dominated hearings of the House of Commons Environment Committee inquiry on VOCs. The Chemical Industries Association (CIA) suggests that under the UNECE and existing UK legislation the industry will face a bill of between £9 and £12 billion to control solvent emissions. As well as lobbying against stricter controls, industrial groups have also called for a relaxation of existing measures. Of particular concern to industry is the reassessment of emission standards under the EPA. These standards, set in LAAPC guidance notes, are currently being reassessed as part of a four-year review process. Each of the notes sets deadlines for upgrading existing processes to new plant standards.

The CIA, which is coordinating a joint trade association VOC Task Force, claims that to meet emission standards under LAAPC, annual expenditure by industry will peak at around £1 billion in 1997 – when spending, according to the CIA, will be "comparable with the profitability of many of the sectors being regulated."[24] It is unclear what underlying assumptions have been made in this industry-calculated figure. In contrast, under the proposed EC Solvents Directive most existing processes would not be required to upgrade until the middle of the next decade, several years later. Consequently, industrial groups maintain that UK firms will be seriously disadvantaged under LAAPC because of these timing differences. Industrial groups have also argued that the timing of the UK provisions will force many companies to go down the abatement – end-of-pipe – route rather than adopting low-solvent, water-based systems.[25]

Possibly to balance its demands for a relaxation of existing or planned VOC controls, the British Chemical Federation (BCF) also proposed a scheme to the House of Commons Environment Committee to halve VOC emissions from decorative paint and called on the Government to press for EC legislation to support their proposal. The inquiry was informed by ICI Paint's Technical Manager that currently available technology can give low-VOC paints with a "highly equivalent performance" to conventional paints – but with an associated increase in costs of 30 to 50 per cent.[26] Because of this cost difference the BCF regard legislation, at the European level, as essential to stimulate market acceptance and ensure a level playing field. In 1988 VOC emissions from decorative paint amounted to 76,000 tonnes. Although these emissions fell to 66,000 tonnes in 1992, the DoE expects no further reduction by the turn of the century.

In June 1995 industry's opposition and lobbying seemed to pay off. The DoE announced its decision to postpone controls on VOC emissions from eight sectors.[27] The decision allows the sectors concerned to delay upgrading their processes until 1 June 1998, a delay of up to 27 months for some of the sectors. The relaxations also apply to emissions of other substances, such as particulates, isocyanates and formaldehyde. Industrial opposition to the EC Solvents Directive has also had some success. The latest draft (number seven), has been amended to reduce considerably the number of solvents to be phased out as soon as possible and to exempt smaller firms from solvent-emission controls. Thresholds under which firms would have become subject to control have been increased from two tonnes per year to five tonnes per year.

According to the Environmental Industries Commission (EIC), the DoE's decision to delay VOC controls caused havoc among suppliers of VOC abatement equipment who literally saw orders cancelled overnight. The international competitiveness of the companies affected is also likely to be damaged. The European market for VOC abatement equipment is growing at 15 per cent per year and was expected to reach £660 million by 1997. In a 1996 report prepared by the EIC on the impacts of the DoE's 1995 decision, the EIC forcefully argued that a solid home market, created by effective legislation which is properly enforced, is essential if UK firms are to compete in export markets. The EIC report also pointed out that in reaching its decision, the DoE did not take proper account of the benefits of reducing VOC emissions from the coatings sector: reduced health, crop and materials damage by ozone, and reduced odour nuisance problems at the local level.

Conclusions

This chapter has reviewed three national environmental issues: acid rain, air quality and road transport, and VOCs. Industrial and government responses to the issues have also been examined. In contrast to the global issues reviewed in the previous chapter, the above problems are already subject to a significant amount of regulation. The effectiveness and adequacy of this regulation, however, varies between the issues. This is discussed below. A common theme running through all three of these examples, once again, is one of industrial opposition and resistance to proposed legislation. At the same time, voluntary action by industry has been unambitious and limited. Both industrial and Government opposition has also served to delay and weaken European initiatives aimed at addressing these environmental problems.

Legislation to reduce sulphur emissions has been effective. The UK is on target to meet its UNECE commitment to reduce its SO_2 emissions by 80 per cent, compared to 1980 emission levels, by 2010. Although this target is largely being met as a result of the UK's 'dash for gas' – the rapid expansion in gas-generated power and the subsequent demise of coal-fired power generation following liberalization in the energy markets – it seems likely that legislation has contributed to encourage this shift. Anticipation of tighter regulatory controls on sulphur emissions may have discouraged investment in coal-fired power stations and encouraged the switch to gas.

The impacts of legislation and other Government initiatives aimed at reducing transport-related air pollution have been mixed. Legislative controls on vehicle emissions have been effective. Ambient lead levels fell by some 77 per cent following 1981 legislation to restrict the maximum lead content in fuels. Current EC emission limits (effectively requiring the use of catalytic converters) are expected to reduce emissions of CO, VOCs and NO_x from the transport sector by 43 per cent, 60 per cent and 64 per cent respectively by 2003.[28] Despite these measures, poor urban air quality remains a major problem and the UK's proposals for an air quality strategy are unlikely to be sufficient to meet national and internationally recommended air quality standards. The restriction of lead in fuel and the imposition of EC vehicle emission limits have also resulted in trade-offs – reduced emissions of some pollutants have been achieved at the expense of higher emissions of other pollutants. For lead, the reduction in emissions has been accompanied by increased emissions of benzene, a known carcinogen. For catalysts, reduced VOCs, NO_x and CO emissions are accompanied by increased emissions of CO_2 and N_2O – two powerful greenhouse gases.

The use of catalytic converters is also very much a technical fix to the problem of vehicle exhaust emissions. Auto catalysts are effectively bolted onto existing, conventional engines to achieve reduced emissions from individual vehicles. However, with a rapidly expanding fleet size, together with an overall increase in the distances travelled, total vehicle emissions are set to increase. Any benefits arising from the wider adoption of auto catalysts may therefore only be short term. This is borne out by experience in the US where growth in vehicle numbers and distances travelled have prevented NO_x levels from falling despite strict air emission standards dating back to the 1970s. UK emissions are also forecast to increase beyond 2010 for the same reason.

Catalysts are also ineffective when cold and therefore make little impact on the 75 per cent of journeys made in urban areas which are less than 3 miles (4.8 kilometres) in length.

Industry's less than proactive response in relation to vehicle emissions is illustrated by reference to vehicle fuel-efficiency. In its report, the RCEP called for a 40 per cent increase in the average fuel-efficiency of new cars sold in the UK between 1990 and 2005 (with smaller improvements of 20 per cent for light goods vehicles and 10 per cent for heavy duty vehicles). European car manufacturers have offered only a 10 per cent improvement in vehicle fuel-efficiency by 2005 – a goal which, says the RCEP "is widely recognized as derisory."[29] The Government, in its Climate Strategy, has already acknowledged that improvements of up to 40 per cent are achievable within the next decade.

Further and more restrictive controls on vehicle emissions would therefore seem inevitable, especially given the scale of the problem, the projected increase in vehicle numbers and the unwillingness of industry to take meaningful action on a voluntary basis. The political will has been absent but ultimately, as the economic, social and environmental costs of transport-related pollution become more acute, such action seems unavoidable. It will also have to deal with the root cause of the problem – the number of cars and the distances they travel – if a truly sustainable transport system, a prerequisite for improved air quality, is to be developed.

Further and more restrictive controls on VOC emissions also seem inevitable. Although the UK appears to be on target to meets its UNECE obligation to reduce VOC emissions by 30 per cent by 1999 (compared to baseline emissions in 1988), the adequacy of this commitment is in doubt. The Government's own Expert Panel on Air Quality Standards suggests that VOC (and NO_x) emissions will need to be cut by some 75 to 90 per cent in order to meet the recommended health-based 50 ppbv ozone standard (rejected by the UK Government). The 30 per cent target has also been criticized since it has no environmental or health legitimacy.

The above reviews suggest that regulatory control, and anticipation of regulatory control, have been the main drivers for industry to address the environmental challenges of acid rain, transport-related air pollution and VOCs. As stated, voluntary action by industry to date has been limited. Industry's opposition to such controls has been based on the grounds of the perceived impacts such regulations may have on international competitiveness and employment; the general argument that "it costs too much" has now replaced industrial opposition on the basis of scientific uncertainty and lack of understanding. It is also clear from the reviews that the win–win outcomes discussed in Chapter 2 are rare and seem remote to the industries affected by these issues. Since transport-related air pollution and VOC emissions (also a major source of transport-related air pollution) are dependent upon industrial activity, consumption patterns and lifestyles, tighter regulation in isolation may not be sufficient or the most effective means of adequately resolving them – especially given the scale of the problems. Consequently, the real challenge now for both industry and government is to develop more innovative, participatory and ambitious approaches to deal with these environmental challenges in partnership with other stakeholders.

CHAPTER 5
Regional and Local Environment Issues

Water Quality

Summary

In general, the quality of the UK water resource is good and, despite recent increases in water bills, the price paid for water is well below that charged in many parts of the world. However, demand for water and the demand for improvements in water quality are increasing. For some regions demand is forecast to rise by as much as 40 per cent by 2021.[1]

Until recently, responsibility for the quality of the water resource, whether directly or indirectly, rested with a large number of bodies including the National Rivers Authority (NRA), Her Majesty's Inspectorate of Pollution (HMIP), the Drinking Water Inspectorate (DWI) and the Department of the Environment (DoE). Overlap in responsibilities and the need for interaction between these organizations may have lead to confusion over who controlled the release of which substances from which processes into which media. Following the establishment of the Environment Agency in August 1995, which took over responsibility for functions previously carried out by the NRA and HMIP in April 1996, this situation should be eased.

The water industry is subject to a substantial amount of both national and EU legislation. With the implementation of the EU Urban Waste Water Directive (UWWD) and ambitious plans for an EC framework Directive on water resources, published in 1997, legislative standards covering the water industry are set to tighten over the foreseeable future. According to the Water Services Association (WSA), the forward capital expenditure programme for the ten years to 2005 exceeds £24 billion. Of this total, the industry suggests that £11 billion will be spent on investments designed to improve water quality.[2] Other commentators have suggested that the industry is forecast to spend in the region of £53 billion in improved facilities by 2010, and the market for the supply of water pollution control for processors is likely to grow to around £1 billion annually.[3] Despite these investment programmes, the water industry (rather than industry) still dominates pollution prosecutions by the NRA. To the end of 1993 since privatization in 1989, water companies have paid over £600,000 in fines and have been prosecuted 168 times. The UK has also been prosecuted by the European Court of Justice over failure to fully implement EC directives relating to water quality. In 1992 the UK was held to be in breach of the 1980 EC Drinking Water Quality Directive and in 1993 in breach of the 1976 Bathing Water Directive.

The UK continues to delay implementing measures designed to meet EU standards. Recent decisions to delay four sewerage schemes in Devon and Cornwall, which the NRA believed to be essential to comply with the Bathing Water Directive, and the decision to reclassify the Humber Estuary as a coastal water under the 1991 UWWD – which would allow Yorkshire Water to avoid anything other than primary treatment of sewage from Hull – could expose the UK to further action by the European Court of Justice. UK Government resistance to tighten any of the existing standards under the 1976 EC Directive on bathing water quality – despite the results of a recent UK study which suggest that significant levels of disease may be caused by exposure of bathers to faecal streptococci at levels well below even those proposed in the amendments – are unlikely to improve the UK's image with regard to environmental matters within the rest of Europe.

The Issue: Water Resources in the UK, Quantity and Quality

The UK water industry supplies over 19,500 million litres of water per day to over 57.7 million people. At least 20,000 million litres of sewage arrives daily at sewage treatment plants, resulting in the production of just over one million dry tonnes of sewage sludge annually.

Quantity
Historically the availability of virtually limitless supplies of good quality water have been taken for granted in the UK. However, despite the relatively cooler and wetter summers of 1992 and 1993 the hot, dry conditions of the 1988–92 drought returned to the UK in 1994 and again in 1995. Soaring temperatures, the reappearance of hose pipe bans in some areas over these years, and Yorkshire Water's high profile and costly (£47 million) tanker operation to replenish dwindling local supplies with 'imported' water (to avoid rota cuts) have reminded people that such an assumption may no longer be appropriate.

In reality, the availability of supply is not necessarily the critical issue, if supply sustainability is simply regarded as keeping use below replacement rates. At present, taking England and Wales as a whole, less than 10 per cent of average annual effective rainfall is authorized for abstraction by the water companies, industry and agriculture.[4] Even when viewed region to region, with rainfall yield based on a one in 50-year drought, only the Thames region appears to be in danger of requiring abstraction rates in excess of drought rainfall. Options do exist for major interregional transfer schemes, and technical supply-enhancement options have already been identified to cope with unmanaged demand within each region until well into the next century.[5] However, the sustainability of supplies encompasses far more than just the quantity of available water. As discussed below, reduced rainfall has contributed to the decline in river quality and in many instances the environmental impacts of using water in excess of natural replacement levels may be unacceptable.[6]

Quality

Since 1958, surveys have been periodically carried out to establish the overall state of rivers, estuaries and canals in England and Wales. More recently, these surveys have been carried out every five years (1980, 1985 and 1990). The most recent five-year survey in 1990 was conducted by the NRA and found that there had been an overall deterioration of rivers, canals and estuarine water. River quality had declined by nearly 4 per cent, canal quality by 8 per cent and estuaries by 2 per cent compared to the 1985 survey.[7] Factors contributing to the decline, according to the NRA, were sewage and storm outflows, industrial effluent and farm pollution. The dry summers of 1989 and 1990 were also a significant factor; reduced rainfall resulted in a reduction of available water to 'dilute and disperse' inputs of contaminating waste. Compared to the 1980 survey, the decline in Class 1A rivers was 6 per cent, with over 1400 kilometres of top-quality watercourses downgraded.

Between 1990 and 1992, the NRA reported an overall 10 per cent improvement in river quality and in their 1995–96 annual report, the organization stated that there had been a net upgrading in quality of 26.1 per cent of the total length of rivers and canals across England and Wales since 1990. However, 1990 was the year in which river quality had deteriorated to its lowest level since the 1970s, and, despite this improvement, it seems likely that river quality remains poorer than it was in 1980 and well short of the long-term objectives set around that time.[8]

Despite the decline in river quality, the overall quality of drinking water remains high. According to the DWI, almost 99 per cent of the 3.75 million drinking-water samples tested in 1993 met all UK and EU standards at the time. The issue of pesticide levels and more recently endocrine pollutants in drinking water have, however, received renewed attention and demand for action. A recent medical study concluded that atrazine, the most commonly occurring pesticide in drinking water, is a potential cause of breast and other cancers.[9] To bring levels of this pesticide to within the allowable limits permitted under the 1980 EU Directive on Drinking Water Quality, the water companies have been forced to invest over £800 million.[10] Over 40 tonnes of atrazine are used in the UK every year.

Box 5.1 The structure of the water industry

Following the privatization of the water industry in 1989, water and sewerage services in England and Wales are provided by ten licensed Water Service Companies (WSC) and 21 Water Supply Companies. The WSCs provide all of the sewerage services and approximately three-quarters of water supply in England and Wales; the remainder is supplied by the water supply companies. In Scotland, water and sewerage are local authority services provided by nine regional and three island councils. In Northern Ireland, these services are provided by the Department of the Environment for Northern Ireland.

The Environment Agency, established by the Environment Act 1995 (EA 1995), is now responsible for water quality and the control of inputs to the water resource. These functions – as detailed below – were previously carried out by the NRA and HMIP. The Agency was formed by the merger of the NRA and HMIP, together with the Waste Regulatory Authorities, and commenced operations in April 1996.

Tasks carried out by the National Rivers Authority (NRA) (until 1 April 1996)
Established by the 1989 Water Act, the NRA had responsibility for consenting and monitoring both abstractions, from surface and groundwater, and discharges to controlled waters, primarily rivers and estuaries. The NRA also had responsibility for flood defence and drainage, freshwater fisheries, nature conservation and recreation on inland waters and some navigation: in total, the management of the nation's water resource.

Tasks carried out by Her Majesty's Inspectorate of Pollution (HMIP)
(until 1 April 1996)
Under the EPA 1990, HMIP had responsibility for discharges to water from processes subject to integrated pollution control (Part A Processes of the Act). All of the substances prescribed for control to water are red list substances – they pose the greatest threat to the aquatic environment because of their toxicity, bioaccumulative properties or persistence. Consequently, when authorizing prescribed processes which involved releases to water, HMIP was required to consult with the NRA. At the very minimum, HMIP had to include in the authorization any consent conditions required by the NRA to ensure discharges did not result in, or contribute to, failure to meet statutory water quality objectives.[11]

Other organizations include the following

The Office of Water Service (or OFWAT)
OFWAT is responsible for the economic regulation of the water industry and the protection of the interests of existing and potential consumers.

The Drinking Water Inspectorate (DWI)
Established within the DoE in January 1990, the DWI is responsible for ensuring that the water companies of England and Wales are fulfilling their statutory requirements for the supply of wholesome drinking water. The DWI carries out annual technical audits of each water company, which include an assessment of the quality of the water in each supply zone (based on information by the company), arrangements for sampling, and progress made on achieving compliance with UK and EC requirements.[12]

Legislation

The water industry is subject to a substantial amount of both national and EU legislation. Certain processes which discharge to water are subject to Integrated Pollution Control under the Environmental Protection Act 1990. Five new Water Acts in 1991 consolidated over 20 main Acts and a large number of statutes dating back to the 1930s. For example, the Water Resources Act 1991 deals with the functions and responsibilities of the NRA, replacing corresponding sections of the Water Act 1989. Regulations within the Water Acts also implement the requirements of EU directives, such as the 1976 EU Bathing Water Directive and the 1980 EU Drinking Water Directive. In the immediate future it seems likely that both the stringency of water quality standards and their enforcement will increase. Future EU directives will also be of a more integrated nature.

European Union Legislation

Over recent years there have been mounting calls for the EC to rationalize and overhaul much of its existing water legislation. The UK has been prominent in urging a review, challenging the scientific foundation of some directives – in particular those relating to drinking water and bathing water – and expressing concern over the cost implications of others, notably the 1991 Directive on urban waste water treatment. Such an overhaul is now nearing completion. After several years' work, the Commission published a draft Framework Directive on water resources in 1997. The Directive's overall purpose is to provide a framework for the protection of surface freshwaters, estuaries and coastal waters, together with groundwaters. Member States will be required to prepare plans for each river basin to ensure that most surface and groundwaters are of 'good' status by 2010 and for the first time, the issue of water quality will also be addressed by European legislation. The Directive will require Member States to promote the sustainable consumption of water based on long-term protection of water resources.

Scarcity of water in some parts of the European Union has become an increasingly significant issue in recent years and, in some instances, a source of regional conflict. As noted in a paper presented by the Environment Commissioner Ritt Bjerregaard to a meeting of Environment Ministers in October 1995, no water quality policy can really be successful without addressing the issue of quantity, and in turn, the availability of quantities of water of different purposes is fundamentally dependent on the quality of the basic resource. Past European policy has failed to address this issue.

Perhaps the most controversial provision in the proposal is the requirement for Member States to ensure full recovery of the costs of providing water services to households, industry and agriculture by 2010. This marks the Commission's boldest foray yet into the use of economic instruments for environmental purposes outside the field of energy taxation. Whilst the UK already has a fairly comprehensive system to recover charges for water abstraction, distribution, wastewater collection and treatment, the Commission's proposals go even further. Where appropriate, the Commission may come forward with further proposals to ensure that the costs of environmental damage and resource depletion caused by water use are also reflected in water charges. It is far from clear how acceptable these provisions will be to countries such as the UK which have traditionally been hostile to EC intervention in national policies on taxation and charges.[13]

The Commission hopes the proposal will be adopted by Member States by the end of 1997 and implemented by the end of 1999. However, with so many strategic and detailed issues raised by the proposal, this is perhaps unrealistically optimistic.

The remainder of this section focuses on three EU Directives that have been a particular source of conflict between the UK and the Commission: the EU 1980 Drinking Water Directive and the 1976 EU Bathing Water Directive – both of which led to prosecutions by the European Court of Justice – and the 1991 EU Urban Waste Water Directive.

The 1980 Drinking Water Directive and 1976 Bathing Water Directive

The UK has twice been prosecuted by the European Court of Justice over failure to fully implement EC directives relating to water quality. In 1992 the UK was held to be in breach of the 1980 EU Drinking Water Quality Directive. The 1992 prosecution related to breaches concerning "formal" compliance – the introduction of necessary national laws and other measures to implement the Directive by 18 July 1982 and the failure to adopt all measures necessary to achieve the minimum standards contained in the Directive by the 18 July 1985 deadline.[14]

Seven months later the UK was held to be in breach of the 1976 Bathing Water Directive. Under Article 4 of the Directive, the quality of bathing water had to conform to certain limit-values by the end of 1985. The case focused on the waters around Blackpool and those adjacent to Southport. For both sites the UK did not deny that the waters failed to conform to the standard.[15] The Government had intended to bring all designated waters into compliance with EC standards by 1995. However, by the end of 1993 only 79 per cent of the 457 designated waters met the EU bacteriological limits. In 1994 delays in a number of clean-up programmes resulted in 49 UK beaches breaching EC standards and by 1995 11 per cent of designated waters still failed to meet EC standards.[16] Although this represents a marked improvement over the failure rate of 21 per cent in 1993, the improvement can only partly be attributed to the efforts and investments made by the water companies. As noted by the NRA, "favourable" weather conditions experienced over the summer were also a factor: "the exceptionally dry summer in 1995 meant that storm sewer overflows operated relatively infrequently during the bathing season."[17] This, together with the beneficial effect of long hours of sunlight – which serves to kill off some of the bacteria present in sewerage discharges – helped to keep bacteria levels down.

In 1994 the EC proposed to tighten standards under the 1976 Bathing Water Quality Directive. The main features of the proposal are a new mandatory standard of 400/100ml for faecal streptococci and a change in monitoring requirements which would make the present, widely disregarded zero limit for enteroviruses binding.[18] The revised standards could add an industry-estimated additional £1 billion to the existing

£2 billion capital investment programme to bring designated waters in England and Wales up to the existing standards.

The 1991 Urban Waste Water Directive

Under the 1991 Urban Waste Water Directive (91/271/EEC) two phases of major improvements in the sewerage and sewerage treatment infrastructure will be required in all Member States by 2005. The Directive sets minimum standards for the treatment of municipal waste water and the disposal of sewage sludge. Depending upon the population size being served and classification of receiving waters, the Directive specifies what level of treatment (primary, secondary and secondary plus nutrient removal) must be undertaken by sewage treatment works before the waste water can be can be discharged. The Directive also applies to waste water discharged directly to water from a limited number of industries, including milk processing, breweries, the meat industry and fish processing.

Tentative estimates suggest that the implementation of the Directive will result in a 56 per cent increase in the volume of sewage sludge between 1992 and 2005. The projected increases among Member States range from 24 per cent in The Netherlands to 540 per cent in Portugal, with the UK being nearer the average figure at 51%.[19] Most of the UK's annual one million tonnes of sewage sludge is disposed of on agricultural land (52 per cent in 1993–94) and at sea (22 per cent). Other disposal methods include landfill (11 per cent) and incineration (9 per cent).

As the volume of sludge production is set to increase, the main disposal routes themselves are also under increasing pressure. Reduced availability and higher standards are forcing up landfill costs. Incinerators are having to deal with tighter emission limits and a rapid expansion in capacity is unlikely in the immediate future in the face of public opposition. The spreading of sludge on agricultural land is also under pressure due to restrictions on its metal content, curbs on nitrate and phosphorus leaching to protect surface waters, and resistance from food retailers to buying produce grown on sludge-treated soils. The Directive also bans disposal at sea by 1998. However, despite public opposition, it seems likely that within the EU as a whole there will be a major expansion in both incineration and disposal on agricultural land and a significant decrease in the direct disposal of sewage sludge to landfill.

Industry's Response

The preceding sections have detailed the water industry's response to demands for improved water quality. This section concludes by briefly reviewing the controversy over the response of the water industry itself to the issue of water quantity. Water quantity, or more precisely, concern over the availability of continuous and uninterrupted water supplies, attracted considerable attention following another hot summer in the UK in 1995 – the third hottest and second driest since records began in the seventeenth century. Drought orders were imposed, 18 million people faced hose pipe restrictions and the privatized water industry became the focus of considerable public and media hostility. Much of this hostility was due to the fact that as supplies were being restricted, the industry was losing over one third of supplies through leakages – a staggering 6.5 billion litres per day. With annual profits in excess of £1.5 billion since privatization, increased dividends to shareholders at a time of rising water bills, and further controversy over the level of directors' pay in the privatized utilities, it was felt that the industry was not doing enough to reduce leakages and maintain supplies.

In response to this criticism, the water industry maintained that the capital cost of reducing leaks was prohibitive. The Water Services Association, which represents the ten Water Service Companies, suggests that an investment in excess of £400 million would be required to achieve a 1 per cent reduction in leakages. To obtain a leak-proof system would require an investment in the region of £20 billion. Instead of concentrating on reducing leaks, the water industry argues that demand-management options such as water metering may be a more effective means of avoiding future supply restrictions. A recent NRA report suggests that with good demand management through the installation of low-flush toilets, metering, domestic water recycling and various other conservation options, 40 per cent of current usage could be saved. Box 5.2 details some of these demand-management options.

Water quantity is likely to become an increasingly important issue in the next century. Some water companies have been forced to compensate consumers for disruptions in supply, and although the industry is required to provide for a one in 50-year drought, such events are occurring somewhere in the UK every four to five years. With demand forecast to increase by as much as 40 per cent in some regions during the next century and the likelihood of further hot and dry summers, water quantity and pricing could become increasingly sensitive issues. Urgent action may be required to balance the competing demands and needs of different users such as industry, consumers, anglers, environment and conservation groups, and the water industry itself.

Box 5.2 Water demand management

In an attempt to decrease the frequency of water shortages and the need for new reservoirs and boreholes, the National Rivers Authority's 1995 *Saving Water* report suggests various demand-management options that could save 40 per cent of current water usage. Measures include setting a maximum standard for all new washing machines of 80 litres per wash, replacing pre-1981 toilet cisterns in households with dual-flush versions – which allow the option of using half the amount of water of a conventional cistern, the installation of lower-volume shower heads and the promotion of domestic water recycling. Spending £300 per family buying dual-flush toilet cisterns would be more cost-effective than building a new reservoir. Supplying the entire country with new toilets could save 13 per cent of the nation's water needs.

The report also called on the water companies to reduce their leakage rates to six litres per household per hour – equivalent to about 18 per cent of total water pumped into the mains being lost. Despite trials on the Isle of Wight, where water meters have reduced demand by 20 per cent and peak demand by 30%, the NRA believes that fitting one in every home is unnecessary. Instead, selective metering in the South, East Anglia and Thames catchment areas would solve the problem of excessive peak demand.

Source: *Saving Water*, NRA, 1995

Contaminated Land

Summary

Contaminated land has recently become a major environmental issue in the UK. Tighter environmental standards, concern within the financial services sector over lenders' liability and mounting pressure to redevelop derelict and abandoned industrial sites, particularly in and near urban areas, is forcing industry to reappraise its approach to land use and development. No comprehensive survey of UK contaminated sites has been carried out. Estimates suggest that a possible 200,000 hectares may be contaminated. The potential clean-up costs of all contaminated sites could eventually be in the region of £10 to £30 billion. Contaminated land was not forecast or anticipated to be such a major environmental issue in the 1990s.

The Environment Act 1995 introduces a new legal framework to deal with contaminated land. Following intense industrial and commercial opposition, plans to introduce contaminated land-use registers, originally proposed in the Environmental Protection Act 1990, were abandoned. The House of Commons Environment Committee viewed such registers as "an essential first step" in tackling the problem of contaminated land. Business opposition centred on the belief that such registers would result in 'blight' and reduce land and property values. Registers or lists of contaminated sites have been used for some time in the US, Germany and The Netherlands.

In terms of liability, those responsible for the contamination are to be held liable for the clean-up: ie the polluter-pays principle is to apply. However, the Government has rejected EC calls for a strict liability regime, which would only require the injured party to prove a connection between the action taken and the damage caused. With no equivalent of the US Superfund (see Box 5.4), it is also unclear as to who will pay for so-called orphan sites or how far liability will extend.

The Issue

Centuries of industrial activity in the UK have left the country with an unquantified but significant stock of contaminated land – land contaminated with a range of chemical and often persistent pollutants. These include toxic metals, such as lead, arsenic and mercury from mines, iron and steel works and the electroplating industry, flammable gases and corrosive leachates from landfills, and a vast array of substances from chemical works, refineries and waste disposal sites.

There is a great deal of uncertainty over the true extent of the problem in the UK. Estimates suggest that somewhere in the region of 100,000 to 200,000 hectares of land may be chemically contaminated.[21] This area may cover some 100,000 to 150,000 sites. The potential health impacts, risks and economic costs associated with such contamination are well illustrated by the Love Canal incident in the US and a similar incident at Lekkerkerk in The Netherlands. In both cases residential houses had been built on land previously contaminated by toxic chemical wastes. Residents became ill, drinking water was contaminated and contaminated leachates were found in cellars and building voids. The Love Canal site was eventually declared a national emergency and both sites required multi-million dollar clean-up programmes (see Box 5.3).

Box 5.3 The Love Canal

Between 1942 and 1952, the Hooker Electrochemical Company dumped 210,000 tonnes of chemical waste, including caustic substances, alkalis and solvents, into the Love Canal in Upper New York State. The dump was sealed with a layer of clay and subsequently used as the site of a school and housing estate. By the mid-1970s the waste containers had begun to corrode and a series of heavy rains washed the chemicals into underground waterways and hence into gardens and cellars. In 1976 chemical contamination from Love Canal was detected in Lake Ontario and in 1980 over 700 families were evacuated. In addition to personal claims, Hooker faced a claim of $125 million from the US Environmental Protection Agency. Clean-up work on the site cost a further $1.3 billion.

Source: *Business Strategy and the Environment* Vol 4. No.2, April–June 1995

Financial liability is at the heart of the contaminated land debate. Dealing with contaminated sites will impose costs on both the public and private sectors. Estimates by the National Rivers Authority suggest that around £500 million per year is already being spent on dealing with contamination in England and Wales alone. Other estimates suggest that the total clean-up costs of all contaminated sites could eventually be in the region of £10 to 30 billion.

Contaminated land became a major environmental issue in the UK during the much debated passage of the Environment Bill (now the Environment Act 1995) onto the statute book in July 1995. The Bill attracted intense industrial and commercial opposition. Building on earlier environmental legislation, such as the Water Resources Act 1991 and the Environmental Protection Act 1990, the Bill set out a new framework to deal with contaminated land. This involved enhancing the powers of the regulatory and enforcement bodies. This tighter regulatory framework, together with increased pressure from the public and capital markets (concerned about potential lenders' liability for environmental damage), may now be forcing industry to reappraise its approach to land-use and valuation, development, and purchase and sale.

This section reviews the UK's new strategy to contaminated land under the Environment Act 1995, and the success of industrial lobbying in weakening the original proposals which called for the establishment of public registers of contaminated land. Alternative methods of contaminated land treatment, to the standard engineering solution of removal and disposal to landfill, are briefly reviewed in the section on *industry's response*. The UK's landfill tax, introduced in October 1996, is reviewed separately in Chapter 9.[22]

What is the UK's Strategy and Approach to Contaminated Land?

The Environment Act (EA) 1995

Building on statutory nuisance laws, the new legal framework established under the Environment Act 1995 seeks to give local authorities, supported by the Environment Agency, the power to serve clean-up notices to the "appropriate persons" (the person responsible for the "nuisance" or, if they cannot be found, the owner or occupier of the site), when there is clear evidence of harm. To identify sites, local authorities are required, "from time to time", to inspect their areas.

The EA 1995 reaffirms the UK's long-term approach to contaminated land clean-up. This approach is based on the concept of 'suitability for use' – land need only be cleaned up to a standard suitable for the intended new use of the site as it comes up for redevelopment or where a site is causing an environmental or health hazard. 'Suitability of use' has been criticized for encouraging a minimalist approach in land remediation. Very different clean-up operations would be required depending upon whether a contaminated site was to become a car park, a hospital, a housing estate, or a market garden. In contrast, other countries – for example, The Netherlands – apply the concept of multifunctionality; land must be cleaned up to a standard suitable for any end-use.

The UK approach is sometimes justified on the grounds that it minimizes, or attempts to minimize, uncertainty among investors about their potential liabilities. Fear of these liabilities, particularly for lenders, stems from the US experience of Superfund (see Box 5.4) and dominated the business sector's lobbying activities during the passage of the Environment Bill (see below). Industry's concern over this issue may also explain why advice on the responsibility for contaminated land, and its clean-up, was the single highest category of environmental consultancy work in 1995, accounting for 15 per cent of the sector's turnover.[23]

Following the polluter-pays principle, in general, those responsible for the contamination will be liable for paying for the clean-up. However, in situations where they cannot be found, the Government's consultation paper *Paying for Our Past* suggested that funds could also be raised from other parties. Regulators "should – in so far as appropriate – be able to pursue lenders, financial institutions, etc for recovery of costs of cleaning up contamination."[24] Not surprisingly, this sent shock waves through the financial services and banking sectors. However, from the wording of the final text of the Act it seems that there will not be 'a deep pocket' regime whereby lenders could be pursued regardless of their responsibility for any contamination, if no directly responsible party could be found. Consequently, with no equivalent to the Superfund, there is still uncertainty as to who will actually pay for 'orphan sites'. The DoE originally wanted to establish a fund from part of the landfill tax proceeds. However, this proposal was rejected by the Treasury.

Box 5.4 The US Comprehensive Environmental Response,
Compensation and Liability Act 1980

The US Government's response to Love Canal was the enactment of the Comprehensive Environmental Response, Compensation and Liability Act 1980 (CERCLA – known widely as Superfund). Superfund enables the federal government, through the Environmental Protection Agency, to respond to emergencies arising from the uncontrolled releases to the environment of hazardous substances. The Act provides for site identification and gives regulators the power to seek clean-up through the courts by the responsible parties or to carry out clean-up and subsequently recover its costs. Under the Act lenders could become liable, in certain circumstances, for any environmental damage caused by their borrowers. The persons potentially liable for the costs of clean-up include current and past owners and operators of the contaminated site. In some cases this may include parent companies; individual shareholders and directors; predecessor companies; and financial institutions that have exercised a degree of ownership and control.

Not surprisingly, Superfund has been surrounded by controversy and created a lot of anxiety among the US business community. A major criticism has been the large proportion of funds used up in litigation and the resulting long delays in clean-up operations. The fund itself was raised, mainly by taxes on the petroleum and chemical industries with 12.5 per cent coming from government, to finance clean-up costs when "potentially responsible parties" could not be identified to pay for the clean-up of 'orphan sites'. Total funds exceeding $15 billion have been raised. However, in a backlash against the 'green lobby' Congress has plans to repeal and scale down many of its 'green laws', including the Superfund legislation.

The Environment Act 1995 also falls short of earlier plans, under the Environmental Protection Act 1990, to establish public registers of contaminated land. Section 143 of the EPA 1990 would have required local authorities to compile public registers of contaminated land uses – both historic and present – using documentary information. A national set of such registers would appear to be a necessary prerequisite to a comprehensive strategy to deal with contaminated land. Such inventories or registers have formed a key step in many countries, such as The Netherlands, with progressive land remediation policies. However, "few if any items of environmental legislation can have attracted such hostility from such a broad coalition of interests."[25] In addition to those with known or potential liabilities on their books, opposition to the proposals was widespread. Bankers, property developers, chartered surveyors, mortgage lenders, insurers and many sectors of industry all argued that registers would cause planning blight, diminish property values and reduce the security on loans provided by land. In March 1993 the proposals were withdrawn.

Under the new framework, only limited information such as remediation notices and appeals, together with other particulars (to be prescribed in regulations), will be available to the public. It seems likely that Section 143 public registers, by raising the profile of contaminated land and hence making individual companies more accountable in the public domain for their actions or inactions, could have acted as a significant incentive for industry to adopt a more proactive and innovative approach to contaminated land issues. Consequently, the legislation is less effective than it might otherwise have been.

Industry's Response

Environmental legislation has posed a series of problems for the financial services sector. Of particular concern is the prospect of lenders' liability – the risk, under legislative provisions or proposals currently being considered in several countries, that lending institutions could be held liable for environmental damage caused by their borrowers. This legislation is most advanced in the US where, under the Superfund legislation, for example, some lenders have been held liable for contaminated land clean-up (see Box 5.4). Some of the losses at Lloyd's of London also relate to US pollution claims.

In addition to lobbying aggressively to limit or weaken proposed legislation, the financial services sector is also adopting a more positive role in environmental protec-tion through its lending and investment practices. Loan applicants may receive detailed questionnaires on their environmental performance, may be required to pay for site audits where more information is required and could have their applications rejected where the risks are considered too high. For investment purposes, lenders are also attempting to develop effective company ratings, in terms of environmental risk and risk-management systems, as a supplement to existing financial ratings. In time, this new aspect of customer ratings could lead to differential interest rates, loan terms, payback periods and so on being available to customers with different 'scores' or ratings under the scheme. Consequently, greater scrutiny of environmental performance by the financial services sector could act as a major driver in forcing industry to reappraise its approach to contaminated land, among other environmental issues.

Responses from the banking and insurance sectors to increased environmental legislation, and concern over lenders' liability, have varied between countries but there is every indication that environmental assessment will become an integral part of normal banking activity. At the 1992 United Nations Earth Summit in Rio de Janeiro, an earlier initiative by the United Nations Environment Programme led to a statement by banks on the environment and sustainable development. The statement has now attracted nearly 70 signatories.[26] Since then, it has held the first of a series of annual round-table meetings for banks from all over the world to discuss environmental issues. On the European level, the Fédération Bancaire de la Communautée Européennée has set up an environmental working group as have most banking associations at the national level.

Remediation Industries Response

Traditionally, land remediation has involved excavation and removal of contaminated soil to landfill. However, these engineering methods cannot be regarded as sustainable solutions to the problem of land contamination. They simply delay potential threats of further contamination and transfer them to another place and time rather than solving them permanently. More recently, alternative and innovative decontamination technologies have been developed. These methods effectively recycle the land or immobilize or destroy any contaminating species through a range of physical, chemical and biological reactions, for example soil washing.

Relatively cheap landfill in the UK has contributed to a lack of incentive for owners of contaminated sites to consider these alternative methods. Not only is it generally cheaper to remove the contaminated soil from the site and dump it in a landfill, but such a strategy also safeguards the site owner against more stringent legislation and tighter standards in the future. Following the introduction of the landfill tax, and the likelihood that rates for the new tax will be increased, pressure on industry to explore and consider these alternative technologies has increased. Possible restrictions on the disposal of treatable soil to landfill, currently being considered in The Netherlands, will also encourage business to consider these alternative technologies.

Alternative treatments are already being utilized (see Box 5.5). Other initiatives include the recent formation by ten major UK industrial businesses of the Soil and Groundwater Technology Association (SAGTA). The main aim of the organization is to stimulate the development of more cost-effective remediation techniques through information exchange and sharing experience of technical aspects of investigating and dealing with land contamination.

Box 5.5 The use of electro-osmosis and thermal
treatment of contaminated land

The use of electro-osmosis could, according to the developers of the technique –
EA Technology – provide a simpler and more cost-effective approach to contaminated land remediation than simply removing the soil to landfill. The
technique involves applying a voltage to electrodes inserted in the ground. The
cathode attracts metal ions dissolved in the soil's water, while the anode draws
acids.

In 1994 Royal Ordnance commissioned the UK's first thermal treatment plant
for soils contaminated with hydrocarbons. Although this form of clean-up and soil
treatment is currently more expensive than landfill, at roughly £30 per tonne
compared to a typical £15 per tonne landfill charge, Royal Ordnance maintain
that their £1 million treatment unit is competitive when the costs of transport and
reimporting clean fill are taken into account.

Emerging Themes from Chapters 3 to 5

The major theme to emerge from the review of industry's response to the global,
national and regional and local environmental issues discussed in chapters 3 to 5 is one
of industry's continuing confrontation with policy-makers. This sits uneasily with the
expanding set of procedures being built up within companies to address the environmental challenges they now face. Proposed legislation and other policy measures aimed
at tackling the issues have generally been resisted by industry. At the same time,
voluntary initiatives by industry have been limited and unambitious. Numerous
examples have been provided in the reviews, demonstrating that industry's opposition
to legislation has often served to weaken, delay and, in some instances, result in the
complete abandonment of the proposed measure. The pay-off from lobbying is still
seen as high, and from the perspective of industry, such lobbying can be a highly
successful activity.

Of the four main drivers for improved environmental performance reviewed in
Chapter 2 – regulation, customer preferences and demand, relations with local
communities, and investor pressure – regulatory control and anticipation of regulatory
control still appear to be the most important motivating influence on corporate
environment-related decisions. As discussed, legislation has been particularly effective
in reducing sulphur emissions, improving and maintaining water quality, and in
reducing the emission levels of certain vehicle exhaust pollutants. In other areas, such
as reducing anthropogenic emissions of greenhouse gases and reducing the levels of
VOC emissions and ground-level ozone concentrations, regulation has been less
effective. However, this largely reflects a lack of political will at this time to take
meaningful and adequate action. As discussed in Chapters 3 and 4, tighter regulatory
control in both these areas seems inevitable.

Regulation, in some instances, has also been used by some companies as a competitive tool. The different approaches and responses by CFC producers to the proposed phase-out of ozone-depleting chemicals provides a good illustration of how regulation can be used in this way. Unified industrial opposition to controls on CFC production eventually gave way to a more fragmented resistance as individual producers attempted to turn the proposed measures to their advantage. There have been clear winners and losers in the industry–environment debate. While industry, furthermore, may not be adequately addressing the environmental challenges it faces, its approach to the environment has developed and changed significantly over the last three decades. Environment units have been established within companies, corporate environmental statements are being produced, and companies are beginning to adopt and develop their own internal environmental management systems. However, given the scale of the environmental problems faced by society, and recognizing that industry's efforts to reduce the environmental impacts of its activities have done little more than reduce the overall rate of environmental degradation, it is far too early for optimism. A few examples help to illustrate this point. Despite curbs on VOC and NO_x emissions, ground-level ozone concentrations are getting worse. Urban air quality remains poor despite improvements in vehicle emissions; sulphur emissions, although substantially reduced, are still causing incremental damage to ecosystems in certain areas as critical loads continue to be exceeded.

The environment is still seen as a threat, and not an opportunity, and small- and medium-sized companies, although more aware of environmental issues, do not appear to have moved beyond meeting minimum legislative requirements. The reviews provide more examples of trade-offs than win–win outcomes, and based on industry's response to the environmental issues considered, enhanced profits and improved environmental performance are not compatible in many circumstances. In some senses the seven issues examined – ozone depletion, climate change, acid rain, air quality and road transport, volatile organic compounds, water quality, and contaminated land – have 'challenged' industry. They have required industry to change the way things were done in the past and compliance has generally involved considerable costs. Initial opposition and resistance were probably inevitable. However, it is difficult to see how any approach other than regulatory control could have delivered and maintained the improvements in, for example, water and air quality. This does not suggest that continued and ever-tightening regulations will be the best and most effective means of delivering and sustaining continued improvements. Sensible and well-constructed regulations will still have an important part to play in future policy strategies. However, as discussed in Chapter 4, future strategies will also require new, innovative and more participatory approaches to environmental policy to deal with the growing importance of consumption-related emissions and wastes.

Some of these approaches are considered in Chapter 6 to 9, which extend the analysis by examining, with case studies, four sets of approaches to environmental management. Chapter 6 is concerned with the traditional approach to dealing with industrial pollution: process regulation through formal, legally sanctioned authorization arrangements. It deals with the introduction of Integrated Pollution Control (IPC) following the 1990 Environmental Protection Act. By way of contrast, Chapter 7 examines an initiative built on a partnership between companies and public sector bodies. The Aire and Calder project demonstrated to companies the existence of cost-effective opportunities to improve environmental performance. This case study considers the project's success in cutting costs and reducing environmental releases and assesses the degree to which companies can be encouraged to take up the win–win opportunities which manifestly exist. Chapter 8 considers attempts within the electrical and electronics sector to establish mechanisms for reducing and recycling post-consumer waste. This is a form of partnership engaging companies which undertake diverse activities related to a single waste stream. The case study considers the establishment and operation of ICER – the Industry Consortium for Electrical and Electronic Waste Recycling. The final case study (Chapter 9) reviews the use of economic instruments for dealing with environmental problems. The chapter covers the EU's attempts to implement a carbon and energy tax, the UK Government's plans for switchable quotas for sulphur, and the successful implementation of the UK landfill tax.

CHAPTER 6

Integrated Pollution Control

Introduction

The Environmental Protection Act 1990 (EPA) introduced a comprehensive reform of the regulatory system of pollution control. Previously, this system had been dominated by a focus on controls of specific emissions to different media by different agencies. Several of these agencies were merged in 1987 to form Her Majesty's Inspectorate of Pollution (HMIP) which, together with the National Rivers Authority (NRA), took over responsibility for pollution control. In turn, these agencies were merged under the Environment Act 1995 to form the new Environment Agency (EA). The Agency came into being in August 1995 and commenced operations in April 1996.

The EPA gave the regulatory bodies a radical new framework for the control of industrial pollution – Integrated Pollution Control (IPC) – and a set of guiding principles governing its implementation.[1] The framework essentially requires a far more holistic and integrated approach to reducing the overall environmental impact of industrial processes and emphasizes the need to minimize impacts across all media: air, water and soil. Some 2100 of the UK's most complex and polluting processes have now been brought under the IPC framework. These *prescribed* processes can no longer be operated without authorization from the EA.

With its overall goal to achieve a high level of protection for the environment as a whole, the EU's Directive on Integrated Pollution Prevention and Control (IPPC) extends and develops the concept of integrated pollution control across industry. Covering some 3500 to 4000 additional processes not currently subject to IPC, and with a much broader list of prescribed substances in liquid effluents compared to the current IPC list, the Directive is likely to require significant changes to the UK's system of integrated pollution control. Not surprisingly, the implementation of IPC has had its problems. It represents a complex innovation in pollution control and with its explicit goal of minimizing or preventing harmful emissions, rather than simply cleaning them up, IPC has forced industry to reappraise its approach to pollution abatement. Of principal concern to many industries, especially those higher up the materials supply chain, such as energy, metals and chemicals, are the potentially huge cost implications of IPC compliance. Although the EA maintains that IPC is good value for money and can also have positive impacts on competitiveness – by encouraging a search for cost-reducing measures or by stimulating the adoption of alternative process techniques – most companies remain unconvinced. The rhetoric of environmental and economic win–win appears remote to their own experience.

IPC has forced operator companies to address the management of their environmental performance. As such, the implementation of IPC may be contributing to the development of industrial environmental-management systems (EMS) such as BS7750. The overlap and degree of shared and common objectives between IPC and BS7750 is recognized by the EA. However, it is perhaps in strengthening the position of company environmental managers when negotiating with resistant departments within the regulated company that IPC is contributing most to the development of EMSs.

This chapter attempts to evaluate the impacts of IPC on UK industry and to assess the environmental effectiveness of the regime – the other key issue surrounding IPC. It is specifically concerned with assessing:

■ the impact IPC has had on the competitiveness of UK industry – taking into account the costs of compliance and any stimulation of lower-cost, cleaner production technologies;
■ the relationship between industry and regulators with regard to both the negotiations and implementation of IPC – has industry embraced tighter environmental regulation or is industry's response more in line with the 'compliance plus' strategies, as discussed in Chapters 1 and 2;
■ how successful the IPC regime has been in delivering the basic objectives set out in the EPA 1990, including the use of best available techniques not entailing excessive costs (BATNEEC) and, where appropriate, the best practicable environmental option (BPEO) principle.

This chapter provides some basic background information on IPC before moving on to consider what the regime has achieved to date and the impacts of IPC on the competitiveness of UK industry. It also considers the implications of the formation of the Environment Agency and the adoption of the EU's directive on IPPC.

Background

The Integrated Pollution Control Regime

Proposals for an integrated approach to pollution control were first put forward by the Royal Commission on Environmental Pollution in 1976. In its fifth report (*Air Pollution: An Integrated Approach*), the Commission drew attention to the cross-media movement of pollution and recognized that reducing the level of pollution released to one environmental medium could well have implications for another. The report also made the case for a unified inspectorate to ensure an integrated approach to pollution control.

IPC was eventually introduced under the Environmental Protection Act 1990. It represented a comprehensive reform of the regulatory system of pollution control and provided the then new regulatory agencies, HMIP and the NRA, with a radical new framework for the control of industrial pollution (HMIP and the NRA, together with the Waste Regulatory Authorities, were merged under the Environment Act 1995 to form the Environment Agency).[2] Unlike previous single-medium regimes, IPC required a far more holistic and integrated approach to reducing the overall environ-mental impact of industrial processes across all media – air, water and soil. With more emphasis on prevention rather than clean-up, the aspirations of the regime are perhaps also more compatible with the whole notion of the *greening of industry* than previous regimes (the new IPPC framework amplifies this emphasis on prevention further and perhaps represents a more significant leap forward in this respect than IPC).

Under the EPA, no prescribed process can be operated without an authorization. Companies whose processes come within the IPC framework must now apply to the EA for authorization for each relevant process (see below). Authorizations must include conditions which are appropriate for meeting the following objectives:

■ ensuring that the best available techniques not entailing excessive cost (BATNEEC) are used to prevent the release of prescribed substances or, where that is not practicable, to reduce their release to a minimum and render harmless any releases that do take place; and to render harmless any other substances which might cause harm if released;
■ where the process is likely to involve the release of substances into more than one environmental medium, operators are required to consider what the best practicable environmental option (BPEO) is – for example, they must ensure that BATNEEC is used to minimize the pollution which may be caused to the environment taken as a whole.

Authorizations must also ensure compliance with obligations under the EU treaties or international law; with limits or environmental quality standards or objectives; and with the requirements of any national plans establishing limits or quotas for environ-mental releases – such as those used to implement the Large Combustion Plants Directive.

Initially over 5000 of the country's most complex and polluting industrial processes were due to be regulated under the IPC framework (Part A).[3] However, a deregulatory review conducted by the DoE in 1993 reduced this total to approximately 3000. Following the receipt of applications for the final group of processes – covering a diverse range of other industries – the actual total number of processes coming under IPC control turned out to be under 2100. These are shown by process category in Table 6.1.[4]

The EA must review the conditions of each authorization every four years. By December 1995 HMIP had completed the first review for technology options for fuel production and combustion processes with the publication of five revised guidance notes for combustion and gasification processes. Six other notes were published in November 1995 – covering the combustion of a range of waste-derived fuels, specialist combustion processes and carbonization processes. Revised guidance notes for gas turbines were produced ahead of schedule in 1994 because of improvements in burner design.

In March 1996, HMIP announced what have been described as ambitious new emis-sion limits for coal- and oil-fired power stations, almost five years after the plants in question had come under IPC regulation. The new conditions will require the remaining 23 coal- and oil-fired stations to cut their SO_2 emissions by 79 per cent from their 1991 level in 2001 and 85 per cent by 2005, and should enable the UK to easily meet its international commitments to curb SO_2 emissions. Under the revised authorizations each station has been set two annual SO_2 limits: an 'A' limit, which cannot be exceeded, has been set to protect local air quality; and a 'B' limit, which has been set to take into account the combined effect of SO_2 emissions in critical loads. Companies can exceed the B limit for a particular station provided that its overall emissions do not exceed the sum of its B limits. The generators have welcomed this flexibility as well as the non-prescriptive nature of the reauthorizations with regard to BATNEEC (it seems likely that the limits will largely be met by the continuing move to gas-fired generation and a continued reduction in the load factor of coal-fired plant).

Table 6.1 IPC authorizations by process category

Industry	Process	Number of Authorizations
Fuel and power	Combustion: boilers and furnaces, and other	372
Waste disposal industry	All	135
Mineral industry	All	86
Chemical industry	Petrochemical, organic, pesticides, pharmaceutical, acids, halogens, fertilizers, inorganic chemicals, bulk storage	1,195
Metals	Iron and steel, smelting	38
Metals	Non-ferrous	118
Other industry	All	146
Total	All	2,090

Source: adapted from *ENDS Report 254*, March 1996

Application and Process Authorization: Implementing IPC

The EA, in an attempt to speed up the regulatory process, has adopted a cooperative approach in its relations with industry. Operators are reportedly seen as *customers* and the EA offers guidance to assist their *clients and customers* in preparing their IPC applications. Operators are now sent copies of the Chief Inspector's process guidance notes, together with other relevant and useful documentation which details information on process definitions, process descriptions, techniques for controlling releases, achievable releases for different environmental media, relevant standards (for instance, ambient air-quality standards) and monitoring techniques. The regulator may also hold preapplication meetings to discuss draft applications prior to final submission and inform applicants about good applications already on the public register which may be used as models. Although application documents vary considerably in structure and in detail, they should all contain the information detailed in Box 6.1.

HMIP had initially adopted a far more 'arm's length' approach to the authorization process. Most communication between HMIP and process operators took the form of formal written communications. This was intended to avoid the provision of advice to operators by HMIP, which would more appropriately have been obtained from external consultants. The new approach is regarded as more efficient since it avoids unnecessary and time-consuming requests for follow-up information which characterized the early years of IPC.

Box 6.1 Required information for IPC process authorization

Information includes:

- a process description;
- prescribed substances released from the process;
- abatement techniques;
- environmental releases;
- effects of environmental releases;
- monitoring techniques;
- BATNEEC/BPEO justifications; and
- an improvement programme.

The operator's chosen approach should be justified in terms of the BATNEEC principle and, where appropriate, the BPEO principle.

Once received, the EA has four months, or an agreed longer period, to determine an application, to refuse it or to issue an authorization containing conditions under which the process may be operated. The EA must also notify statutory consultees of all applications. These include: the Health and Safety Executive (HSE), the Ministry of Agriculture, Fisheries and Foods (MAFF) and English Nature; the NRA, prior to the merger with HMIP to form the EA, was also a statutory consultee. All applications and subsequent authorizations are advertised in the local press and are placed on the public register unless information is withheld on the grounds of commercial confidentiality.

The authorizations, which follow a standard format, provide a brief description of the process and then list the conditions which the operator must meet. These cover the requirements for keeping records and notification of any unauthorized releases and the conditions the operator must meet with regard to implementing an improvement programme. The authorizations also specify air emission limits, aqueous discharge limits and the conditions for *preventing, minimizing and rendering harmless* releases to land. The improvement programme is the most important element of the authorization. It not only requires operators to investigate and implement environmental improvements to their process, but it is also used by Inspectors to generate important information missing from the original application, such as monitoring details and environmental assessments.

What has IPC Achieved?

This section attempts to assess how effective IPC has been in delivering the basic objectives of the EPA 1990 – to reduce the overall impact of industrial processes across all media – including the use of BATNEEC and, where appropriate, the BPEO principle. It covers monitoring and environmental information and the environmental effectiveness of IPC. The section also considers the relationship between industry and regulators.

Overview

To date, the application, or even the acknowledgement, of BATNEEC and BPEO principles on the part of operators has been limited. There has also been little assessment of environmental impacts in process applications. New authorizations have paid more attention to BATNEEC and BPEO, and it seems likely that greater attention will be paid to these principles in the second round of authorizations. With an ambitious timetable to complete IPC implementation, given the available resources, it is perhaps understandable that the regulators did not devote more attention to ensuring greater adherence to BATNEEC and BPEO in the first round – the priority being to get processes authorized and IPC implemented within the timetable. Consequently, it is too early to measure the success of IPC against a criterion which supposes the full and consistent application of the BATNEEC and BPEO principles. It is also not yet possible to use measurable reductions in environmental releases as a criterion for assessing IPC. Nevertheless, there are important achievements associated with the regime:

- There has been a major improvement in the basic monitoring regime for industrial pollution.
- A comprehensive set of release limits covering air and water has been established, though there has been, as yet, little tightening of release limits to reduce pollution burdens.
- The EA and operators have developed a more sophisticated and confident approach to implementing the regime. Both Inspectors and operators have learned from experience and developed techniques for instituting the legal framework.

Another positive development – as outlined above – concerns the relationship between industry and the regulators. Over the six years that IPC has been operating, there appears to have been a move away from formal, distant relationships between industry and the EA (the 'arm's length' approach) to a more flexible, consultative relationship. This more cooperative and proactive approach is reflected in the increase in preapplication contacts between the EA and operators, a fall in the number of formal requests for more information because of inadequate returns, and reduced determination periods. However, the degree to which this change in approach reflects a conscious decision on the part of the regulators, rather than being forced on them as a result of inadequate funding, is uncertain.

Monitoring and Environmental Information

Improvement of the Knowledge Base

One of the greatest achievements of IPC to date has been the way in which it has stimulated the more rigorous monitoring of environmental releases (not surprisingly, this has been welcomed by suppliers of monitoring equipment). Historically, operators have had little idea of their releases, especially those to air. Sampling of discharges to water took place as a means for controlling site effluent-treatment processes or as a check against NRA sampling. However, little systematic monitoring of releases appears to be have been carried out prior to IPC. Many of the release figures provided in applications are either asserted without any reference to methodology or are deduced from theoretical calculations.

In a review of 80 site authorizations, we found that prior to IPC, only 33 per cent of air releases were sampled, 3 per cent were monitored continuously and 29 per cent were estimated, while the remainder were not monitored at all. As a result of authorization, and if operator proposals and improvement programmes are followed through, virtually all prescribed releases to air will be brought within a monitoring regime. Similarly, the SPRU survey revealed that only 30 per cent of releases of prescribed substances to controlled waters were sampled prior to authorization. As a result of authorization, it appears that all releases in this sample will be monitored by operators if proposals made in applications are included.

Requirements of operators to design and implement monitoring regimes have played a very important role in IPC improvement programmes. Only when reliable information is available can reauthorization procedures be used to secure soundly based reductions in releases.[5]

Chemicals Release Inventory

The establishment of a comprehensive monitoring regime has enabled the construction and maintenance of the Chemicals Release Inventory (CRI) administered by EA central staff. The CRI is built up from individual IPC process authorizations and from the Environment Agency's monitoring reports. It contains year-by-year data on release limits and actual release levels (both measured in annual flows of pollutants). The data is broken down by authorization, substance and receiving media. There are certain limitations inherent in the CRI: it covers only releases of prescribed substances; it covers only release points specified in the process authorization (fugitive emissions are not covered); and it does not contain concentrations as opposed to pollutant flows. Nevertheless, the CRI has the potential to provide meaningful indicators pointing to the effectiveness of IPC. This potential value will not be realized until several years of data have been built up. Methodological problems could arise with the CRI if individual release data based on different monitoring or estimation techniques are aggregated.

Environmental Effectiveness

Overview

IPC to date has been about establishing a baseline of releases and ensuring patterns of future improvements. Any attempts to assess IPC's impacts by measuring reductions in releases must be treated with caution. Very few direct assessments about the environmental effectiveness of IPC can yet be made. However, effectiveness may be judged indirectly – for example, by assessing the content of improvement programmes.

Release Limits

IPC release limits do not yet provide a suitable indicator of the success of IPC, though the fact that they are now being established on a more comprehensive basis is a positive sign. Limits have been set for most releases of prescribed substances to air, controlled waters and sewers. However, these limits largely reflect the position before IPC; in general, existing industrial processes coming into IPC were authorized as they stood. Limits were set according to operator statements in IPC applications. In some cases, estimated emissions were based on calculations which, in the light of subsequent monitoring, proved to be optimistically low. Authorization limits were then varied upwards to accommodate the status quo more comfortably. In other instances, Inspectors have deferred setting limits until more monitoring information becomes available through improvement programmes. For example, limits relating to the majority of releases to controlled waters have simply been 'grandfathered' in from previous consents which predate IPC. Only in a few cases of releases to controlled waters and to air have lower limits been requested or are appraised.

For new plants, Inspectors will use release limits in their process guidance notes as minimum standards, and may occasionally ask for tighter controls if there is an environmental quality argument to be made. For existing plants, the new plant emission standards and upgrading timetables in the process guidance notes provide a baseline for negotiating with operators. However, many operators have been able to justify less onerous standards using BATNEEC-based arguments.

Improvement Programmes

Improvement programmes are central to the implementation of IPC and provide a very strong indicator of the effectiveness of the regime to date. Up to this point, they have provided a useful vehicle for Inspectors to bring operators up to a point where they can begin to be regulated – for instance, where they can require operators to establish adequate monitoring regimes. If followed up during reauthorizations, improvement programmes can move operators towards a release profile close to BATNEEC for new processes.

In practice, many improvement programme items require operators to assess the feasibility of meeting a generic achievable release level mentioned in guidance notes. Inspectors ask for feasibility studies because they must be certain that the achievable release level is realistic in a specific context and that, therefore, it is BATNEEC. Often Inspectors feel that they lack sufficient information to require the operator to meet given release limits. Asking the operator to carry out a feasibility study creates the necessary information and requires operators to justify their conclusions. The Inspector plays an auditing role, checking that operators have produced satisfactory feasibility reports and have considered alternative options. If a report concludes that action is needed, the operator may proceed with the work. In other cases, a variation notice may have to be issued to prompt the operator into action. The approach is pragmatic. Operators are shown draft authorizations, including the improvement programme, and invited to comment. In this way minor problems can be ironed out without resorting to appeal procedures.

In principle, when existing plant is upgraded, any deviation from the limits in the process guidance notes have to be justified to the Chief Inspector. This rarely happens in practice. Inspectors do, however, have some flexibility over the timing of upgrading. Most Inspectors focus their improvement programmes on areas where the greatest reductions in release can be secured.

Environmental Assessments

For processes involving cross-media releases, operators are required to ensure that their choice of BATNEEC adequately reflects the best practical environmental option. This requires the completion of an environmental assessment in order to evaluate the wider effects and impacts of their releases and, consequently, to determine the 'best option' for the environment as a whole. However, to date, environmental assessments have proved to be one of the weakest elements of process applications. In initial applications, the environmental impacts of processes were generally ignored or dismissed. Work carried out by SPRU revealed that only two-thirds of applications had given any consideration, no matter how briefly, to any aspect of the environmental impact of their processes. Very few mentioned ecosystem impacts.

In later applications, operators have begun to refer to dispersion modelling or to compliance with NRA consents as evidence that ambient standards are being met. One problem is that there are few environmental quality benchmarks against which to judge impacts. WHO guide values for SO_2, NO_x and ozone are exceptions. In developing proposals for a BPEO index, the EA had to synthesize environmental assessment levels for many pollutants by adjusting exposure limits employed in an occupational health context. The four-yearly reauthorization cycle may provide an opportunity for operators to raise the quality of their analysis in this respect.

Best Available Techniques Not Entailing Excessive Costs (BATNEEC)

Few operators have justified their process applications using BATNEEC arguments. Although work carried out by SPRU suggests that about two-thirds of applications acknowledged BATNEEC, justification of BATNEEC was provided in only 8 per cent of the cases reviewed. The principle was entirely ignored in a third of applications. Inspectors generally insist on a much more explicit evaluation of alternative options than BATNEEC in applications for new plants.

Inspectors, for example, typically infer costs rather than factor them explicitly into their decision-making. Many Inspectors rank releases according to their significance. Improvements are then negotiated with operators at what are deemed to be a feasible and affordable rate. Inspectors can check feasibility by consulting with colleagues regulating similar processes. Alternatively, Inspectors may ask for financial data in order to assess the relative significance of upgrading costs. In practice, the following broad principles appear to be followed:

- Plant upgrading requirements are often based upon assessments of wider industry practice.

■ To the extent that 'excessive cost' is considered explicitly in relation to existing plant, excessiveness tends to be considered in light of the resources available to the particular enterprise rather than the sector as a whole. The practical guide to IPC issued by HMIP, however, follows the EU 1984 Air Framework Directive and suggests that inspectors should have regard for "the economic situation of undertakings belonging to the category in question."[6]

Best Practicable Environmental Option (BPEO)

Developments at a policy level with regard to the BPEO methodology are intended to facilitate a more uniform approach. The BPEO methodology is intended to provide common tools for Inspectors and operators. However, there are large gaps in the knowledge base needed to apply BPEO, especially in relation to environmental quality and the level of harm caused by substances.

The BPEO principle has been applied even less than BATNEEC by operators making applications. BPEO was acknowledged in just over half of applications but justified in only a handful of applications. Again, where applicable, such information is required as part of the IPC application process. BPEO has also been employed less by inspectors. Although HMIP consulted on a methodology for implementing a BPEO index, this has not yet been brought into operation by the EA.[7] The fact that the index is not yet operational has led to several varying speculations about its impact:

■ It will make operators more conscious of the environmental impact of their activities rather than having their responsibility end at the top of the chimney.
■ By doing so, it will draw attention away from pollution prevention and minimization of releases at source.

These two views of BPEO reflect an inherent tension between an effects-oriented approach to pollution control (what do you need to do) and a technology-based approach (what can you do). The utility of BPEO may differ for new and existing plant. For existing plant, inspectors clearly prefer to assess an operator's ability to implement marginal improvements. For new plant, a wider range of process options may be available and, in this context, the BPEO index may have more applicability.

IPC and Competitiveness

Overview

In principle, IPC forces industry to invest to "prevent the release of prescribed substances, or to reduce their release to a minimum and to render harmless any releases that do take place." Consequently, by raising industry's private costs, compliance with IPC, at least initially, would be expected to have a detrimental affect on competitiveness. However, in a similar fashion to the process of waste minimization (as discussed in Chapter 7), IPC could also have a positive impact on competitiveness by encouraging a search for cost-reducing measures or by stimulating the adoption of alternative process techniques. These benefits can be substantial. Consequently, it is by no means certain what the net effect of IPC on industrial competitiveness may be. The overall effect is also likely to vary between firms – both within and between different industrial sectors – depending upon the characteristics of the individual businesses involved and the approaches and attitudes of their managers.

The impact of IPC on competitiveness is uncertain. Few investments are undertaken solely for IPC compliance. In addition, much of the cost information relating to IPC remains the private knowledge of those companies involved in the IPC process and many firms may also be unable to actually establish what IPC authorization has actually cost them.

Costs

The specific costs of obtaining an IPC authorization include the *application charge* – which relates to the cost of determining an application; an annual *subsistence charge* – to cover the costs of monitoring, inspection and enforcement; and a *substantial variation fee* – to cover subsequent changes to an authorization.[8] These costs are payable to the EA. Other costs incurred by industry include the commitment of internal company resources (management time); monitoring and investment costs (compliance costs); and changes in operating costs. Many operators also make use of external consultants.

With the exception of IPC authorization and subsistence fees, which can be obtained from application and authorization documents, these costs are essentially the private knowledge of the regulated companies themselves. For reasons of commercial confidentiality, companies are often unwilling to disclose these costs. It is also difficult to estimate the cost of IPC compliance. Few investments which lead to reduced environmental releases are undertaken solely for regulatory reasons. Capital investment may be undertaken to replace obsolete plant, expand capacity or to reduce unit production costs. Compliance with regulations may therefore be only one of several factors influencing companies' investment decisions. Similarly, changes in operating practices may involve changes in the amount of time that operators spend on particular tasks. As a result, it can be very difficult to define the precise changes in operating costs attributable to IPC.

Table 6.2 shows estimates of IPC compliance costs obtained from a small sample of 30 operators. The information was obtained from telephone interviews conducted by SPRU.

As shown, investment costs, even when modified to take account of the fact that IPC may not have been the sole motivation, dominate in all sectors except minerals. On average, investments account for 90 per cent of costs. Investment in monitoring accounts for a further 6 per cent and internal management time for 3 per cent. Although the fees charged by the EA to recover the costs of authorizing and policing processes under IPC have been somewhat contentious – with industry resenting the level of charging – authorization fees appear to account for only 1 per cent of costs. The total cost per process is estimated to be typically around £1.6 million.

Table 6.2 Average costs associated per regulated process (£000s/process)

	Investment	Monitoring	Internal costs	Authorization	Consultancy	Total
Combustion	1015	20	50	25	5	1110
Other Fuel	N/A	N/A	N/A	10	N/A	N/A
Waste	750	25	100	10	0.0	885
Minerals	0	0	5	20	10	30
Chemicals I	5325	165	60	15	10	5570
Chemicals II	1625	20	45	15	5	1700
Chemicals III	635	55	95	10	0	800
Other	175	10	15	10	5	210
All Processes	1430	85	55	15	5	1590
Proportion of total	90%	6%	3%	1%	-	100%

Internal company costs estimated on the basis of £500 per person per day.

Investment costs are adjusted according to the degree of dependence on IPC regime. If IPC was 'decisive', 100% of costs are included; if it was 'a factor', 50% of costs are included.

N/A = no company interviewed.

All figures have been rounded up to the nearest 5000.

The cost data presented in Table 6.2 are broadly compatible with data collected from other sources.[9] The total cost per process of entering the IPC system appears to be of the order of £1 to 2 million, though this varies greatly from one sector to another and from one site to another. With some 2100 processes now authorized, this would suggest total costs of the order of £2 to 4.5 billion.[10] However, there are huge uncertainties associated with any figures of this nature. As discussed above, investments might have been undertaken in the absence of regulation or under an alternative single-medium regulatory approach.

Benefits

The EA maintains that IPC is good value for money. It would seem that the requirement for increased and improved monitoring has helped operators to identify areas where potential savings can be made. As part of their '3Es' project – the EA's scheme to assess the impact on process *emissions*, *efficiency* and *economics* of applying a culture of 'operator responsibility' – significant emission reductions and financial-savings opportunities have been identified from two processes at Allied Colloids' chemical works in Bradford. The 3Es project had originally been instigated by HMIP before the transfer of responsibilities to the EA in April 1996.

Allied Colloids had agreed to work with HMIP to identify savings from two of its IPC-authorized processes, together with its effluent treatment plant. Following initial work, the firm believed that savings of £300,000 per year could be made.[11] An interim report published in 1995 identified potential savings of between £1.25 million and £1.5 million per year for an outlay of just £250,000 (representing investment costs and operator and HMIP time). These savings related to one process and the site's effluent treatment works. Similar savings opportunities have also been identified on the third process. In 1996 the final report suggested that potential savings could exceed £4.5 million and concluded that "BATNEEC may not necessarily require expensive 'end-of-pipe' solutions."[12] A significant benefit from the project, as noted by Allied Colloids' Production Director, was the demonstration to both Allied Colloids and many other companies in the process industry that "cost savings and productivity gains – both bottom-line benefits – run in parallel with environmental benefits."[13] The company now intends to apply the 3Es approach elsewhere on the site.

Several staff members of Allied Colloids worked with HMIP to identify deficiencies in existing processes and operational practices. In a similar fashion to the waste minimization initiatives discussed in the next chapter, many of the savings opportunities related to 'upstream' issues, such as material and energy inputs, together with operating practices and procedures. At one plant it was discovered that most emissions to air occurred during plant downtime and change-over between products. Downtime alone, a third of which was caused by inefficient inventory control of raw materials or product storage, was costing the company £1 million annually. Improved batch scheduling and inventory control offered both financial savings to the company and reduced releases to the environment. The 3Es project is now being extended as a joint initiative with the organisation Business and the Environment to five firms in the north-east of England. It is hoped that similar cost-saving opportunities resulting from IPC will be found.

Other potential benefits arising from participation in the IPC authorization process are detailed in Table 6.3. These indirect, less tangible benefits were identified by the same operators involved in the telephone interviews and survey detailed above. As shown, only a quarter of operators interviewed perceived no benefit resulting from IPC authorization.

Table 6.3 Benefits derived from IPC authorization

Benefit	Proportion of sample mentioning
Improved environmental awareness and more effective management	37%
Reduced costs and improved process control	16%
Good publicity and licence to conduct operations	11%
Improved housekeeping	8%
Less burdensome than single-medium control	3%
No benefit	25%

By raising the profile of environmental issues within companies, IPC has forced operators of prescribed processes to address the overall management of their environmental performance. It is from this broader, more process-oriented and holistic approach to the environmental challenges facing industry that many of these less tangible but nonetheless worthwhile benefits have been identified. As demonstrated by the 3Es project, these wider benefits can be substantial.

There are also significant overlaps between IPC and various environmental management systems, such as the European Environmental Management and Audit Scheme

(EMAS) and the UK's BS7750. For example, both IPC and BS7750 require the derivation of baseline environmental releases and impacts; both seek targets for continuous improvement; both seek organizational capabilities for meeting targets; and the emphasis is on operators to demonstrate compliance to third parties. Activities required for IPC authorization place industrial operators in a good position for securing BS7750 accreditation. Similarly, the adoption of environmental standards and environmental management systems by operator companies provides a mechanism for control comparable with much of the work required for the full and effective implementation of IPC.[14]

As industry's attention is increasingly focused on environmental improvement, pollution prevention and cleaner technology, IPC, together with other environmental initiatives and industry voluntary schemes, may now be playing a part in the overall process of the 'greening of industry'. The significance of this role, however, will be very dependent upon the stringency of IPC reauthorizations and adherence and interpretation what constitutes BATNEEC and BPEO.

The Way Forward: the Environmental Agency and the EU's Directive on Integrated Pollution Prevention and Control (IPPC)

The Environment Agency (EA)

The Environment Agency was created by the merger of HMIP and the NRA together with the Waste Regulatory Authorities (WRA) by the Environment Act 1995. The Agency came into being in August 1995 and commenced operations in April 1996. It is still early days for the Agency but already the EA Chief Executive Ed Gallagherhas stated that the Agency does not wish to see a continuation of the "old battle lines" between environmentalists and industry, "but will treat the regulated companies as 'customers'."[15] At a CBI conference in October 1995, Mr Gallagher explained that the Agency can be expected to engineer "a shift from prosecution to prevention". In the water control field this had been made possible by the Environment Act 1995, which gave the agency new powers to serve enforcement notices to correct an actual or impending breach of a discharge consent, as well as works notices to prevent the entry of polluting matter into water.

At the same conference Mr Gallagher went on to explain that he would be keen for the Agency to introduce a system of incentive charges. As pollution levels are reduced, this will result in the Agency receiving lower revenues. There are also plans to streamline and simplify relations between industry and the regulators. In addition, the Agency will eliminate duplication of monitoring with industry, so as to reduce the charges paid and hence the cost of IPC to industry. Where the Agency feels sure that firms will invest some of the savings in environmental improvements, 'deals' may be reached. The Agency will also explore the greater use of economic instruments and adoption of a more 'pragmatic' approach to pollution prevention and control over the next few years.[16]

It is too early to tell what impact this change in approach and emphasis on pollution prevention implies for UK industry. However, the creation of a single agency with overall responsibility for pollution prevention and control can be expected to overcome many of the bottlenecks and inefficiencies associated with the multi-agency system prior to April 1996.

IPPC

The EU's Directive on Integrated Pollution Prevention and Control (IPPC) was adopted in 1996. The introduction of IPPC is likely to have some specific impacts on the UK's current system of IPC. For example, the Directive covers some 3500 to 4000 additional processes not currently subject to IPC and has a much broader list of prescribed substances in liquid effluents, compared to only 23 named items on the current IPC list. However, in other respects, as discussed below, little may change. Both IPC and IPPC employ regulatory principles (BAT and BATNEEC) with the same site-specific caveats.

The Directive's overall goal is to achieve a high level of protection for the environment as a whole by means of measures "designed to prevent or, where that is not practicable, to reduce emissions" to air, water and land. Although the IPC rules have a somewhat different emphasis – requiring the release of prescribed substances to be prevented or, where not practicable, minimizing and rendering them harmless – this difference is regarded as less important than the divergences between the substances prescribed under IPC and the equivalent annexes in the Directive.

The main additional processes that will come under the new regime include intensive livestock units and food and drinks plants.[17] Several hundred manufacturing processes which are currently subject to local authority air pollution control, or are outside the scope of control altogether, will also come under IPPC control. The Department of the Environment has yet to decide whether to apply the IPC system to these additional processes or to take advantage of provisions within the Directive to allow the involvement of other regulatory authorities. Consequently, the Environment Agency together with local authorities and, in cases where the process involves discharges to sewer, the sewerage authority, may all be involved.[18] If this route is taken, legislation will be required to ensure that regulatory decisions incorporate two key principles of the Directive – that limits for releases to all media are based on best available techniques (BAT), and that the various permits "achieve a high level of protection for the environment taken as a whole." The Directive will also require competent authorities to take into account raw material consumption and energy efficiency and the need to promote low-waste technology when defining "best available techniques" in general or in specific cases.[19] While all permits and authorizations will have to contain conditions to ensure compliance with BAT and other obligations on operators (such as to ensure no significant pollution is caused and where waste is produced, that it is recovered), permits will not prescribe the use of any technique or specific technology.[20] This is intended to give operators flexibility in deciding how to comply.

The issue that most divided Member States during negotiations on the Directive concerned the setting of emission limits and the degree to which plants subject to IPPC should be allowed to operate at less-stringent environmental standards than those achievable with BAT – for instance, the degree to which local conditions should be taken into account when determining permit conditions. Many Northern States believed that if authorities were allowed to set standards less stringent than BAT, industry would be encouraged to relocate and this would prevent the possibility of creating a level playing field. Southern states, in contrast, favoured such an approach, and maintained that they lacked the North's financial resources to pay for BAT. Under the original IPPC proposal, it would have been possible to imagine the European Commission systematically collecting BAT information from Member States, synthesizing it and issuing daughter Directives which would specify emission limits permitting arrangements at the Member State level.

The final draft for the Directive addressed the question of EU emission limits much more explicitly, but also bound the circumstances in which Community-level limits might be used. Any requirements will have to emerge from systematic exchanges of information (to be published every three years) and the Council can only act if the Commission proposes. UK policy-makers are adamant that this does not set up a system of Community emission limit-values. However, the Directive can be used for such a purpose if the political climate allows it. The final compromise reached requires permits to be based on BAT but allows authorities to take account of the technical characteristics of processes, their geographical location, and local environmental conditions. It therefore preserves the UK's site-specific approach to authorizations.

Another major concern for UK industry has been the excessively generous timescale for existing processes to be upgraded to BAT. Under IPC, most plants will have to upgrade to new plant standards over the next few years. In contrast, under IPPC, processes need only be upgraded as often as is necessary – Member States were unable to reach an agreement on a specific upgrading period. This may put UK industry at a competitive disadvantage (according to some within industry). The Directive will enter into force in 1999, three years after it was adopted, and Member States will then have eight years to authorize existing processes.

Conclusions

The above discussion has outlined the key features of IPC to date. Despite the limited use of environmental assessments or justification of BATNEEC, and where appropriate BPEO, there have been important achievements associated with the regime:

- There has been a major improvement in the basic monitoring regime for industrial pollution.
- A comprehensive set of release limits covering air and water has been established, though there has been, as yet, little tightening of release limits to reduce pollution burdens.
- The EA and operators have developed a more sophisticated and confident approach to implementing the regime. Both Inspectors and operators have learned from experience and developed techniques for instituting the legal framework.

It is difficult to assess the overall impact of IPC on the competitiveness of UK companies. By raising the profile of environmental issues within companies, IPC has forced operators of prescribed processes to address the overall management of their environmental performance. This, argues the regulators, could have a positive impact on competitiveness by encouraging a search for cost-reducing measures or by stimulating the adoption of alternative process techniques. As demonstrated by the 3Es project, these benefits can be substantial. However, as outlined in the review of the impacts of IPC on the competitiveness of UK industry, compliance costs, dominated by investment expenditure, can also be substantial. Since one of the objectives of IPC, although not expressly stated, is to apply the principal of the polluter pays, it is perhaps somewhat unrealistic to expect win–win type outcomes for all companies affected. It is hard to see, for example, how National Power or PowerGen could gain any private benefit, let alone financial savings, from retrofitting multi-million pound desulphurization equipment to their Drax and Ratcliffe power stations.

One of the principal difficulties in assessing the competitiveness implications of IPC revolves around methodological difficulties in, first, identifying and, second, estimating both costs and benefits which can be directly attributable to IPC compliance. Many of the benefits, such as improved environmental awareness, good publicity, and more effective management are difficult to quantify. Similarly, quantification of compliance costs can be equally difficult. These costs often remain the private knowledge of the regulated companies. Difficulties include: obtaining accurate, rather than ballpark cost estimates from companies; the problem of defining the unit of inquiry – company, site or process; and the variety of motivations, not all regulatory, for undertaking environmental investments – the major cost of compliance for most sectors.

It is also difficult to assess the environmental effectiveness of IPC at this stage. Although all scheduled processes have now been brought inside the IPC system, authorizations have reflected the position before IPC – as declared by operators in their applications. In some instances, adjustments (upwards and downwards) were subsequently made if monitoring proved that initial operator statements were inaccurate. Consequently, with no real attempt to reduce pollution burdens at this stage, release limits as they stand do not yet provide a suitable indicator of the success of IPC. The real challenge, and credibility test, for IPC will come with the first round of reauthorizations – the first of which took place during 1995 – which will need to build on the new monitoring data to implement the BATNEEC and, where appropriate, BPEO principles to reduce overall emissions. By the end of the 1990s, once sufficient data has been built up from operator returns, the Chemicals Release Inventory (CRI), despite a number of limitations, should be able to assess whether IPC is delivering reduced emissions.

It is perhaps also too early to fully assess the wider benefits arising from IPC. Implementation of integrated pollution control has certainly raised the profile of environmental issues within industry. The fact that IPC is a legislative requirement has meant that companies, who may otherwise have chosen not to devote company resources to dealing with environmental issues, are now being forced to address their environmental impacts in a more systematic fashion. Many company environmental managers have used the statutory power of IPC to secure funds from their boards to complete improvements to their processes that have been recognized for years.[21] Consequently, the regulatory push or catalyst provided by IPC is beginning to contribute to the overall 'greening of UK industry'.

Over the six years that IPC has been operating, the relationship between industry and regulators also appears to have improved. Industry, perhaps understandably, still continues to adopt a resistant position to tighter regulations, illustrated by often lengthy and protracted negotiations between operators and industrial organizations and the regulators. However, at the same time there has also been an increased level of cooperation between operators and the regulators. A retreat from the arm's length approach adopted in the early stages of IPC appears to have improved the quality of applications, shortened authorization-determination times and reduced the reliance on formal Schedule 1 notices to gather adequate regulatory information. This increased level of cooperation – for whatever reason – together with a more systematic management of environmental issues with industry could help to facilitate the more widespread realization of the elusive double dividend.

CHAPTER 7

Waste Minimization: A Route to Profit and Cleaner Production

Of the many polluting liquids which now poison the rivers there is not one which cannot be either kept out of streams altogether, or so far purified before admission as to deprive it of its noxious character, and this not only without unduly interfering with manufacturing operations, but even in some instances with a distinct profit to the manufacturer.

1868 Royal Commission on River Pollution

Introduction

The above nineteenth-century observation from the Royal Commission reflects the idea that pollution and waste represent economic inefficiency within the production system. Not only should it be possible to reduce the level of industrial pollution, and therefore reduce industry's burden on the environment, but such reductions may also be achieved at a profit. The experience of a number of recent and successful waste minimization initiatives – the Aire and Calder project, Project Catalyst and the Leicestershire Waste Minimization Initiative (LWMI) – has clearly demonstrated the validity of this idea. Pollution prevention can indeed pay and the elusive double dividend – reduced environmental impacts and increased profits – can be won. Financial savings in excess of £3.3 million a year are now being achieved by the 11 companies participating in the Aire and Calder project. Savings of £2.3 million a year have been achieved by the 14 companies participating in the DTI's Project Catalyst, and after just six months, potential savings of £2.6 million have been identified for the ten companies in the LWMI. However, despite the overwhelming financial case, and logic, for adopting a philosophy of waste minimization, take-up of the idea by UK industry has been limited.

A major reason for this situation is that many companies have very little idea of what their waste actually costs. The ten firms participating in LWMI, for example, estimated their combined annual waste bill to be in the region of £500,000. Following waste audits by consultants Orr & Boss, it was established that the actual figure was closer to £13 million – 4.5 per cent of their total turnover. Other reasons include lack of time and human resources; lack of funds and cashflow available for investment; lack of commitment and resistance to change; lack of information and, for some companies, process and legislative constraints relating to their particular industries. With many companies focusing more on short-term survival rather than future opportunities, it is also perhaps not surprising, given recent economic conditions, that adoption of waste minimization strategies has not been more widespread.

Despite this lack of appreciation of the potential of waste minimization strategies, the seeds of a new culture of waste minimization are starting to take root in the UK. There are now 16 regional *club* approach initiatives being planned or at various stages of implementation across the UK, involving 80 companies. This chapter provides a summary of the Aire and Calder project and outlines how this successful initiative, the UK's first waste minimization demonstration project, has provided both a model and lessons for subsequent waste minimization initiatives. This chapter, furthermore, provides some background information on the project, details the project results, and considers what the implications are for the replication of such initiatives elsewhere in the UK. A number of mini-case studies on individual companies involved in the Aire and Calder project, and other waste minimization initiatives, are also provided to illustrate the benefits achieved by individual companies. A word of caution is voiced in the chapter's conclusion. While the adoption of a waste minimization philosophy can offer the potential for substantial savings, the scale of these savings needs to be kept in perspective. Not all measures which are designed to make industry internalize costs previously inflicted on society will have a positive rate of return for industry. There is a danger that by focusing attention on the idea that pollution prevention pays, industry's expectations may be raised unrealistically. Similarly, the adoption of waste minimization strategies alone, although an important step in the process of reducing industry's environmental burden, does not equate to a sustainable system of industrial production.

Background

The Rivers Aire and Calder drain densely populated industrial catchments in West Yorkshire. Water for public supply, including industry, is abstracted from reservoirs in the headwaters or imported from catchments further north. The river systems have a long history of serious water pollution. A significant investment programme is now underway to restore the water quality of both rivers.

The Aire and Calder project was launched on 25 March 1992 in response to a recommendation in the CEST report *Water: Resource and Opportunity*.[1] The rationale for the project was that many companies, in response to increasing environmental regulation and rising costs for waste disposal, were opting for treatment or end-of-pipe solutions rather than reducing the scale of the problem through waste minimization and cleaner technology. This latter approach appeared to offer the double benefit of reducing emissions and costs, but there was still a need to demonstrate that the technique worked in an industrial context. The initiative was broadly based on the Dutch PRISMA scheme (Project Industrial Successes with Waste Prevention). The PRISMA study, carried out in 1988–90, identified ways of preventing waste emissions in ten companies within five industrial sectors. Of the measures identified by PRISMA, 82 per cent were considered feasible and 27 per cent could be implemented immediately. Of these, almost 80 per cent either cost nothing or had a pay-back of less than one year.[2]

Unlike the Dutch scheme, the Aire and Calder project required participating companies to make a financial contribution to project expenses (to cover half the costs of the external consultants). It was hoped that by making such a commitment, participating firms would develop a greater sense of ownership and commitment to the initiative. The other main difference to the Dutch model was the Aire and Calder's focus on a river catchment rather than on an industry sector. This approach was thought to confer a number of advantages by:

- providing a common interest for participants;
- ensuring a reasonable mix of industries;
- providing a link between industry and the local community; and
- allowing the use of local channels for dissemination.

The project was managed by the March Consulting Group, who were also responsible for carrying out the initial site surveys and waste audits. It was divided into the following three phases:

- recruitment of the participating companies;
- training of staff in waste minimization techniques; identification of measures to reduce waste; assessment of feasibility of measures; installation of monitoring and targeting systems; implementation of selected measures; and
- further implementation, assessment of progress, dissemination and replication.

Each of the 11 participating organizations (Table 7.1) appointed a 'project champion' to coordinate the work and to take responsibility implementing those waste reduction measures identified as feasible. The project made use of a *club* approach, bringing the project champions together regularly to review progress and exchange ideas. Although the focus of the project was limited to liquid effluent, with the proviso that the polluting load should not be transferred to other media, savings were also achieved in both solid and gaseous waste.

Table 7.1 Companies participating in the Aire and Calder project

Company	Business Activity
British Rail	Railway maintenance and engineering
CCSB	Soft drinks
Croda Colours	Dyes and pigments
Crystal Drinks	Soft drinks
DuPont Howson Printing Systems	Printing plates
Hickson and Welch	Organic chemicals
Horsell Industrial Graphics	Printing plates
Lambson Speciality Products	Speciality chemicals
Rhône Poulenc Chemicals	Speciality chemicals
Spring Grove Services	Commercial laundry
Warwick International Specialities	Speciality chemicals

Project Objectives and Support

The project's primary objective was to demonstrate that a systematic and fundamental approach to pollution control pays dividends in the long run (Table 7.2). Attention was focused on prevention through changes to procedures and fundamentally cleaner technology. The controlled nature of the experiment enabled accurate data on benefits and costs to be collected, and gaps in the supply of products and processes to be identified as well as gaps in knowledge which could be satisfied through development or research.

Table 7.2 Objectives of the Aire and Calder project

Objectives are to:

- demonstrate the benefits of a systematic approach to emission reduction;
- focus on procedural changes and cleaner technology;
- collect accurate data on costs and benefits;
- identify gaps in supply, technology and science;
- examine the utility of the IChemE waste minimization manual in practice;
- act as a showcase for UK expertise.

A further tangible output were comments on the Institution of Chemical Engineers (IChemE) Waste Minimization manual.

It is important to appreciate that the primary objective of this project was *not* to improve the quality of the rivers, which is determined by many factors outside the control of those participating in the project. Widespread uptake of waste minimization by other companies will, however, help improve river quality. Support for the project was substantial and a total of £300,000 was raised from The BOC Foundation for the Environment,* Her Majesty's Inspectorate of Pollution, The National Rivers Authority and Yorkshire Water Services. A further £100,000, representing 50 per cent of the consultancy costs, was contributed by the 11 participating companies. A steering group of the sponsors' representatives, chaired by CEST, oversaw the project. The role of the consultants was to enable personnel within the participating companies to undertake some of the assessments and to identify options for change so that they owned the solutions and were committed to them. This also ensured that the process of minimizing waste and substituting cleaner processes continued after the consultants had completed their task.

Project Results

The first encouraging finding was that once a waste minimization philosophy had been adopted, more and more waste minimization opportunities became evident as the project progressed. By 31 August 1994, participants had identified 900 measures which

---

* The BOC Foundation for the Environment is a charitable foundation established by BOC PLC, formly known as the British Oxygen Company.

could reduce waste, improve efficiency and save money (Table 7.3). This represented an increase of 20 per cent on the number identified twelve months earlier at the end of the intensive stage of training and support. After accounting for the double counting of measures from each monitored area, the total identified measures were reduced to 671.

Table 7.3 Savings opportunities identified

Source	To 31 August 1993		To 31 August 1994	
	No.	%	No.	%
Inputs				
Water	140	19	175	19
Raw materials	163	22	199	22
Energy	93	13	119	13
Subtotal	396	54	493	54
Outputs				
Liquid waste	239	32	259	29
Other	108	14	149	17
Sub Total	347	46	408	46
Total	743	100	901	100

Boxes 7.1, 7.2 and 7.3 detail the sorts of savings opportunities identified following the waste audits by the consultants and individual firms participating in the project. These include energy-related savings from improved maintenance procedures and general awareness of energy efficiency and costs; reduced water consumption from improved metering, recycling and improvements in operating practices; and reduced raw material requirements resulting from product- and raw-material recovery from effluent streams.

To the surprise of some participating firms, in excess of two-thirds of the savings arose from reductions in the use of inputs, such as raw materials, energy and water (Table 7.4). This reinforces the oft quoted but rarely believed saying that "pollution is simply material (or energy) out of place." Most of the savings were achieved through relatively simple process changes. However, the study did identify opportunities for the supply of cleaner technology. These are detailed in Table 7.6.

Box 7.1 Reduced effluent production: Hickson Fine Chemicals –
the Aire and Calder project

Hickson Fine Chemicals, a division of Hickson International PLC, occupies a site near the confluence of the Rivers Aire and Calder in Castleford. The site produces organic chemical intermediaries and chemicals which are constituents of many familiar industrial and household products, including paints, dyes, washing powders and weedkillers. Twenty-seven waste minimization opportunities identified during the project resulted in annual savings in excess of £92,000, which were made from an investment of around £35,000 – giving a payback of about four months.

Most savings were obtained from reducing company's liquid waste volume following the installation of a closed-loop cooling system. The company had previously used standard vacuum distillation techniques for purifying product, which made use of a 'direct conduct' condenser. This method resulted in the production of large volumes of contaminated water. Before being discharged back into the river, contaminated cooling water would have to be treated in an on-site effluent treatment works. In contrast, the closed-loop system utilizes an 'indirect contact' condenser which greatly reduces the volume of contaminated waste.

Other savings were made by reducing water consumption following the fitting of triggers on hoses. Energy consumption and raw material usage were also reduced from improved awareness of waste minimization amongst the 800-strong workforce.

Source: *The Aire and Calder Experience, Reducing Costs and
Improving Environmental Performance through Waste Minimization,*
Case Studies (available from CEST)

Box 7.2 Waste minimization opportunities identified by
firms participating in the Aire and Calder project

Rhône-Poulenc Chemicals occupies a 6-acre site (2.4 ha) south-west of Leeds. There has been industrial activity on the site since 1866, with chemical manufacture beginning in the 1930s. Today manufacturing operations concentrate on the production of surfactants which are used in shampoos, detergents and a variety of beauty products. The company has implemented a number of measures aimed at reducing the loss of product and subsequent release of chemical oxygen demand (COD) to effluent. These include improved sampling methods, which reduce product spillage, and changes to product runs and schedules to reduce the requirements for 'boiling out vessels' – which results in the loss of product and the use of washing aids. One year after the start of the project, the company has cut the COD of its effluent by 88 per cent and its effluent volume by 83 per cent – over the same period production had increased by 7.3 per cent.

Horsell Graphics is one of the UK's largest producers of lithographic printing plates. Plate production involves the manipulation of aluminium in acids and alkalis and extensive rinses. The 11-acre site (4.5 ha), employing over 300 people, had annual water and effluent bills of £140,000 and £137,000 respectively. Over 100 waste minimization opportunities were identified at the works. Replacing nitric acid with hydrochloric acid recovered from several points in the plant saved £12,000 per year. Improved pH control at the site effluent treatment plant saved a similar sum. Replacing scrubber liquor for process acid saved an estimated £44,000.

British Rail was involved in the project through its depot at Neville Hill, Leeds, where the main activities are train washing and engine refuelling. One of the site's main problems was an ageing and poorly understood drainage system which results in inadvertent mixing of effluent streams from the two processes. The resulting emulsified, high-COD liquid can cause serious difficulties for the local sewage works. More than 50 waste minimization measures were identified. A modification of diesel fuelling arrangements could save an estimated £50,000 per year and reduce liabilities resulting from ground contamination. Recycling of water containing powerful detergents, which are used in body work cleaning, could save a further £60,000.

Source: *Aire and Calder Case Studies* and *ENDS Report 221*, June 1993

Box 7.3 Cooker sterilization losses: H J Heinz – Project Catalyst

The Problem: HJ Heinz utilize steam-heated cookers and sterilizers for its canned food products. The cans are carried through sterilizers on greased and lubricated conveyors. The steam condensate can become contaminated from the conveyor grease and products from defective cans, which discharge through the expansion of the contents during the cooking and sterilization process. Blockage of steam traps by this contaminated waste prevents the discharge of the condensate, resulting in operatives by-passing steam traps. This action allows steam to discharge continually into the working environment.

■ Changes made: A containment baffle to prevent contaminated waste entering the traps was devised by the utilities team and fitted into the condensate chamber of one of the cookers for trials.

■ Savings and Benefits: £50,000 per year from reduced energy costs associated with steam losses from all cookers. Working environment will also be improved.

■ Cost: £25,000, giving a payback of just six months.

Source: Project Catalyst: *Report to the Demos Project Event, Manchester Airport*, 27 June 1994 (available from the DTI)

In the year to 31 August 1994, the implementation of waste minimization methods continued unabated and resulted in a 55 per cent (from £2.1 million to £3.3 million) increase in savings over the previous year (Table 7.4). Savings in water consumption and, therefore, the production of liquid effluent have been substantial as have savings attributable to improved utilization of energy. Not surprisingly, much of the reduction in emissions to the environment has been indirect, through reductions in the volume and strength of trade effluent going to sewer.

Table 7.4 Financial benefits of measures implemented (£000s)

Source	Savings achieved to 31 August 1993		Savings achieved to 31 August 1994	
	£000s	%	£000s	%
Inputs				
Water	186	9	512	15
Raw materials	1,310	61	1,565	47
Energy	112	5	327	10
Subtotal	*1,608*	*75*	*2,404*	*72*
Outputs				
Liquid waste	197	9	462	14
Other	351	16	484	14
Subtotal	*548*	*25*	*946*	*28*
Total	2,156	100	3,350	100

Of the 671 waste minimization measures identified to 31 August 1994, 60 per cent had been implemented, a further 23 per cent were regarded as feasible and studies had begun on the majority of remaining measures. Only 15, or 2 per cent, of the measures were regarded as unfeasible. Most of those measures regarded as feasible, 148 or 22 per cent of all measures, were scheduled to be implemented over the 12 months to 31 August 1995.

Excluding those measures solely concerned with legislative compliance, just under 90 per cent of measures implemented to 31 August 1994 had pay-backs under two years. Only 3 per cent had pay-backs in excess of three years. Table 7.5 provides an overview of the savings opportunities according to the prevention technique. The relative importance of the techniques used to achieve these savings has changed little during the 12 months since the end of Phase 2. Good housekeeping techniques account for nearly 40 per cent of savings opportunities, and technology modifications – many only minor – account for a further 42 per cent of saving opportunities. Modifications to products have become more important over the two years and on-site reuse of materials still accounts for about 12 per cent of savings.

The major reason for the rapid implementation of these measures and the quick pay-back they provide is that most were extremely simple measures requiring relatively minor changes to working practice, or modest investment in changes to processes and technology. These have sometimes been dismissed as simply 'good housekeeping' and concern has been expressed that participants should have been more ready to install new, fundamentally cleaner technology. However, it usually makes financial and economic sense for companies to opt for the easier and most cost-effective options first. It is less easy to understand why managers, in their day-to-day operations, had not identified and implemented these simple cost-saving opportunities earlier.

Table 7.5 Overview of savings opportunities according to prevention technique

Prevention Technique	Savings achieved to 31 August 1993		Savings achieved to 31 August 1994	
	No.	%	No.	%
Product modifications	2	0.5	24	3.5
Substitution of input materials	23	4.5	33	5
Technology modifications	223	41	282	42
Good house-keeping	226	41.5	256	38
On-site reuse	68	12.5	76	11.5
Total	**542**	**100**	**671**	**100**

This missed opportunity is illustrated by the experience of food company RF Brookes, one of the participants in the LWMI. According to Harry Hallam, the *project champion*, "managers were astounded" to find that the company had been throwing £750,000 of materials into skips each year. There were "several red faces" following the screening of a video, produced to prove the point, which tracked the course of material through the company. A further and striking example is provided by Colgate Palmolive, one of the firms participating in Project Catalyst. A survey at the company's soap factory at Salford revealed a tremendous amount of water wastage from several easily corrected sources. The initial survey revealed that good-quality town water, rather than borehole water, was being used to spray condensers and barometric equipment in a soap-drying plant. Water was also wasted through hose pipes left on after cleaning yards, a cold tap left running continuously to cool milk for operatives' tea breaks, and an emergency eye-wash fountain left on continuously and used as a drinking fountain. Actions to remedy this wastage cost nothing and cut town water consumption by 140,000 cubic metres per year and saved over £80,000 per year in effluent treatment charges.[3]

Having achieved all they can by picking the 'low-hanging fruit', it is hoped that management will have greater confidence to invest more effort and capital in measures which are likely to show a longer pay-back. However, a greater willingness to invest in measures with longer pay-backs has not materialized, as yet, amongst the project participants. In terms of the original objectives, the Aire and Calder project has clearly demonstrated the environmental and economic benefits of a systematic approach to emission reduction based on the principle of waste minimization. The project further emphasized that reductions in emissions can be achieved most profitably from efficiency improvements. Other benefits also arise from this more holistic approach, which might more accurately be described as 'total process efficiency', including:

- a better understanding of processes;
- improved product quality;
- opportunities for new or modified products and processes;
- a better working environment.

Table 7.6 Summary of technological needs

Cleaner technology	surface preparation of plates
	coating of printing plates (low solvents)
	nitration without sulphuric acid
	more efficient bromination
	radio-frequency drying
	dry-seal vacuum pumps
	easy-clean coatings for trains
Process control	deaeration with nitrogen
	sampling of batch processing
Membrane separation involving analysis	dyestuffs, salts, solvents, organic intermediates, sulphuric acid, total organic-carbon chemical-oxygen demand, toxicity

The message that reducing emissions can save money has been demonstrated. This is mainly because the controlled nature of the project enabled collation of accurate data on costs and benefits. Indeed, most participants discovered that costs attributable to waste far exceeded estimates, once they were actually measured. Gaps in the supply of products and processes have been identified and the project has certainly pushed the UK further to the front of European activity on waste minimization, with another six projects now running and ten planned. However, these opportunities have yet to attract suppliers or engage the imagination of the science base. There is no doubt that this project has also affirmed the value of local demonstrators of waste management techniques and environmental improvement. The club nature of the project and the close proximity of participants facilitated regular meetings, the exchange of ideas and the inspiration and encouragement to continue. The local media provided good coverage of the project and favourable publicity for participants.

The project also showed that the regulated and the regulators can work together without conflict of interest. In addition, both the regulators and Yorkshire Water have made considerable use of the results of the project to encourage others nationally and, more especially, at a local and regional level. The Environment Agency, for example, is now sponsoring a number of other demonstration projects (these are briefly discussed below).[4] A further achievement of the project has been to demonstrate that industry can reduce water consumption. This is not only a benefit to companies financially, and a reduction of waste water, but also of environmental benefit because of the detrimental effect of abstraction. Before the project, participating companies spent approximately £1.7 million per annum on water and £0.8 million per annum on trade effluent (Table 7.7). Since the start of the project, however, companies have reduced water consumption by 20 per cent and the emission of trade effluent by 28 per cent, leading to annual savings of over £0.5 million.

Table 7.7 Annual cost of water used and effluent discharged by
participating companies

Water				Liquid effluent		
Metered (m³ × 10³)	Saved	River (m³ × 10³)	Cost (£000s)	Volume (m³ × 10³)	Saved	Cost (£000s)
3,410	661	16,000	1,730	2,400	661	791

In addition, the waste minimization process provides a rigorous method for identifying pollution hazards resulting from leaks, spillages, accidents and other escapes, which could result in one-off pollution incidents. The challenge now is to encourage widespread implementation of total process efficiency in manufacturing and service businesses throughout the UK. Awareness is improving and there is a considerable amount of assistance and guidance available. The key requirement is to establish effective mechanisms for delivering practical support, training and motivation to companies without the need for subsidy.

Factors of Success

According to the final report on the Aire and Calder project, the companies which gained most from the project adopted many or all of the principles in Box 7.4.[5] A strong steering group, which met regularly and to whom the project manager reported, was another significant factor in the success of the project. The knowledge and experience that the group contributed was of enormous benefit, and the sponsors consider that the project benefited greatly from the leadership of CEST and the expertize of the March Consulting Group. In particular, there is work which still needs to be done even if the project manager takes on the burden of recruiting and training the participants. Although one or more of the sponsors could, theoretically, absorb this effort, there is an efficiency gain in leaving this to another body, in this case CEST. A strong collaborative approach between the regulators, HMIP and the NRA, and Yorkshire Water also contributed to the success of the project.

Box 7.4 Aire and Calder success factors

Success factors include:

- senior management commitment and support;
- effective project champion;
- a supportive culture or a change to one;
- mutual support and encouragement of the club;
- consultant with appropriate knowledge of waste minimization and the industry.

At a more detailed level, it is clear that companies which follow a structured approach to waste minimization have most to gain and that the most important elements are:

- engagement of production staff in the project from the start;
- accurate determination of a baseline before improvements are assessed;
- appropriate metering of resource consumption and waste generation;
- rigorous identification, characterization and quantification of waste streams;
- adoption of formal monitoring and targeting techniques to record and quantify improvements.

Replication

Despite the overwhelming financial case for adopting waste minimization strategies, industry appears to remain far from convinced about the potential benefits, or relevance, of waste minimization for their own particular sectors or businesses. A major barrier to the development of further schemes seems to be lack of awareness and lack of information on waste minimization technologies, particularly amongst small- and medium-sized enterprises (SMEs). Other barriers and constraints to the adoption of waste minimization strategies, identified from interviews conducted as part of the final phase of the Aire and Calder project, include: lack of time and human resources; lack of capital and cashflow to pay for investments; lack of commitment and resistance to change; and for some companies, process and legislative constraints relating to their particular industries. Some companies, no doubt, are conducting unpublicized waste minimization initiatives on their own as part of their day-to-day operations. They may not, however, regard or describe them as such. In addition, without the benefit of the expertise of external consultants and waste specialists, or the shared experience gained from the club approach, they may not be maximizing the potential savings available.

In an attempt to overcome some of these constraints and to ensure that the waste minimization message takes route, a series of regional waste minimization club schemes have been, and are in the process of being, established across the UK. The schemes build on the success of the Aire and Calder project and are detailed in Box 7.5.

Box 7.5 Regional waste minimization initiatives

Regional waste minimization club schemes are run by the following:

- the Dee, North Wales;
- the Don, Rother and Dearne catchments, South Yorkshire;
- the Medway, Kent;
- the Humber Estuary;
- Merseyside;
- Leicestershire Waste Minimization Initiative;
- Morecambe Bay;
- the Severn Estuary;
- the Thames Valley;
- the Tees;
- the West Midlands;
- Project Team.

Summaries for both Project Catalyst and the LWMI, the first two initiatives to follow the success of the Aire and Calder project, are provided in Boxes 7.6 and 7.7. In contrast to the Aire and Calder project, both Project Catalyst and the LWMI broadened the scope of the projects to address all types of waste: liquid, solid and gaseous. As detailed in the boxes, both schemes have also reinforced the results of the Aire and Calder project by demonstrating the scale of the potential savings available from waste minimization. Savings of £2.3 million a year have been achieved by the 14 companies participating in the Department of Trade and Industry's Project Catalyst, and after just six months, potential savings of £2.6 million have been identified for the ten companies in the LWMI.

Box 7.6 Project Catalyst

Building on the success of the Aire and Calder project, Project Catalyst was initiated in the summer of 1993 and involved 14 firms in the UK's largest waste minimization project. Participating businesses included an airport operator, a food processing company and a brewing firm together with large and small manufacturers of equipment and chemicals. The project cost in the region of £1 million, funded by the DTI, the BOC Foundation for the Environment and the participating companies themselves. The project ran for 16 months and identified opportunities for reducing emissions and discharges to air, soil and water. Announcing the results in June 1994, the Corporate Affairs Minister said they showed that "much could be achieved with existing technology and better housekeeping; all that is needed is the will to do something."

Financial Savings

The project identified potential savings totalling £8.9 million per year, of which over £2.3 million had been implemented before the end of the project. Opportunities included measures to reduce raw material requirements, to reduce operating costs, to cut water consumption and to reduce the demand for electricity and gas. Almost £2.5 million of the savings identified could be achieved at a zero cost and just under £3 million had pay-back of less than one year. Estimated annual savings ranged from £2.19 million from 67 measures at HJ Heinz, to £107,500 from nine initiatives at Lever Brothers.

Environmental Benefit

The identified opportunities involved a potential reduction of over 12,000 tonnes to landfill, a reduction in demand of over 1,900,000 cubic metres of water and a potential saving of 1,800,000 tonnes of liquid effluent. Of the total value of the 399 opportunities identified, 55 per cent involved technology modifications; 19 per cent were good housekeeping; 23 per cent involved recycle and reuse and 3 per cent were from product modification. All of the participants reported a range of benefits in addition to the cost savings achieved and improvements in environmental performance.

Source: Project Catalyst: *Report to the Demos Project Event,*
Manchester Airport 27 June 1994

> **Box 7.7** The Leicestershire Waste Minimization Initiative (LWMI)
>
> Set up in January 1994, the LWMI aims to demonstrate the technical, financial and environmental effectiveness of better waste management compared to end-of-pipe treatment methods for emissions and waste materials. The scheme was set up and funded by a working group operating under the umbrella of the East Midlands Advisory Group on the Environment – a partnership of local organizations formed to provide small- and medium-sized businesses with free specialist advice on environmental matters. The group comprises Leicestershire County Council, the Leicestershire Training and Enterprise Council, the DTI, the EA, the BOC Foundation for the Environment and Severn Trent Water. A key feature of the scheme is its emphasis on deriving upfront figures for the cost of waste for the ten firms involved. The participating companies – including firms in the food, building materials, engineering, brewing and textile sectors – were required to contribute 25 per cent of the project costs. Waste audits were carried out by the consultants Orr and Boss who were also responsible for identifying opportunities and assisting companies with implementation where necessary. After six months, potential savings of £2.6 million were identified.

It is partly because of this success – the financial returns from such initiatives have been proven – that the DTI, amongst others, has argued that industry should bear much more, if not all, of the costs of future projects. Some commentators, however, believe that the provision of seedcorn funding is essential to get projects off the ground. Without such funding many companies, particularly SMEs, are unlikely to turn up to preliminary meetings on new initiatives, let alone get involved. Firms participating in the latest schemes are now expected to bear a greater part of project costs. Innovative funding arrangements, however, such as paying for consultants out of cash savings achieved – 'pay as you save' arrangements – can be fraught with difficulty. For example, unlike the previous three schemes, the consultancy costs in the West Midlands scheme are planned to be met from the cash savings achieved. The project has attracted £50,000 of funding from the Government's Environmental Technology Best Practice Programme, and a further £130,000 from the BOC Foundation for the Environment and the NRA. These funds will be used to support project management and to subsidize audit costs for the firms involved. Although originally expected to include some 15 firms, the project got underway in the autumn of 1995 with only six firms.

Conclusions

The Aire and Calder project together with Project Catalyst and the LWMI have demonstrated that the potential savings available to UK industry from the adoption of waste minimization initiatives are substantial. Estimates by CEST suggest that UK industry could save £1 billion by adopting those techniques successfully used in the Aire and Calder project. This does not take account of the potential savings from tackling emissions to air and solid wastes, which were outside the scope of the Aire and Calder project. Consequently, the true figure could be much higher.

The scale of these savings, however, should be kept in perspective. Following the implementation of the measures identified in the waste audits, savings by the companies participating in the LWMI are predicted to be only worth perhaps 1 per cent of combined turnover. Taken together, potential savings for the participants of all three projects were predicted to be worth even less, perhaps only 0.27 per cent of turnover.[6] Although these sums do represent real savings, and are undoubtedly worth pursuing, they are relatively modest. On the basis of the results of the three projects taken together, a project costing in the region of £6000, for example, would only be financially worthwhile for sites with incomes of £2.2 million or more. It is therefore, perhaps, not surprising that scarce management time has not always been devoted to the search for waste minimization opportunities.

Similarly, the adoption of a waste minimization philosophy alone, although extremely important in the process of 'greening industry', does not equate to a system of sustainable industrial production in itself. Cost savings and not environmental considerations, together with legislation, are typically the main drivers for implementing waste reduction and minimization measures. While reduced, the environmental burden of those companies adopting a waste minimization philosophy remains significant. Focusing attention on the idea that pollution prevention pays may also raise industry's expectations unrealistically, especially the expectations of SMEs. There is a danger that such a focus may draw attention away from those measures that do not have positive returns or short pay-backs – for instance, those that are unlikely to be taken by industry without legislation or the threat of legislation in the absence of realistic voluntary initiatives by industry.

For many companies the price paid for consuming energy, water and raw materials and for dispersing wastes into the environment still remains too low to attract management attention to the potential of waste reduction. Legislation to correct unrealistic price signals in the market may still be necessary. Given that the 'greening of industry' requires polluters to internalize costs previously inflicted on society, it would be foolish to expect this to be achieved without cost to industry.

CHAPTER 8

Voluntary Approaches to Environmental Management: End-of-Life Electrical and Electronic Equipment Recycling

Introduction

As illustrated in the previous chapter, voluntary approaches to environmental management, often based on new partnerships, can be successful. However, the degree to which such approaches can substitute for either traditional regulatory controls or market instruments is not clear. Similarly, there is uncertainty over the degree to which self-regulation or voluntary approaches can actually deliver meaningful or adequate results and within a reasonable timeframe.

Experience would suggest that in the absence of potential cost savings, from energy efficiency or waste minimization measures, or the threat of tough legislation (that will actually be implemented and enforced), voluntary initiatives in isolation will not work. At the very least some form of legislative framework is required to support such initiatives and to overcome the problem of free riders. Successful initiatives are also likely to require the application of some type of economic instrument – such as a levy or tax – to provide partial funding and finance to support the initiative. For example, the packaging industry's Producer Responsibility Group (PRG) argued that its plan to meet the Government's 1993 challenge to recover 50 to 75 per cent of all packaging waste (industrial, commercial and household) by 2000 would require both legislative support (to prevent free riders) and the introduction of a levy on packaging to provide funding for the scheme.

Reflecting the inherent difficulties in consortia approaches such as this, the packaging industry's attempts to meet the Government's challenge have been dogged by intense infighting, delays and backtracking over targets. However, agreement was eventually reached in December 1995 over how to share the legal responsibility for the recovery of packaging waste among the four main sectors in the chain – raw material producers, converters, packers and fillers, and retailers. Draft regulations were published in July 1996 for consultation and legislation was passed in 1997. The regulations are intended to implement the EC directive on packaging waste which requires Member States to recover 50 to 65 per cent of packaging and to recycle between 25 and 45 per cent – with a minimum of 15 per cent for each material – by 2001.

Under the UK's regulations, all companies who contribute towards the production, use and sale of more than 50 tonnes per year of packaging will be legally responsible (from January 1998) for meeting waste recovery and recycling targets.[1] The regulations have set an interim target of 40 per cent recovery and 8 per cent recycling by 1998/99, rising to 50 per cent recovery and 25 per cent recycling by 2001. The obligation is to be shared amongst the four main sectors in the packaging chain as follows: raw-material manufacturing; 6 per cent; converting; 11 per cent; packing and filling; 36 per cent; and retailing 47 per cent.[2]

The packaging industry's partnership initiative with the Government is perhaps the most advanced and developed of its kind in the UK. However, the compromise deal over how to apportion responsibility for packaging recovery was only reached under the threat of a Government-imposed settlement. Many problems remain to be resolved, not least the development of an infrastructure and administration capable of implementing the initiative. Businesses covered by the regulations will either have to join a registered *compliance scheme* or register with one of the environment agencies (the EA or the Scottish Environment Protection Agency).[3] Whether the regulations can be effectively implemented remains to be seen. Despite the Government's optimism, the complexity of the regulations, together with the practical difficulties associated with data gathering, monitoring and ensuring compliance with the targets across so many businesses, may make the initiative unworkable. This has lead some within the industry to believe that the whole initiative will collapse within a few years.

To explore the feasibility of self-regulation or voluntary approaches further, this chapter provides a case study on the UK electronics industry's attempts to develop a framework strategy for end-of-life (EOL) electronic-equipment waste – one of six priority waste streams identified by the European Commission in 1991. Like the packaging waste initiative, negotiations to develop an industry-lead solution to the problem of EOL electronic-equipment waste and recycling have been dogged by infighting and delays – particularly over funding mechanisms and the need for legislation to underpin producer-responsibility schemes of this nature.

Background

Close to six million large items of electrical and electronic equipment (EEE) are disposed of to landfill each year in the UK. These end-of-life (EOL) items include personal computers and workstations, photocopiers, televisions, video recorders and microwaves. Half of this total, some 500,000 tonnes, comes from households.[4] This is equivalent to about 3 per cent by weight of the domestic waste stream.

EOL electronic equipment represents a potentially valuable and reusable resource – possibly worth in the region of £50 million per year.[5] Despite this, equipment recovery for refurbishment and repair prior to reuse, or for the recovery of component parts and materials for reuse and recycling, is currently very limited. Materials available for recovery include plastics, printed circuit boards, gold, silver, aluminium, tin and copper.

There is mounting political and economic pressure to increase the recovery of used electronic goods. In 1991 the European Commission identified electrical and electronic equipment (EEE) as a priority waste stream and several Member States are currently in the process of developing and implementing their own domestic legislation, ahead of any agreement on a European-wide initiative. The UK Government clearly favours an industry-led voluntary approach. Higher landfill costs, reflecting reduced availability of landfill space, the imposition of landfill levies in several European Member States, including the UK (see Chapter 9), and stricter environmental standards for landfill, have also focused attention on the need to reappraise this waste stream and consider alternative options.

There are three key issues surrounding EOL electronic equipment recycling. First, there is a great deal of uncertainty over the scale of the waste stream, the content of EOL electronic equipment and the existing level of recovery and recycling. All these factors have implications for the potential economic viability and optimal structure of any proposed recovery and recycling schemes. Second, there is uncertainty over the size of the market for recycled goods and materials. Third, and not surprisingly, there is a great deal of controversy surrounding the issue of costs and finance. Questions which need to be addressed include: will recycling and recovery schemes require legislation and a subsidy to be effective, and if so, who should pay and how?

A distinction should be made between commercial and domestic EOL electrical and electronic equipment waste. The former waste is likely to be newer and to include items such as PCs and telecommunication equipment. This sort of equipment is likely to be of greater value with both a market for reuse as whole units and for component parts and spares. In contrast, domestic EOL electrical and electronic equipment waste is likely to be older, invariably broken and to consist of items ranging from old teasmades and electric irons to fridge-freezers and televisions – dominated by low-value electrical goods. In addition to the practical difficulties and cost of collecting domestic electrical waste, and separating items from the rest of the waste stream, such items may have only limited value.

This chapter reviews industry's response to the challenge of EOL electrical and electronic equipment recycling. Although industry appears to be taking a more positive and proactive approach to the issue, compared to the sometimes hostile and sluggish response to the issues considered in Chapter 3 to 5, progress to date has remained limited. The chapter covers the formation of the Industry Consortium for Electrical and Electronic Waste Recycling (ICER), and various other UK industry initiatives. The prospects for European legislation and experience in other countries is also considered.

Industry's Response: Uncertainty and the ICER and EOL Electronic Equipment Recycling Trials

With mounting pressure to address the issue of EOL electronic equipment recycling, and to be seen to be doing so, and in response to recommendations made in a CEST report on the subject, the electronics industry established ICER, the Industry Consortium for Electrical and Electronic Waste Recycling, in 1993. ICER is a voluntary initiative with a cross-sectoral membership which includes suppliers, manufacturers, retailers, recyclers, waste management companies, and local authorities.[6]

In January 1994 the DTI challenged ICER to develop a framework waste strategy for electronic goods – both domestic and commercial – and to begin pilot recycling schemes to test collection and recycling methods by the end of 1994.[7] One of the principal reasons for establishing recycling trials was to address some of the uncertainties over the content and scale of domestic EOL electronic equipment waste.

Based on sales data and average product lifetimes, estimates of the quantity and quality of EOL electronic equipment entering the waste stream have varied considerably. CEST, for example, in their 1991 report, suggest that the annual volume, based on current consumption and disposal patterns, could be in the region of six million items per year.[8] Other estimates suggest a much lower figure. The Warren Spring Laboratory (WSL) has calculated that the annual weight of electronic equipment waste is perhaps only 100,000 tonnes (Table 8.1). While these estimates may not be directly comparable, because of the underlying assumption adopted and inclusion or exclusion of particular product categories, these uncertainties have major implications for the economics and viability of any proposed recovery and recycling schemes.

Table 8.1 Annual arisings of EOL electronic equipment (by weight and quantity)

	Annual arisings (tonnes)	Number of items (million)
Televisions	60,000	3
Video	10,000	1
Personal stereos	500	2.5
Radios/cassettes	5,000	2
Computers (less monitors)	5,000	1
Calculators	500	7.5
Telecommunications	4,000	5
Hi-fis	no data	no data

Source: Warren Spring Laboratory (in *ENDS Report 215*)

In an attempt to address this issue and to gather more accurate data on how much and what type of equipment households dispose of, ICER had initially planned to set up recycling trials at three locations: Cardiff, West Sussex and the Lothian region. The trials would have covered some 230,000 households and involved kerbside collections and drop-off points at civic amenity sites for bulkier and heavier items. However, because of difficulties in raising the required level of funding (the DTI made it clear that it expected industry to pay for the trials themselves), ICER was forced to scale down these plans.

A single trial, involving 5000 to 10,000 households; was eventually started in the autumn of 1995 in the Worthing area of West Sussex. In the trial, householders in Worthing are given grey plastic bags in which to deposit small items of electronic waste. The bags are then placed in *grey boxes*, provided by the Council for other recyclable material under an existing scheme, to be collected as part of the normal kerbside collection service. The waste is then delivered to a materials recovery site in Sompting prior to be taken to three recycling centres for separation and analysis. The trial also covers 3000 householders in the Midhurst area of West Sussex. Instead of kerbside collections, participating householders in the Midhurst area were asked to take their electronic waste directly to civic amenity sites. Householders were also asked to detail what they took to the sites on prepaid cards for return to the Council. ICER plans to use the information generated from the trial to help formulate a national plan which will limit the volume of equipment currently going to landfill.

Funding Options

The issue of funding and the requirement for legislation to support EOL electronic equipment recovery and recycling schemes has split industry. While ICER has stated a preference for either a visible levy, on new products at the time of purchase or a local authority tax, backed up by legislation, other industry groups remain violently opposed to any form of levy since it could affect market share. Other funding options include a general increase in the price of electronic goods; increases in council taxes and business rates to pay for collection and recycling; an additional landfill levy; national taxation allocated to the scheme; or payment by the last user at the time of disposal. Not all of these options reflect 'producer responsibility' and, not surprisingly, it is the last of these options, payment by consumers of a fee at the time of disposal, which has considerable support in industry – from the European Association of Consumer Electronic Manufacturers and the UK trade association BEAMA (the British Electrical Appliances Manufacterers Association). Such a strategy would minimize manufacturers' and retailers' involvement and keep down the price of new products. However, a system requiring consumers to pay at the time of disposal could also act as a fly-tipper's charter, encouraging irresponsible disposal and other abuses. Other manufacturers and industry groups are backing a local authority tax as a funding mechanism.

The most appropriate option is likely to vary between products or sectors and could involve a combination of measures. In terms of administrative ease, however, a product levy may be the only feasible method for all types of EEE. This method is also likely to be favoured by other European Union Member States since it would require consumers to pay in advance for waste management costs.

With regard to the need for legislation, ICER has stated that in the absence of legislation any scheme would be open to abuse and evasion. The organization has welcomed the Government's promise to introduce legislation to underpin voluntary producer responsibility schemes. Legislation could also provide a structure to collect funds for recycling schemes.

Other UK Initiatives – Reuse or Recycle

Perhaps frustrated by the lack of progress being made by ICER, a number of separate electronic waste recycling initiatives have also been started by groups and partnerships involving producers, suppliers and waste management companies – many of whom are also ICER members. Unlike the ICER trials, however, most of these schemes are predominantly concerned with commercial and business electronic waste. These are essentially commercial ventures and are able to operate without subsidy, since there is greater potential to recover collection and recycling costs for this type of waste from the resale of recycled materials – whether as whole systems or component parts.

When possible and practicable, reuse following repair and refurbishment of recovered and collected electronic equipment would seem to offer a more efficient strategy to EOL electronic equipment recycling than a system involving the complete break-up of recovered items to their base materials. Again, this is more likely to be viable for commercial and business electronic waste (it is easier to imagine the commercial viability of a scheme refurbishing PCs and telephones for resale, rather than one attempting to the same with teasmades and toasters). This is illustrated by the experience of a partnership involving the waste management business UK Waste and the reclaimers R Frazier (both ICER members). The partnership is attempting to set up a national collection and recovery system for electronic waste with the intention of ensuring that collected components, as far as possible, are reused as complete systems. In the joint venture, UK Waste provides a nation-wide network of collection depots and R Frazier provides the remanufacturing and marketing capability to return unwanted and repaired items to their former uses. Most of the equipment is collected from large manufacturers of electronic scrap, such as British Telecom, and consists mainly of telecommunications equipment and computer hardware. Other types of electronic wastes, such as televisions, are collected where there is a reuse market. Of items collected, nearly 90 per cent are resold as complete systems or components, with the rest sold to the scrap trade.[9]

The companies state that it makes economic sense for their customers to send their waste to be reused rather than to recycle it destructively. An example is provided by R Frazier who returned £2.5 million to a customer who normally would have paid to have the waste removed. The expansion of company business also lends support to this. In 1993 the UK Waste – R Frazier partnership recovered 400 tonnes of electronic waste. In 1994 the figure increased to 3000 tonnes and the estimated figure for 1995 was 10,000 tonnes. This contrasts with the 250 tonnes of waste equipment expected to be collected in the Sussex trial.

Figure 8.2 Estimated value of EOL electronic equipment waste

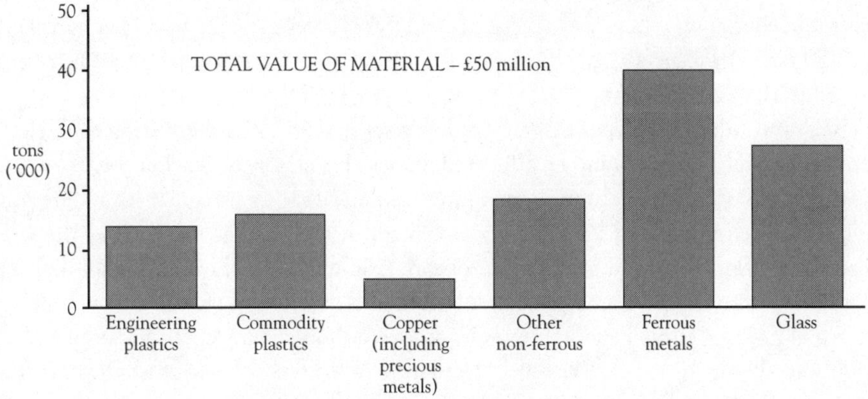

Source: R. Roy, *End-of-Life Electronic Equipment Recycling*, CEST, London, 1991.

Reflecting the disagreement within the industry over the issue of funding and legislation, another industry group, the Electronic Manufacturers Equipment Recycling Group (EMERG), was formed in 1995. The new group involves the recycling firm the Mann Organization together with 17 electronic manufacturers (many of which are also ICER members).[10] EMERG intends to promote "environmentally responsible" and "economically viable" recycling of used equipment. Like the UK Waste and R Frazier project, the initiative concentrates on the more lucrative commercial and business electronic waste as opposed to domestic electronic waste; however, in contrast, the emphasis of EMERG's system will be on recycling used equipment back to the raw materials for use in new products. According to the group, the organization aims to establish an industry-standard recycling scheme that will be highly cost-effective and environmentally appropriate. This, it argues, will negate the need for legislation concerning EOL electronic equipment recycling.

Other initiatives include a feasibility study by the Corporation of London on providing an electronic waste recycling service and a free collection service for used electronic items set up by the Lothian and Edinburgh Environmental Partnership. The scheme covers 800 workplaces in the region.

European Union Initiatives

Electrical and electronic equipment (EEE) was identified as one of six priority waste streams by the European Commission in 1991. Reporting in July 1995, the EEE working group outlined a range of recommended targets for minimization, diversion of waste from landfill and incineration, recycling, and reuse by 2010. Products were divided into 12 categories with targets set for each. With the exception of telecommunications equipment, the targets for the prevention, recovery and disposal of electronic equipment waste were set at around 5 to 10 per cent, 40 to 50 per cent and 40 to 50 per cent respectively. The target for telecommunications equipment recovery was set at 70 to 85 per cent.

The group failed, however, to agree on how responsibilities for recovering EOL electronic equipment waste should be allocated. It was also unable to reach a consensus on whether legislation or voluntary measures are needed to integrate the different approaches being adopted across Europe. Several Member States are set to impose national legislation ahead of any European Commission scheme. These include Germany, Denmark, Sweden and The Netherlands.[11] The group was also unable to reach a consensus, or make any proposals, on overall targets; instead, it recommended that these should be set at EU level "to identify a common level of environmental ambitions."[12] At the end of 1995 it was agreed that it should be left to the Commission to decide who would be responsible for collection and recycling, what mechanism would be used and who would pay. There was also a great deal of uncertainty over what action, if any, would be taken.

In 1996 the Commission clarified the situation with an announcement that the priority waste stream programme had been abandoned. Five years after its launch, despite the belief that getting the main interests involved would actually speed up the regulatory process, only one draft proposal (on end-of-life vehicles) was made. The Commission attributed the lack of success to inadequate data on waste generation, incomplete representation of interested parties on priority waste stream groups, and the difficulty of agreeing targets and objectives when participants did not have a mandate to negotiate them.

While the priority waste stream programme failed, the European electronics industry – spurred on by the prospect of legislation – has been very active on an industry-lead collaborative basis in attempting to address some of the issues involved in EOL electronic equipment waste. This activity stemmed partly from recognition by the industry that it needed to address, and be seen to be addressing, these issues but also from the realization that such action offered the prospect of real cost savings through improved resource efficiency. Such action, perhaps, could also negate, or at least delay, the need for legislation. Box 8.1 provides an overview of CARE Vision 2000, the umbrella programme which contains many of these collaborative initiatives. The programme's broad aim is to improve the efficiency of electronic equipment recycling and to reduce the amount of electronic scrap going to landfill.

> **Box 8.1** CARE (Comprehensive Approach to the
> Recycling of Electronics) Vision 2000
>
> CARE Vision 2000 developed from a single research project concerned with electronics recycling to become the environmental research umbrella of the electronics industry in Europe. It currently has 125 participants – major manufacturers and research institutes – and 17 different projects. These cover technical subjects such as eco-design, recycling technologies and design for disassembly; logistical issues such as take-back and reverse logistics; and economic and marketing topics such as life-cycle costing and consumer behaviour in the second-hand market.
>
> The overall objective of this research programme is to find a comprehensive solution to the problem of electronic scrap by promoting and encouraging reuse and recycling of electrical and electronic products. The approach is very much based on the notion of *shared responsibility* and consequently involves producers, recyclers and consumers. The immediate goal is to develop practical solutions, reflecting technological together with marketing, logistical and economic considerations, which can be directly implemented and applied.
>
> Source: L G Scheidt & H Stadlebauer, *CARE Vision 2000*
> *The Environmental Research Platform of the Electronics Industry in Europe*,
> Sony Environmental Centre Europe, Fellbach, Germany.

Barriers

Although what is and is not economically viable or profitable depends very much upon whose perspective is being considered – and what externalities are included and at what value – industry can go a long way in improving the economics of EOL electronic equipment recycling. Careful attention to product design and choice of materials, with regard to minimizing environmental impacts throughout the product's life-cycle, could minimize the generation of waste at source and enable easier material recovery and reuse and recycling. This is achieved, for example, by using one type of plastic only instead of several in a particular component. With increasing demand for electrical and electronic goods, these upstream activities may be essential, since rising sales may counter any savings in material usage from product minimization and disposal from only limited EOL equipment recovery.

A more liberal approach taken by some manufacturers to the resale of used equipment could also assist in establishing markets for refurbished equipment; this would help to improve the viability of recovery and recycling and refurbishment schemes. Many manufacturers prefer that material does not enter the second-hand and maintenance markets because of the potential impact on the sale of new equipment.

Conclusions

Industry appears divided over the issue of EOL electronic equipment recycling. The response to the Government's challenge to develop a comprehensive *framework strategy*, encompassing domestic and commercial electronic waste, has been incomplete; in a similar fashion to the evolution of the packaging waste plan, industry is now haggling over who should foot the bill for collection and recycling costs. Although various industry groups have been formed, progress on the more challenging half of the waste stream – the collection and recycling of domestic EOL electronic waste, where collection costs can outweigh financial benefits, remains limited. Recycling trials had to be scaled down due to an inability to raise adequate funds and the scale of the single trial started in West Sussex remains modest. Only 5000 to 10,000 households are covered in the collection trial in Worthing – equivalent to the work of one or two "refuse freighters for one week."[13]

EOL electronic equipment recovery and recycling, like waste minimization, offers industry the prospect of the elusive double dividend – reduced environmental impact and the potential of enhanced profits. At the very least, for commercial and business electronic waste, recovery and recycling schemes should offer some return on the disposal of items which, in the absence of such schemes, would normally have been subject to disposal costs. R Frazier provides an example of £2.5 million being returned to a customer who would normally have paid to have their electronic waste disposed of. Not surprisingly, under these circumstances, profitable recovery and recycling schemes are beginning to take off. They represent sound business opportunities and have very little to do with the environment.

EOL electronic equipment recycling has become something of a political issue in Europe. In the UK there appears to be a degree of uncertainty and stalling. While Government waits on industry to meet the challenge and come up with its own solution, industry remains uncertain about what exactly is required and what would be acceptable. With the prospect of European legislation at some future date, and with many Member States implementing their own domestic policies, legislative action in the UK, encompassing some form of funding mechanism, now seems inevitable unless industry can come up with a credible voluntary initiative, with meaningful and defendable environmental targets. To date, this has not happened.

CHAPTER 9
Economic Instruments

Introduction

Pollution and environmental degradation is simply the result of imperfections in the market system that have allowed private and social costs to diverge. Since these imperfections have resulted in economic decisions being made which do not adequately reflect the costs of environmental damage, and as such tending to promote the overuse of natural resources and those very activities which cause the damage. This divergence results in suboptimal and inefficient outcomes. Industry is able to pollute and impose the external costs of its activities, such as contamination of water and land resources, on the rest of society because the market is sending out the wrong price signals.

Government must therefore intervene to align private and social costs and, essentially, to force industry (as well as consumers) to internalize costs previously imposed on the rest of society. This intervention could take the form of standards and regulations, of the type embodied under Integrated Pollution Control (discussed in Chapter 6), or could be implemented by the use of economic instruments, such as 'green' charges and taxes. Voluntary initiatives by industry, as discussed in the previous chapter, may also form part of a balanced policy mix. According to the World Business Council on Sustainable Development, "getting the prices right" is perhaps the most important factor in the pursuit of sustainable development.[1] The idea of internalizing environmental costs and encouraging full cost pricing is not new. The concept builds on the polluter-pays principle (PPP), adopted as a guide to proper environmental polices by the OECD in 1974. The principle states that the polluter should bear the full costs of abating pollution caused by the production of goods and services.

Without getting drawn into a lengthy debate about what the true costs of environmental damage are and how to measure and apportion them equitably, this chapter looks at the use of economic instruments as a means to extend the PPP and thereby to encourage industry to adopt full cost pricing in their business decisions. After a brief review of economic instruments and their use in the OECD, the chapter provides three case studies. These cover the European Commission's attempts to introduce a carbon/energy tax; tradable sulphur quotas (advocated as a means to implement the EU Large Combustion Plant Directive); and the implementation of the UK's landfill tax – the only potential success story out of the three.

The Appeal of Economic Instruments

All economic instruments involve some type of government intervention in the market, through various mechanisms such as taxes, charges and subsidies, which aim to alter the costs and prices of goods and services and to get the prices right, by providing incentives and encouraging changes in both producer and consumer behaviour. Box 9.1 lists the principal types of economic instruments.

Box 9.1 Different types of environmental economic instruments

Economic instruments include:

- charges and taxes;
- deposit schemes;
- subsidies;
- market creations;
- enforcement incentives.

Source: *The Use of Economic Instruments in Nordic Environmental Policy*,
Nordic Council of Ministers, Copenhagen, 1994

The appeal of economic instruments is that they can provide a flexible, cost-effective and market-based solution to the problems of environmental degradation and pollution. As such, they tend to appeal to industry more than traditional command-and-control type policy interventions – at least in theory.

They have two primary advantages over standards. In the short term, they can provide a given level of environmental improvement at a lower cost to society than is achievable by the introduction of standards. This is because, again, at least in theory, producers will have an incentive to reduce their pollution and waste for as long as it is less expensive to do so than to pay environmental charges.[2] In addition, such an approach also allows industry the flexibility to use the technology they judge to be most efficient and appropriate for their circumstances. Second, in the long run, economic instruments can provide incentives for continual improvements beyond those demanded by fixed standards. This could encourage innovation by encouraging polluters to change to cleaner technologies, and to develop new technologies since it pays to clean up more.

Other advantages of economic instruments include lower compliance costs for industry. Some American studies suggest that the difference in the cost to the community between typical regulation and well-designed economic instruments may be as much as five or ten times.[3] The administrative costs for government may also be lower.

Experience with Economic Instruments

Although there appears to be growing interest in the use of economic or market-based instruments in the OECD, the actual use of such instruments – with the exception of

Scandinavia – remains limited. The OECD average is about six or seven instruments in use per country, with perhaps two or three water and waste user charges, a deposit-refund system and a tax differential on unleaded fuel as the standard spread.[4] Green taxes or charges appear to be the most widely used and the oldest economic instruments for environmental protection.[5] Examples of other instruments in use include the imposition of charges on artificial fertilizers in several Nordic countries; taxes on disposable batteries; scrap car levies; charges on the emission of NO_x and SO_2, again in Scandinavia; and the imposition of a 100 Lira charge on plastic bags in Italy – which resulted in an initial fall in their use by 40 per cent. However, to date, industry within much of the OECD remains largely unaffected by economic instruments. Many of the taxes that have been introduced have been implemented principally to raise revenues and have been set at too low a level to affect polluters' behaviour.

The remainder of this chapter is divided into three sections. The first reviews the development of the EU's proposal to implement an carbon and energy tax and industry's role in effectively preventing the introduction of a community-wide scheme. The second assesses another abandoned attempt to introduce a market instrument, in this case a 'tradable permit' (or 'switchable quota') scheme for sulphur dioxide (SO_2) emissions. The third looks at the introduction of the UK's landfill tax which, to date, represents the most significant market-based instrument facing UK industry.

The European Carbon/Energy Tax

The European Commission's proposal for a combined carbon/energy tax ranks as one of the most controversial in the history of EC environmental policy. The original proposal, which called for a phased introduction of the tax from $3 to $10 per barrel of oil over a seven-year period – split 50/50 between the carbon and energy components – met with intense and hostile industrial opposition. Despite industry's apparent acceptance of market-based solutions and generous exemptions for energy intensive industries, business groups were very active in opposing the Commission's proposals. Although the failure to introduce a tax perhaps owes more to political debates about Member State sovereignty over fiscal policy, industrial opposition was a very striking feature of the debate.[6]

Background: Why a Carbon/Energy Tax

A detailed account of the science of global warming and development of the United Nations Framework Convention on Climate Change is provided in Chapter 3. This section focuses solely on the development of the EU's strategy to address the challenge of global climate change. EC interest in climate change began in 1988–89 and coincided with a number of hot summers and a strong performance by the Green parties in the European elections. Following a review of the latest scientific evidence and wider global diplomatic activity, the Commission started a formal programme of policy studies in 1989. By 1990 it was clear that the Commission intended to sign the Framework Convention on Climate Change at the United Nations Conference on Environment and Development (UNCED), popularly known as the Rio Earth Summit, in June

1992, and also to take a proactive role in treaty negotiations. In October 1990, an unprecedented joint EC Council of Environment and Energy Ministers agreed a Community-wide target of stabilizing carbon dioxide emissions at their 1990 levels by 2000. However, there was no agreement regarding either the means for achieving this target or distributing the target around individual Member States.

Development of the EU's Climate Strategy

It took until May 1992, just a few days before the UNCED, for the Commission to develop its formal policy strategy. It consisted of four draft measures covering monitoring mechanisms for CO_2, a set of conventional measures relating to the promotion of energy efficiency (SAVE and ALTENER), the use of 'cohesion funds' to stimulate development in economically less favoured regions of the Community, and proposals for the carbon/energy tax. The logic behind introducing a tax was simple: taxing fuels according to their carbon content will, in principle, lead to the selection of a cost-effective set of abatement measures through the operation of the market. For all the reasons detailed above with regard to the advantages of market-based instruments, the implementation of such a tax would allow business and individuals to make the decisions about which pollution abatement measures to take. It would favour the selection of less carbon-intensive fuels and technologies and, where no alternative fuels or production technologies exist, costs would rise and the demand for such products would decline.[7]

The use of market-based instruments also fitted in with the Commission's aim to move away from the traditional command-and-control policy interventions which had characterized past environmental action. The new approach to environmental policy-making, detailed in the Commission's Fifth Environmental Action Programme, places greater emphasis on the participation and involvement of all stakeholders – shared responsibility – and the use of a wider range of policy instruments.

The Policy Process

Although the Maastricht Treaty enabled the majority of new environmental policy measures to be agreed on the basis of a qualified majority vote in the EC Council of Ministers, there were three important exceptions to this rule. These were:

- provisions primarily of a fiscal nature;
- measures concerning town and country planning, land use and management of water resources;
- measures significantly affecting a Member State's choice between different energy sources and the general structure of its energy supply.

Any environmental policy measures falling within these categories still required unanimous agreement by Member States. The proposals for a tax, impinging on both taxation and energy, therefore required unanimous agreement.

Before reviewing industry's response to the Commission's plans for a carbon/energy tax, it is worth noting that the proposals were first made amid complex and often heated debates within the EC over the role of Community institutions, the issue of subsidiarity and negotiations for fiscal harmonization. Several Member States, most notably the UK, were opposed to the idea of a mandatory EU-level tax on principle, reflecting political concern about a perceived loss of sovereignty. The EC was also in the middle of a recession and, not surprisingly, rising unemployment and European competitiveness were seen as more urgent issues than concerns about the environment.

Safeguards for Vulnerable Industries

In order to safeguard international competitiveness, the Commission's proposal contained various safety nets to protect vulnerable industries. These included the following provisions:

- If specific firms were to be disadvantaged by an increase in imports from non-OECD countries, they could be granted graduated exemptions, ranging from 25 to 90 per cent from the tax.
- Firms which were very dependent upon external trade would receive a full exemption, as long as they could demonstrate substantial efforts to save energy or reduce CO_2 emissions.
- Member States would also be required to allow companies to set a proportion of investment in energy saving and CO_2 reductions against the carbon/energy tax.

Implementation was also conditional upon main competitors within the OECD introducing a similar tax – or measures resulting in similar financial effects – in order to ensure the maintenance of a level playing field, at least within the OECD. The generosity of these provisions was criticized by some commentators and environmental groups as undermining the whole credibility of the tax. If the most energy intensive industries were to be largely exempted from the tax, why have an energy tax?

The Business Response to the Proposal

Industry's principal objection to the Commission's proposal for a carbon/energy tax concerned the potential impacts such a tax would have on their international competitiveness in global markets – especially for energy-intensive industries. Although economic analysis of the $10 per barrel carbon and energy tax has shown that the aggregate effects would be small, as long as the tax was phased in gradually and the principle of revenue-neutrality was observed (the tax should not result in increased revenues for government but should, instead, be recycled back into the economy), the impact on specific, vulnerable sectors would have been considerable – despite the safeguards.[8]

Direct energy costs, for example, although only making up 2 per cent of industrial production costs on average, make up to 10 to 20 per cent of costs in high-impact industries, such as iron and steel and cement production, and some 5 to 10 per cent of total direct costs in moderate-impact industries, such as chemicals, paper and ceramics. These industries stood to lose substantially if the commission succeeded in implementing its proposals. Not surprisingly resistance to the tax was fierce and the intensity of the anti-tax campaign waged by industry surprised some national governments and parts of the Commission.[9] Predictably, resistance has been greatest amongst these high-impact industries.

When the formal tax proposal appeared in May 1992, industry seemed surprised at how serious the proposals looked. The reaction was a concerted attempt to kill the tax idea, not to modify or delay it.[10] In carrying out this strategy, industry employed a number of different tactics. Discussions were held with the administrators of national governments who were potentially hostile to the tax and with sympathetic Directorates within the Commission – DGXVII (Energy) and DGIII (Industry) for sectors such as chemicals. Less official representations from high-level company officers were also made to politicians. The lead was taken by European-level industrial associations such as EurElectric, EuroPIA (petroleum refiners), CEFIC (European Chemical Industry Council), EuroMetaux, IFIEC (International Federation of Industrial Energy Consumers) and Brussels-based company officers who could exploit their contacts within the Commission. International and national federations also voiced their objections and criticisms of the tax, including the UNICE (Union of Industrial and Employers' Confederations of Europe) and the UK's Confederation of British Industry (CBI).

Following the formal proposal of the tax in May 1992, tactics switched away from broadly based criticisms towards detailed aspects of the proposal. Proactive suggestions for alternatives to the tax – conventional command-and-control regulation and voluntary initiatives, such as sector-specific reduction targets – were also made. Industry's position was strengthened by the absence of a strong pro-tax lobby. Environmental groups backed away from the debate, conscious of the unpopularity of tax measures and the uneven impact of tax on different social groups.

Lessons from the Carbon/Energy Tax

The carbon/energy tax story illustrates that there are still circumstances in which it will be in the interest of industry to adopt a highly negative approach to proposed environmental measures. In this case, political lobbying activity of the simplest and most traditional kind offers pay-offs which are well in excess of either the direct costs or any loss of public image. The central objective of this strategy is not to adapt or anticipate the policy agenda – it is to modify it radically.[11]

The strategy paid off. Having virtually abandoned the whole idea of a Community wide carbon/energy tax, the Commission eventually re-proposed the tax in a very weakened and modified form in March 1995. The re-proposal specified that the tax was an optional measure which could be adopted at the discretion of individual Member States. The tax would have to be adopted using the same structure as the original 1992 proposal (50/50 carbon/energy mix), but Member States could adopt it to any degree they wished – for example, 0 to 100 per cent of the $10 per barrel rate (this ensures that any parallel national taxes are compatible and could be harmonized at a later date).[12] In the event, the Commission was obliged to withdraw even the weakened 'optional' measure in March 1996. A more substantially revised proposal which would harmonise excise duties on fuels now sits with the Council of Ministers.

The carbon/energy tax story also illustrates that when the economic consequences of policy are large and manifestly obvious to stakeholders, the negotiation of economic instruments can be as difficult and fraught, if not more so, than negotiations of more traditional command and control policy interventions. However, industry's response to the proposals also illustrates that business's strategy in dealing with such policy challenges has evolved and become more sophisticated. Keen to demonstrate a more proactive approach to environmental policy making to a more informed, and perhaps more concerned general public, very few firms or sectors attempted to use the strategy, employed extensively during the debate on acid rain, of exploiting ambiguities in scientific evidence and denying that there was any environmental problem in the first place. Instead, industry broadly accepted Community policy goals and proposed alternative measures which the Community and national governments might adopt – such as measures aimed at encouraging energy efficiency and voluntary measures by industry in place of economic instruments.

Switchable Quotas for Sulphur

During 1994–96, the UK Government gave careful consideration to the introduction of a limited 'switchable quota' scheme for sulphur dioxide (SO_2) emitted from large combustion plants – that is, traditional fossil-fuel-fired power stations, petroleum refineries and boiler plants located at larger manufacturing facilities.[13] The ideas under consideration were essentially variations on the concept of 'tradable emission permits' which have been implemented in the US under the 1990 Clean Air Act Amendments.

There were several reasons for this drive: a political desire to restore lost momentum in the push towards the greater use of economic instruments; the need for policy instruments which would provide assurance that international obligations would be met; emerging difficulties with the underlying system of traditional regulatory control; and the development of competition in the all-important power generation sector. The Government has decided, at least for the time being, not to proceed with the 'switchable quota' proposals. Even the uninspiring title of switchable quotas symbolizes a certain degree of lukewarmness about the concept in the policy community. This section traces the origins and attractions of this policy instrument in the UK context and assesses why the measure did not come to fruition.

Background

Meeting international obligations with regard to SO_2 emissions was the ultimate driver of the 'switchable quota' concept. Under the 1988 Large Combustion Plants (LCP) Directive (see Chapter 4), the UK undertook to reduce emissions from 'existing' (pre-1987) plants by 20 per cent by 1993, 40 per cent by 1998 and 60 per cent by 2003 from the 1980 baseline. Under the UN Economic Commission for Europe convention on transboundary air pollution, the UK has also agreed to reduce SO_2 emissions from all sources by 70 per cent by the 2005 and 80 per cent by the year 2010, again from a 1980 baseline.

In order to implement the LCP Directive, the 1990 Environmental Protection Act enabled the Government to establish national plans for emissions reductions. A national plan issued in 1991 allocated separate sets of sulphur quotas to three sectors (power generation, refining and manufacturing) and the three regions of the UK

(England and Wales, Scotland and Northern Ireland). In addition, the power quotas for England and Wales were distributed directly to the two main fossil generators: National Power and PowerGen. The quota system was implemented through the integrated pollution control system (see Chapter 6). Her Majesty's Inspectorate of Pollution (HMIP) allocated annual sulphur quotas to sites under its control in such a way as to ensure consistency with the overall national plan. The quota system was therefore overlaid on the IPC system. Individual sites had to meet their quotas and also to meet 'best available techniques not entailing excessive cost' (BATNEEC) and 'best practicable environmental option' (BPEO) criteria.

For National Power and PowerGen, which each had a company quota, the situation was more complex. They wanted flexibility to switch their sulphur quotas between individual power stations, in order to take account of changes in plant availability and developments in the newly liberalized electricity market. They succeeded in agreeing with HMIP a simple administrative procedure for transferring sulphur quotas from one station to another. However, the unfettered use of this administrative procedure would have risked the breaching of the BATNEEC-BPEO principles at sites located in sensitive areas.[14] For power stations, a second sulphur quota which would reflect site-specific factors was therefore allocated. The generators had freedom to switch national plan quotas from one site to another. But their ability to do so was constrained by the generally higher BATNEEC quotas set at the site level.

Emerging Regulatory Problems

Interest in quota switching derived partly from the rigidities inherent in the allocation system. The initial national plan quotas set in 1990 proved to be inappropriate. Rapid investment in clean gas-fired generating plants in England and Wales caused traditional coal-fired generation to decline, and National Power's and PowerGen's sulphur emissions fell far below their quota levels without the need for specific emission abatement measures. PowerGen abandoned plans to fit desulphurization plant at its Ferrybridge power station.[15] Furthermore, National Power and PowerGen were forced into selling some of their mid-load power stations (those which are particularly influential in setting electricity prices) by the electricity regulator. These are all 'dirty' coal stations. To operate under new owners, these stations would require sulphur quotas.

On the other hand, other sulphur emitters were facing difficulties. A high proportion of Scottish electricity is nuclear in origin. Declining emission quotas in Scotland started from a low baseline and, without investment in new gas-fired plant, Scottish Power would struggle to meet its quotas without investing in desulphurization plant at its large Longannet plant. Ironically, Longannet burns low-sulphur coal and is far cleaner than the Ferrybridge plant at which PowerGen has abandoned desulphurization plans. The UK national plan was modified to switch some sulphur from Scottish industry to Scottish power generation to relieve Scottish Power's difficulties. At the same time, there was growing pressure on industry in England and Wales because sulphur emissions were not declining as quickly as had been anticipated when the national plan was framed. It was assumed that older combustion plants would progressively be retired and make way for new cleaner plants. With the recession of the early

1990s and low fuel prices providing no incentives, plants were retained and emissions failed to go down.

Finally, a number of manufacturing companies – for example, ICI and British Sugar – had several sites covered under the national plan. They aspired to the flexibility which National Power and PowerGen already enjoyed and wanted to switch quotas from one site to another. For an accumulating set of reasons – quota surpluses in some sectors, deficits in others and demands for greater flexibility – the policy attraction of a switchable quota system was considerable.

Agreeing Switchable Quotas

Any scheme which did emerge would have to assure the UK that its international obligations would be met and would be compatible with the pre-existing integrated pollution control system. Politically, there was no question of new primary legislation to bring a scheme into being. Within these constraints, the basic outline of how a switchable quota scheme might operate was reasonably clear. Plant operators would be free to exchange quotas – within companies or between companies for an agreed sum of money – within any given year. Banking quotas for use in a subsequent year would provide no assurance about meeting international obligations on a year-to-year basis – and would not necessarily be compatible with BATNEEC-BPEO principles. To prevent BATNEEC being breached, it would be necessary to set two sulphur quotas for every plant, as was already the case for the England and Wales power generators. One would be a national plan quota which could be switched, the other a backstop BATNEEC quota to ensure that site-specific environmental impacts were taken into account. Government had no plans to become involved in creating a market for sulphur quotas in an institutional sense. It would be up to those involved in transactions to make their own bilateral arrangements.

All that was needed in order to have an operational switchable quota scheme was to agree a system of allocating quotas and, if necessary, to make some adjustments to the national plan for sulphur. The negotiation (consultation) needed to involve the Department of the Environment, the Scottish Office, the Northern Ireland Department of the Environment, three corresponding sets of regulators and all the affected companies. The views of environmental NGOs and wider interests would also need to be taken into account. This negotiating community was far from single-minded in its purpose.

The Failure of Quota Switching

There were four distinct obstacles to the introduction of quota switching. First, if the pre-existing national plan were to be used as the basis for switching, the pattern of switching was clear. National Power and PowerGen would sell quotas to Scottish Power and manufacturing industry. The England and Wales generators would earn windfall profits from the introduction of a switchable quota system while others would have to pay. Also, sulphur emissions would probably be higher than they would otherwise have been because the National Power and PowerGen paper sulphur quotas would be converted to real sulphur in the hands of other operators. Some operators, notably the Scottish generators, were determined to obtain redress for what was seen as the inequitable distribution of quotas under the original national plan. They wanted switchable quotas only if the baseline distribution was renegotiated. The England and Wales generators, on the other hand, did not want the introduction of quota switching to be used to trigger tighter regulatory controls.

A second obstacle was the distribution of national plan quotas to industrial operators. Two extreme possibilities could be imagined. In one, the distribution would closely reflect existing patterns of emissions – but then why make quotas switchable? At the other extreme, quotas would be distributed evenly according to the energy content of fuels burned. This would mean that users of dirtier fuels, such as coal and oil, would need to pay gas users to obtain sufficient quotas in order to operate. In an abstract economic sense this might make sense – operators would have incentives to switch to cleaner fuels and a price premium would be established between low- and high-sulphur fuel oil – but in a political sense it was almost impossible to negotiate. This second point is related to a third obstacle. Legally, the quota allocation would be in the hands of the relevant regulators, set up to implement a traditional command-and-control system – the very bodies which would lose discretion as a result of the introduction of a switchable quota system. These regulators did not have any incentives to come up with a politically credible allocation of quotas to underpin a system of switching. Finally, actors outside the inner circle of government, regulators and industry are profoundly mistrustful of market approaches. English Nature, for example, opposed the introduction of switchable quotas because of the risk of quotas being switched to sites where environmental criteria would not be met.

Against this background, a *winning coalition* for the introduction of a switchable quota system could not be constructed. The problems of emissions trading and quota allocation proved to be too complex and intertwined. In March 1996, HMIP, just before it was subsumed into the new Environment Agency, announced a renegotiated set of emission quotas for the electricity generators in England and Wales. Two sets of quotas were agreed – a fixed site-specific BATNEEC quota and a set of quotas that could be switched only within a company. These will involve substantial reductions in sulphur emissions by 2005 and should make a proportionate contribution to the UK's obligation to reduce sulphur emissions from all sources by 70 per cent by 2005. With this settlement, the prospect of having a fully switchable quota system has receded to the far horizon.

Lessons

The strongest message to emerge from this case study is that the problem of *allocating* tradable quotas is much less tractable than setting up a trading system. Problems of trust between operators – exacerbated in the UK because of the market dominance of National Power and PowerGen – mean that everyone wants a sufficient number of quotas to place themselves in the position of selling rather than buying. In the UK, the initial quota allocation took place in 1990–91 and the question of trading did not arise until later. By that time, the initial allocation had become manifestly inappropriate and there were inevitable disagreements about the legitimacy of a reallocation. In the

US, the allocation and trading decisions were taken simultaneously – not without vigorous debate, but they were taken.

There is also a question concerning the appropriateness of trying to implement a relatively radical policy innovation by grafting it onto the back of a pre-existing command-and-control regime. Implementation was the responsibility of the very bodies which stood to lose influence through the introduction of trading. In the end, higher-level political support, absent in the case of switchable quotas, was probably necessary. The question of how to handle more local, site-specific environmental problems within a quota trading framework is also an issue. The BATNEEC quotas partly met this concern, but not necessarily in a way which would satisfy environmental organizations. Finally, in spite of the current rhetoric about partnership, the inconclusive debate about switchable quotas was an insiders' affair for government departments, regulators and companies. A wider debate may be needed to give the process a sufficient degree of legitimacy.

The UK Landfill Tax

The landfill tax, introduced in October 1996, represents the UK Government's first real attempt to *green* the tax system. The Government had originally proposed to introduce an *ad valorem* tax based on the charges made by landfill operators. However, after much haggling and industrial opposition, the Government made a policy U-turn and introduced a two-tiered levy based on the weight of material to be landfilled. The tax is currently set at £7 per tonne for 'active' waste and at £2 per tonne for 'inert' waste. It is expected to raise some £450 million per year.[16] To ensure the revenue neutrality of the tax, the proceeds are being used to reduce employers' national insurance contributions by 0.2 per cent.

The *ad valorem* tax was opposed, virtually unanimously (by industry and other groups), on the grounds that such a tax, by exacerbating existing differentials between the prices charged by landfill operators, would divert waste to cheaper, and often less-well engineered and operated sites. In addition, such a policy would also encourage the transportation of waste over longer distances, breaching the Government's policy of promoting regional self-sufficiency in disposal and increasing transport-related environmental impacts. The Government also plans to establish private-sector environment trusts to pay for the clean-up of orphaned landfill sites and to promote sustainable waste management practices. The trusts are to be funded mostly by landfill operators who will be able to claim a rebate of 90 per cent of their payments into the trusts (up to a maximum of 20 per cent of their total tax payments). It is hoped that up to £100 million per year will be made available through the trusts in this way.

Background

With over 100 million tonnes of waste going to landfill every year in the UK, the scarcity of landfill space has become an increasingly important issue over recent years. More stringent waste management regulations and the demand for higher landfill standards have further highlighted the scarcity of suitable sites and prompted the need for policy action. In essence, the UK has been running out of holes in which to bury its rubbish (although the situation does vary quite significantly between regions). The idea behind the introduction of the tax was to encourage industry (and others) to reduce the volume of waste going to landfill. Higher landfill prices should encourage the promotion of recycling and the reuse of materials. In addition, the tax could also provide funds for the clean-up old landfill sites.

Industry's Response

Resigned to the inevitability of some form of tax, industry's principal concerns, apart from the actual tax rates themselves, centred on which types of waste would qualify for the lower rate: what could be classified as 'inert' or 'inactive' waste and whether or not there would be any exemptions from the tax. In a statement made after the November 1994 budget, UK Customs and Excise stated that there would be no exemptions.

A major concern for the waste industry itself was a clause, subsequently removed, which provided that the landfill tax would be "recoverable jointly and severally from the company and any director of the company." The industry successfully argued that this would be an unacceptable breach of the convention of limited liability which protects directors from company debts. Intense lobbying by other industries resulted in further concessions. Despite the Government's initial insistence that there would be no exemptions, most contaminated soils will now be exempt from the landfill tax. The logic behind this change of heart partly stems from the Government's desire to encourage the development of brown field sites rather than green field sites. The imposition of the tax on contaminated soils could work against this.

Some industries, however, were in favour of the tax being applied to contaminated soils. The Environmental Industries Commission (EIC), in a bid to strengthen the UK's land clean-up industry, campaigned vigorously against the granting of the exemption. The EIC maintain that the UK's land clean-up industry is weakened by the current practice in this country to remediate sites by removing or encapsulating polluted soil; there is little encouragement for the use of more advanced techniques. Consequently, UK firms are poorly represented in the expanding $4 billion per year European market for land clean-up. Most mine, quarry and dredging wastes will also be exempted.

Intense lobbying by the electricity generators, steel manufacturers and parts of the chemical industry also won last-minute concessions from the Government. Wastes from these industries, such as fly ash from power stations, furnace slags and numerous low-activity inorganic compounds, such as titanium oxide and aluminium oxide, were originally excluded from the Department of the Environment's classification of 'inactive' wastes. Lobbying eventually forced the Government to apply the lower tax rate to these substances which, together with the exemption of contaminated soils, is likely to result in a 10 per cent shortfall – if not more – in anticipated tax revenues. National Power and PowerGen, for example, will pay about £25 to 30 million per year less in landfill tax than originally expected. Primary iron and steel producers and foundries will also have a much smaller tax liability – perhaps £10 to 13 million per year less.[17]

Will the Tax Work?

In submissions to the Government's March 1995 consultation paper on the tax, which received over 700 responses, the Advisory Committee on Business and the Environment (ACBE) and Friends of the Earth (FoE) both doubted whether such a low tax rate would achieve the desired market effects. Concern was also expressed that the current low tax levels would not have much of an impact on the disposal costs of incineration residues and ash, and consequently the tax would be insufficient to shift waste away from incineration.

Just into its second year, it is clearly too early to assess whether or not the tax will prove to be a success. However, it has the potential to become an effective policy instrument. In response to comments made by ACBE, amongst others, the Government has indicated that raising the tax annually is a possible option that will be considered. ACBE urged the Government to commit itself to increasing the tax rates in subsequent years to provide added incentives for waste minimization, reuse and recycling.

Box 9.2 Other European landfill taxes and the proposed EU Landfill Directive

Five other European countries also have landfill taxes. All are weight-based regimes and some have tax bands for different types of waste. Charges vary from about £20 per tonne in Denmark for all waste to £1 to £3 for municipal waste in Belgium. German and Dutch taxes are both about £10 per tonne.

The European Commission is currently considering proposals for a landfill Directive. A number of key issues under the proposal have yet to be decided. These include the likelihood of the European Parliament's call for a phased ban on co-disposal landfills – sites where hazardous, non-hazardous and municipal wastes are dumped in the same site – and whether pressure from some Member States will force the requirement for mandatory pre-treatment of all degradable waste prior to landfilling. In contrast to the UK's waste management licensing regulations, the proposed Directive is also likely to require operators of existing landfills to provide financial cover for liabilities arising from their licences. The original proposals had required Member States to set up aftercare funds, financed by levies on waste, to ensure that damage could be rectified where the polluter was unable to pay. However, largely as a result of UK opposition, this provision was abandoned.

Conclusions

The use of economic or market-based instruments is assumed to achieve the same level of environmental protection at less overall cost to business than regulation and to encourage continuous improvement by business beyond minimum environmental standards. These instruments offer business greater flexibility of response, create markets which reward efficiency and encourage innovation.[18] Despite this and the UK Government's and EU's reported enthusiasm for the greater use of such instruments – as part of a balanced policy mix – their actual use remains limited at this time.

While the UK's landfill tax has the potential to be a success, especially if the tax rates are increased in subsequent years, both the attempts to introduce a Community-wide carbon/energy tax and a system of tradable sulphur quotas have failed quite spectacularly. All three cases illustrate that industry can be as hostile to proposed market-based solutions as they are to more traditional command-and-control type policy interventions; negotiating economic instruments can be as fraught and difficult, if not more so, as negotiating environmental standards and regulations. Economic instruments, despite their intrinsic appeal, do not offer a panacea for resolving the myriad of environmental challenges facing industry. Indeed, inappropriate measures, such as subsidized fossil fuel and tax breaks for land clearance, can actually encourage resource waste and environmental degradation. In the light of the detailed reviews of industry's response to environmental challenges (Chapters 3 to 5), and from the discussions on policy options and mechanisms to address these challenges (Chapters 6 to 9), it seems clear that no generic conclusions about the right policy mix can be made. However, implementation of the polluter-pays principle will require sufficiently ambitious action to deliver meaningful results. In the case of economic instruments, this means that tax levels, or subsidies, will have to be set at rates that will actually lead to changes in behaviour – of both consumers and producers. As noted by the World Business Council for Sustainable Development (WBCSD), we ultimately have to accept that the move towards sustainable development will cause far-reaching changes in the structures of business and industry. This will create both winners and losers.

CHAPTER 10
Next Steps

Introduction

In this final part of the book, we return to the larger themes outlined in the two introductory chapters. In Chapter 1, we accepted the premise that current industrial practices are not compatible with sustainable development. Whether industrial activity organized as it is, with its primary focus on profit, regulated by fallible political institutions, can ever be compatible with sustainable development cannot be answered on the basis of the evidence in this book. If sustainable development is not compatible with current patterns of economic, social and political organization, then the only answer is in radical social change. At the end of this chapter, however, we do turn briefly to this question.

What this book can do is to indicate what might be possible given the current organization of society and business. Specifically, what can be expected from business in terms of reduced environmental impact? Have environmental challenges been as successfully absorbed and mastered by business as was hoped? What is the role of public policy in relation to business activity? Can technology succeed in squaring the environmental–economic circle and generate win–win situations which promote sustainability? Using the evidence set out in Chapters 3 to 9, the first part of the chapter deals with several common ideas about industry and the environment which have attained common currency, if not consensus, during the 1990s:

- Environmental challenges are growing ever more complex and larger in scale.
- Corporate environmental management goes through several stages in which companies proceed from resistant adaptation to compliance-plus or even sustainable enterprise.
- Clean technology can help to solve environmental problems by providing opportunities to reduce environmental impacts and production costs.
- Environmental regulation, far from damaging the competitiveness of firms, enhances it by stimulating innovation.
- Alternatively, that environmental regulation almost inevitably destroys value in companies because win–win clean technology opportunities are quickly exhausted and companies must devote large proportions of their investment budgets to unproductive compliance projects.

The second part of this chapter considers ways forward in terms of dealing with the environmental impacts of industry. The discussion covers three topics: what industry can do itself; the role of public policy; and the nature of the links between business and government. Finally, the chapter returns briefly to the compatibility of current patterns of industrial activity with sustainable development.

What Has Been Learned?

The Environmental Agenda

Writing in *The Independent* in May 1996, Tom Burke, a special advisor to the UK Secretary of State for the Environment, divided environmental issues into two categories: those characterized by easy politics – air and water quality, contaminated land, endangered species, chemicals and radioactivity; and those posing unfamiliar challenges – food security, fish stocks, climate change and transport policy.[1] His thesis was that the easy issues had largely been solved – the future environmental challenge lay with these larger-scale, more systemic issues.

The evidence of Chapters 3 to 9 provides a sobering perspective on the Burke thesis. The hard issues were, indeed, identified by industry and others as major challenges for the 1990s. In the event, the politics has, in a sense, proved to be too hard. Progress in dealing with large-scale problems such as climate change has been painfully slow, both in the corporate sector and in terms of public policy. Lack of progress has meant that climate policies have had little direct impact on industry. Early CEST work projected an expenditure of £40 billion during the 1990s as a result of UK climate policies.[2] In the event, this has turned out to be a significant overestimate. This is not simply the outcome of a remote and difficult political process beyond industry's control. Key industrial sectors have played an active role in the relevant policy-making processes, generally acting to slow progress rather than to speed it up.

The evidence that industry has dealt mainly with the easy issues, such as air pollution and contaminated land, during the 1990s is clear. Policies and regulations have had real impacts, affecting both the cost structures and the competitiveness of industry. However, the easy issues themselves are far from resolved. While the environment continues to be a key issue, the evidence is that tackling tangible, local and regional environmental problems has real attractions for policy-makers and industry alike. Tough policies and strategies to deal with the more abstract global issues remain – as Burke describes them – a challenge for the future. One trend which was not explicitly predicted at the beginning of the 1990s was the shift in emphasis from environmental problems associated with production (traditional pollution-control problems) to problems related to consumption and post-consumption (the management of consumer waste). One of the drivers has been the European waste crisis, first manifested in German producer responsibility legislation. However, policies to deal with waste have developed in tandem with a growing perception that managing the flow of materials through the economic system – closing the materials loop – is the key to making society more sustainable. This mode of thinking draws attention away from specific environmental *issues*, focusing more on the *means* for reducing waste and environmental releases. It also reduces the emphasis on global environmental problems, highlighting instead tangible techniques and practices for reducing material flows. The problem of reducing post-consumer waste also calls for innovative organizational solutions, as Chapter 8 makes clear.[3]

Has Industry's Approach Changed?

Notwithstanding the lack of progress on many specific environmental issues, the world of corporate environmental management has changed greatly. It is ironic that, when viewed through the lens of public policy-making and specific environmental issues, industry can appear to be an obstacle to progress. When corporate strategies, management systems and environmental reporting are considered, a more positive impression is gained. Exploring this apparent paradox is the key to understanding the problem of industry, technology and the environment. For most of industry, environmental issues are perceived as a commercial threat rather than an opportunity. There are, however, exceptions, notably suppliers of environmental goods and services. This is not to deny the significance of win–win measures which improve both economic and environmental performance. But to the extent that the agenda is set by pressure groups and policy-makers, the environment represents, to industry, a loss of predictability and control over profit-making activities. If corporate environmental strategies can be viewed as an attempt to reassert control over a difficult and complex agenda, the phenomenon of obstructive approaches to regulation and policy-making, on the one hand, and proactive environmental strategies, on the other, becomes less of a paradox.

The evidence from Chapters 3 to 9 is that many sections of industry have begun to take more control over their environmental performance, their relationships with regulators and the way that they are perceived by wider stakeholder communities. Most larger companies have adopted formal environmental policy statements, corporate environmental strategies and environmental management systems. Most have environmental managers or even units to coordinate environmental management within the organization. It is equally clear, however, that most parts of industry are not on an inevitable progression towards an ever-closer embrace of the aspiration of environmental sustainability. The dream of the sustainable enterprise – the final stage of the corporate journey, apparently characterized by the subordination of profit to environmental performance – appears to be just that.[4] Many larger companies appear to have reached a stage which the management writers would characterize as compliance-plus – proactive environmental management keeps companies a few steps ahead of regulators and provides some control over the environmental agenda. A few companies, for example Dow, appear to be even one stage further, drawing potential competitive advantage through the application of concepts such as eco-efficiency. Most SMEs, however, have been almost completely untouched by the changes taking place in larger companies. To the extent that they have been affected, it has been mainly through regulation. Most SMEs are simply at the compliance stage of environmental management, and some are regrettably non-compliant. The management resources needed to run more sophisticated environmental strategies are not available in most SMEs.

There is also considerable variation in the level of sophistication and quality of environmental reporting in larger companies. The take-up of EMAS and other certified environmental management systems appears to be very limited. There is some evidence that environmental issues are even shifting down the agenda within some companies, and environmental managers are finding it hard to sell environmental concern to colleagues operating in line-management functions. Industry has changed during the 1990s and in some companies the changes have been very considerable. This, however, does not imply the beginning of a uniformly harmonious relationship between industry, policy-makers and society at large. Although much of industry has recognized the strategic significance of environmental issues, there remains ample scope for legitimate differences in point of view. The basic divergence between the goals of environmental policy-makers and those of industry will guarantee that.

Technology and the Double Dividend

Clean technology, with its promise of improved economic and environmental performance, is an alluring concept. It is an important guiding principle for government initiatives such as the Clean Technology Programme operated by the National Environmental Technology Centre (NETCEN). Most companies recognize the clean technology concept, but almost none use it consciously as an operational principle or management tool.

Clean technology means different things in different contexts. NETCEN's Clean Technology Programme aims to persuade companies to adopt well- (or reasonably well-) established waste-reduction techniques which are incremental and essentially non-innovative. Industry shows an interest in such techniques because they will lead to lower production costs, often for a small initial investment. On the other hand, the former Clean Technology Unit of the Engineering and Physical Sciences Research Council (EPSRC) had a remit to promote more fundamental process change and was specifically precluded from supporting innovations which could be considered near-market. In this context, clean technology implies more fundamental process change to the research and development manager than to the production engineer.

The clean technology concept is necessarily abstract in nature. It is perhaps a drawback that it does not map readily onto industrial decision-making procedures. From the case study work covered in this book, it appears that there are three principal routes through which firms invest in technology leading to changed environmental performance:

- compliance investments undertaken simply to meet environmental regulation;
- cost-saving investments of a relatively modest nature, usually funded from cash-flow; and
- more fundamental process and product change undertaken for strategic reasons, usually with significant research and development requirements.

Depending on the perspective taken, clean technology can refer to investments falling into either the second or third categories. In both these categories, environmental improvement is seldom the primary motivation for expenditure. In most companies, especially those working in high-impact sectors such as energy, metals and chemicals, compliance investments dominate the profile of environmental expenditure.

This categorization of investment highlights the fact that companies are seldom faced with a direct choice between an end-of-pipe technology and clean technology *per se*. When responding to environmental regulation, companies seldom face a multiplicity of choices, and often the obvious solution is end-of-pipe clean-up. Cleaner production and eco-efficiency are best seen not as technology selection, but as a broader strategic move where greater emphasis is placed on environmental factors in making cost-saving investments and undertaking fundamental product and process changes. In the long run, this will lead to reduced compliance investments and give a company more control over the environmental agenda.

The extent to which the cleaner production route is available will vary between sectors and firms. There has arguably been underinvestment in waste reduction in the past, but tighter environmental regulation and rising waste disposal costs have created new opportunities and drawn attention to those opportunities which are already available. In companies where environmental management is well developed, opportunities for cost-effective waste reduction investments become depleted after the most attractive opportunities (the 'low-hanging fruit') are taken up.[5] Companies which have been able to obtain high rates of return on waste reduction measures identified on a first round of environmental auditing, find it much harder to identify similar measures on the second round. No company will fund investments of this type from cashflow unless they earn an acceptable rate of return.

In mature sectors, some basic processes may operate close to the theoretical limits of their efficiency. Research and development, relating to basic process change, may yield at best incremental improvements, particularly in relation to environmental performance. In such circumstances, it may be possible to meet regulatory demands only through end-of-pipe investments. It is only to be expected that there will be business resistance to rising environmental pressures in sectors with these characteristics. These also happen to be the sectors from which Walley and Whitehead have drawn their examples of value-destroying environmental investments driven by regulatory factors.[6]

We conclude that the scope for adopting win–win clean technology measures is case-specific. It would be foolish to ignore the possibility of win–win situations – but it would be equally foolish to rely on them to create a more sustainable industrial sector.

Regulation and the Double Dividend

The previous discussion about clean technology and the economic and environmental double dividend is reflected in an even more intense debate about regulation and the double dividend. The Walley and Whitehead thesis about the value-destroying nature of environmental regulation is confirmed in some sectors where regulation inevitably involves a trade-off between production costs and environmental performance. In such circumstances, it is not surprising that companies will try to block, delay or modify environmental rules. However, there are sectors and companies which stand to gain. The Integrated Pollution Control case study in Chapter 6 shows how some companies can be stimulated to search for cost-saving clean technology opportunities when regulation brings cost-saving opportunities to their attention. The waste minimization case study in Chapter 7 shows that regulators may have a role to play in helping companies to identify these opportunities.

In the longer term, social demands for higher environmental quality give companies an incentive to steer fundamental process and product innovation in more sustainable directions. Companies may gain if, in the longer term, they face lower compliance costs as a result. To the extent that some companies can influence the direction of policy, they may also be in a position to influence future regulations in favour of the technologies in which they have invested. The case study of CFC replacement in Chapter 3 provides a concrete example of this phenomenon.

The preceding arguments apply to companies with existing businesses which are directly affected by regulation. There are other companies which stand to gain:

- Companies which supply emission-abatement technology, generally end-of-pipe in nature, will benefit from environmental regulations which are applied to sectors where clean technology solutions are not readily available. Here, one company's cost is another's opportunity. The tighter the regulation, the more business there is to be done. The activities of the UK Environmental Industries Commission (EIC) are designed to further these types of business opportunity.
- Equipment suppliers who focus on cleaner technology solutions are likely to pick up business from customers. There is evidence, for example, that chemical plant suppliers are beginning to emphasize energy efficiency and low-pollution characteristics.

It has been argued, notably by Porter, that strict domestic rules can help to promote an environmental industry which is competitive in international markets.[7] The examples of Germany and Japan in relation to air pollution control are often cited. However, in both these countries there are basic competencies in chemical engineering which underlie the ability to develop and refine pollution control technologies. German and Japanese companies could well have competed successfully in international markets without the support of strong domestic regulation. The evidence as to whether regulation promotes competitiveness in this way is ambiguous.

Structural Change

Developed economies as a whole are undergoing structural changes which have implications in terms of environmental impacts. On the whole, the high-impact sectors which have traditionally been the source of pollution problems are not the main contributors to economic growth and, in some cases, are in decline. Regulation which adds to costs may accelerate this type of structural change. On the other hand, firms which ride the wave of radical technological innovation in information, communications and biotechnology may contribute to a more sustainable society through the development of their core businesses. This is probably the largest and most imponderable win–win opportunity of all. Structural change does not, however, automatically lead to environmental improvements. For example, the growth of just-in-time deliveries using light vans in the distribution sector adds to the environmental burdens associated with road transport.

The Way Forward

The complexity of the industry and environment agenda undermines general statements about how companies and policy-makers might develop their future strategies. Few prescriptions will work across all sectors and in all circumstances. Manufacturing chemicals is different from marketing personal computers; the problem of reducing greenhouse gas emissions is not the same as organizing the recovery of post-consumption waste. Specifics matter. The range of experience set out in the earlier chapters of this book does not in itself map out a blueprint for the future, but it does provide some useful guidance.

Most companies still see regulation and the anticipation, or avoidance, of future regulation, as the main driver for taking environmental measures. However, this perception has led to anticipatory strategies and sophisticated corporate management systems which will, by themselves, lead to further improvements in environmental performance. These improvements would probably take place for some time, even in the absence of new environmental rules. The momentum behind evolving corporate environmental strategies is testimony to the degree of conviction in industry that the environment is a key social demand which has to be accommodated rather than fought.

It is equally certain that, in the longer term, the momentum behind business environmental management will falter if there is no tangible expression, through public policy, of the desire for a more sustainable society. This is evident from the case studies covered in this book. There is a need for environmental regulation, taken in the broadest sense to cover all forms of government control or influence over industry, whether in the form of market-based or administrative instruments. Unless environmental factors are internalized in markets and incentive systems, it is inconceivable that the profit motive will lead to more sustainable practices. However, if the cost of environmental degradation is internalized, then the profit motive becomes a powerful engine of sustainability.

Taking as a basic premise the need for an interplay between public policy and company strategy, the second part of this chapter assesses ways forward for both business and policy-makers. There is a considerable degree of consensus within industry, and between industry and policy-makers, that the environment is a key issue. This suggests strongly that partnership between government and business could, in the future, play a stronger role in underpinning environmental strategy than it has done in the past. The final section of this chapter assesses the role of business and government relationships.

Industry Strategies

Many larger industrial companies have well-developed strategies for dealing with environmental challenges. As argued below, there are always going to be circumstances in which commercial logic will lead companies to oppose or modify emerging pieces of environmental legislation. But today there are many actions which companies can take to reconcile higher standards of commercial and environmental performance and even enhance profitability. These include:

- Building up the company infrastructure for dealing with environmental issues: this would include developing a policy statement, an internal network of individuals with environmental responsibilities, and a formal environmental management system. It might also be appropriate to aim for a certified environmental management system – such as EMAS – which will create confidence outside the company.

- Communicating environmental information to stakeholder groups – communities, employees, investors and customers – in order to build up trust and credibility: this will probably involve producing a corporate environmental report, but may include other measures such as setting up a citizens' advisory committee.

- Seeking out cost-effective measures which reduce waste and environmental releases: this might involve tilting the internal playing field in favour of investments which relate to strategic issues of wider social concern, or where future regulation affects company activities.

- Building environmental criteria into research and development and the appraisal of new products and processes: this will not generate results in the short term, but will gradually place a company on a more sustainable course and make it more resilient in the face of external demands. The Dow eco-efficiency philosophy represents a very strong example of this kind of proactive strategy. In the long term, this feature of strategy will perhaps be the most important of all.

- Extending the environmental impact of production processes to cover product stewardship (taking account of the environmental impacts of goods and services over their life-cycle). For consumer goods this would involve consideration of the environmental impacts of a product in use, such as the energy efficiency of a washing machine, and after disposal. The latter consideration has become particularly pressing for industry, as illustrated in Chapter 8.

- Maintaining a good public affairs capacity with respect to environmental issues: inevitably, public affairs divisions will end up fighting rearguard actions in an attempt to protect companies from policies and regulations which will have a negative impact on business. Sometimes, this may result in otherwise desirable environmental policies being stillborn. However, there are countervailing advantages even from a wider social perspective. In many cases, public affairs activities may actually serve to improve the quality of regulation, allowing it to attain the same environmental goals in a more effective way. Public affairs divisions are also a company's window on the world. They can convey the extent of external concern about issues such as the environment back to the organization, stimulating internal change. They can also alert the company to external developments which might create business opportunities with positive environmental consequences.

- Considering the types of business in which a company operates: this involves moving out of environmentally problematical businesses – for example, the manufacture of ozone-depleting substances. In effect, it is a company-level manifestation of wider structural changes which may ultimately deliver substantial environmental benefits. However, moving out of environmentally difficult areas is not always beneficial at the wider level. Challenging activities may be contracted out to smaller companies which devote less attention to environmental matters. If this happens, the reputation of the larger company may be enhanced while standards of environmental management fall.

These strategies are particularly appropriate for larger companies. For the largest multinationals, these prescriptions may appear self-evident or even old hat. Small- and medium-sized companies, however, may not have the necessary management resources to implement these measures effectively. Other mechanisms in the business sector can foster the transfer of environmental good practice from one company to another. For example, bringing environmental criteria into purchasing decisions may eventually help to transfer good practice up the supply chain. In this respect, the larger company which attempts to procure environmental performance from a smaller company faces the same choices as a regulator – whether to threaten (terminating contracts), cajole or positively assist (providing free environmental advice to suppliers). The choice will depend on broader purchasing strategy. If companies have other reasons for cutting the number of suppliers, then terminating arrangements on environmental grounds may be feasible. But companies which wish to consolidate their supply base may well prefer the more positive approach; this will help to pull up the environmental performance of their smaller suppliers.

Trade associations have an important role to play in representing small companies externally and in providing them with information about best practice. The Chemical Industries Association's Responsible Care Programme is a good example of a programme which has helped small companies and benefited the sector as a whole.

The Role of Policy

Public policy can impinge on industry in several ways. This section draws together conclusions about more traditional regulatory methods, market-based instruments and support in the form of information dissemination and consciousness-raising.

Regulation
What is termed command-and-control regulation is still seen by government and industry as a key component of environmental policy. The 1996 report on the UK's Sustainable Development Strategy notes that regulations may be more appropriate than market instruments, where the object is to prevent unacceptable health risks or to protect an important environmental resource.[8]

Industry, too, can see the benefit of regulation in certain circumstances. The development of Integrated Pollution Control a decade ago shows industry asking for a more credible regulatory system which would convey legitimacy and a wider licence to operate. Industry requested a legal framework for the Producer Responsibility initiative dealing with packaging waste in order to deal with the problem of free riders on what would otherwise have been a voluntary initiative.

However necessary regulation is in a general sense, it is inevitable that individual sets of rules will be irritating or downright perverse from an industrial perspective. The choice of a regulatory policy depends critically on the balance between different sets of goals. At a generic level, the key issue in any regulatory policy is the proportionality between the environmental benefits and the costs incurred. This casting of the problem, of course, implicitly assumes that environmental regulation is concerned with an economic and environmental trade-off rather than possible win–win situations.

The precise nature of the balance to be struck between costs and benefits depends on the relative importance attached to various aspects of standard-setting. Is the regulatory philosophy related to technological capability (best available technology) or environmental goals (an effects-based policy)? What priority is attached to continuous environmental improvement, the maintenance of competitiveness, the forcing of technological change, or the stimulation of the environmental services industry? Different regulatory philosophies serve different interests and can be agreed upon only at the political level. At the moment, UK regulatory style emphasizes competitiveness criteria and environmental effects through the use of site-specific negotiations under the IPC system.

Whatever the regulatory philosophy, there are some general considerations which may lead to better systems of control. One principle is that the task best suited to regulators is the setting of environmental targets, whether in the form of emission limits, emission quotas or environmental quality standards. Determining how targets can best be met is a task that should be left to industry, which has better information about abatement techniques and costs. Regulators must also consider timescales for meeting environmental targets. Timescales should ideally take into account the rhythm of plant replacement as well as environmental criteria so that companies have an opportunity to take up clean-technology solutions. Regulators can also seek to exploit synergies between regulatory targets and internal company environmental management procedures, which may provide a suitable means for assuring compliance.

These approaches are reasonably well suited to British traditions of administrative discretion and site-specific environmental controls. Other European countries, for example Germany, have traditions which place greater emphasis on uniform standard-setting across a single class of site, taking less account of the specific environmental context. This has obvious disadvantages, but it can help to foster a stronger environmental services industry by providing a greater degree of assurance about potential markets. The choice is essentially a political one. The tension between the two approaches will be manifested most strongly as different national regulatory styles come into contact during the negotiation of EU environmental directives.

Different types of companies have different regulatory preferences. Larger companies which operate processes with the potential for high levels of environmental release – costly to control – will inevitably prefer regulatory regimes which lend themselves to flexibility – for instance, site-specific negotiations with regulators or perhaps tradable emission permits. Companies operating standard processes with lower environmental impacts may prefer clear, uniformly applied guidelines which minimize the input of management time and create a competitive level playing field. Small companies tend to find all regulations burdensome but, again, would generally prefer clear rules. Regulatory regimes could usefully take account of different approaches for different types of industry.

When developing regulatory strategy, the apparently countervailing deregulatory philosophy must be a key consideration. The desire for higher standards of environmental performance and deregulation need not always be in conflict. Chapter 6 showed how deregulation was an important factor in underpinning the establishment of the UK's Integrated Pollution Control system. Deregulation focuses attention on the need to choose appropriate and efficient means for implementing higher environmental standards. Flexible regulatory approaches, an appropriate split of responsibilities between the regulator (setting objectives) and industry (determining compliance methods), and the wider adoption of market-based instruments will help to merge the environmental and deregulatory agendas.

Market instruments

The UK Government has placed great store on the use of market-based environmental instruments, while the European Community has expressed its desire to move in that direction through its Fifth Environmental Action Programme. In spite of these aspirations, the promise of market-based approaches remains largely unfulfilled. The two practical successes in the UK are the new landfill tax and the progressively increasing taxation on road fuels, which has less of a direct impact on industry.

As discussed in Chapter 9, there have been two rather high-profile policy failures – the EU carbon/energy tax and the trading of sulphur quotas as a means for implementing the EU Large Combustion Plants Directive. This double failure signals a generic set of difficulties facing market instruments which may extend beyond the specificities of individual cases:

- The *process* of negotiating a market-based instrument appears to be just as tortuous, if not more so, than the process of negotiating a traditional regulatory instrument. A greater number of actors are involved, even on the policy-making side of the fence where environmental, industry and finance ministries may be concerned.
- In the case of environmental taxes, industry is nervous about ceding more revenue-raising powers to government.
- In the case of tradable permits, there is nervousness about the financial implications associated with acquiring sufficient permits. Industry appears anxious to acquire sufficient numbers of permits during the bargaining which surrounds their initial distribution, so as to avoid the need to participate subsequently in a permit market.

In general, there is a problem of trust; industry appears not to trust government and, in the case of tradable permits, companies appear not to trust each other. With traditional regulation, companies can enter a common cause against government; with tradable permits, companies are also set against each other.

There is a considerable degree of consensus that market instruments *in principle* offer a constructive way forward. When *specific* market instruments are under discussion, consensus can evaporate. Market-based approaches are well worth adding to the canon of public policy instruments. However, in furthering their development, it must be acknowledged that market-based approaches raise problems of equity and new procedural problems concerning their negotiation. A further problem is that most sections of industry appear to oppose all forms of new taxation, whether they bring wider benefits or not. Experience with market-based approaches must be built up gradually in the hope of capitalizing on early successes and building up confidence about the efficacy of the approach.

Voluntary agreements

Interest in the concept of 'voluntary' agreements, as an alternative to traditional regulatory controls, has been much more recent than interest in market-based instruments. Interest is growing because they appear to be the only way forward with respect to environmental problems – such as waste stream management – which present complex organizational challenges; and they allow industry the maximum opportunity to structure solutions. The sense in which voluntary agreements are truly 'voluntary' is of course limited. Such solutions are emerging only as an alternative to more traditional controls. There is considerable interest in voluntary agreements both at the European level, under the Fifth Environmental Action Programme, and in the UK where the Advisory Committee on Business and the Environment (ACBE) is now giving them active consideration.

Voluntary approaches have had their most marked success in relation to the management of waste streams. Here, new partnership approaches have proved necessary in order to allow companies, operating at different points along the same supply chain, to collaborate with each other. In practice, these new partnerships embody features of both traditional legislation and economic instruments. Legislative controls are needed to prevent free-rider problems while quasi-economic instruments, in the form of levies, appear to be necessary in order to generate sufficient revenue to finance expanded waste collection and recycling activity. Traditional trade associations, the membership of which is usually horizontal across a sector rather than up and down a supply chain, have not dealt well with these challenges. The VALPAK packaging waste consortium is the furthest developed in the UK and analogous bodies will be needed with respect to other waste streams.

There are two principal challenges associated with waste stream consortia. The first involves the appropriate definition of a coherent waste stream – which materials and product categories should be included? The ICER example in Chapter 8 shows that collaborations may become unstable if incompatible industrial partners are forced together through inappropriate definitions of waste streams. The second challenge relates to compatibility with competition law. How is fair competition ensured when individual companies have the freedom to choose whether or not to enter a consortium? It is at this point that the legislative framework for waste stream management becomes critical.

Another type of voluntary agreement which may become more common is when a 'contract' is struck between a government and a trade association representing a single sector. This approach has been pioneered in The Netherlands where legally binding agreements incorporating quantitative targets for emission reductions have been struck between the government and a number of sectors. This approach can work in The Netherlands because of the stronger legal status of trade associations and a tradition of close links between government and industry. There is active interest in the UK, but there will be difficulties because trade associations, such as the Chemical Industries Association, do not necessarily represent all of the major firms operating in a sector. To operate in a UK context, voluntary agreements of this sort may need either a firmer legislative framework to avoid free riding or an extraordinary degree of voluntarism.

Partners and Adversaries: Business and Government Relationships

The traditional model of the government and business relationship concerning environmental questions has been adversarial. The very term 'command-and-control', used to describe traditional regulatory arrangements, signals the fact. There will inevitably be specific occasions and circumstances when government and business relations will remain adversarial – for example, when an individual firm persistently breaches environmental rules or when a controversial environmental measure with severe cost implications is being negotiated.

A striking feature of the environmental agenda of the 1990s has been a tendency towards partnership between business and policy-makers. Instances include:

■ the development of a more negotiated site-by-site approach within the framework of the Integrated Pollution Control system;
■ the development of waste minimization initiatives, such as the Aire and Calder project, discussed in Chapter 5, which have involved fruitful collaborations between regulators and firms in a range of industries within a single river basin; these have resulted in economic benefits for firms involved, as well as environmental gains;
■ waste stream consortia, constructed through close collaboration, albeit fraught on occasions between government and business groups; this has resulted in an unprecedented blurring of the line between the public policy and business spheres.

Quite apart from the general positive feelings that may flow from a constructive and cooperative approach, partnership arrangements bring tangible benefits. Groups with different objectives obtain a clearer sense of each other's goals and methods of operation; a greater sense of trust is engendered; the freer exchange of information allows the development of more effective and efficient rules; technology transfer is facilitated; and regulatory and other procedures may be shortened to everyone's benefit.

The growth of partnership is not without risks, however, particularly in the context of regulation. Both industry and regulators have incentives to enter into partnership arrangements. Industry believes that better-informed and well-disposed regulators will create rules which are more compatible with commercial logic. Regulators, frustrated by failures to push through new rules as a result of industrial opposition, see advantages in having industry contributing to the regulatory process itself. These mutual perceptions underpin the emphasis on partnership expressed in the EU's Fifth Environmental Action Programme. What regulators and industry may view as a constructive partnership may, however, be seen as a cosy relationship by members of the wider public. Such perceptions may undermine public trust, both in companies and regulatory institutions themselves. It will also weaken one of the more important benefits of regulation from industry's point of view – the legitimization of its activities through democratically accountable bodies. Partnership approaches must grow in light of the ever-more complex agenda which industry faces. But care must be taken that the automatic adoption of cooperative modes of conduct does not undermine the effectiveness of arrangements which derive their legitimacy partly from their adversarial nature.

Sustainable Development: The Ultimate Challenge

Defining Sustainable Development

Neither this book, nor any other, can answer the ultimate question – is industrial activity, with its primary focus on profit and regulated by fallible political institutions, compatible with sustainable development? In principle, that would require an objective operational definition of sustainable development. There are sustainability indicators in abundance, but each is inevitably partial in nature.[9]

The classic definition of sustainable development, "meeting the needs of the present without compromising the ability of future generations to meet their own needs", begs an enormous number of questions.[10] The environment is seen as instrumental in meeting human needs rather than as something that is valued for its own sake. In a sense, this is a definition with which the corporate sector should be comfortable. The principal rationale for profit-motivated enterprise is that it represents the most efficient and effective way of marshalling resources – natural, financial and human – to meet needs. If this is the case, then do sustainable development and the enterprise system not simply form different parts of the same category?

There are several reasons why the reconciliation between sustainable development and business is not quite so simple. "Meeting the needs of the present without compromising the ability of future generations to meet their own needs" embodies many conceptual elements. How is the issue of equity between this and future generations to be approached? Within the current generation, human needs in different societies scattered across the globe are met to vastly different degrees. Even within societies, the satisfaction of human needs is unevenly spread. Does the Brundtland definition refer only to basic needs, such as food, shelter and security, or to higher-level needs relating to quality of life and the appreciation of landscape and wilderness? Whose needs have priority? How does the environment fit into this needs-driven scheme? Sustainable development clearly has multiple social and environmental dimensions which will not always be easy to reconcile.

The impact of any practical business decision will have different consequences for the various dimensions of sustainable development. A decision which leads to improved local air quality may increase emissions of greenhouse gases. Switching business to a supplier that operates less environmentally damaging processes may result in longer freight hauls and higher levels of emissions from transport. Sustainable development cannot, therefore, conform to a simple set of rules and guidelines which will inspire 'correct' decisions in every circumstance. Sometimes there will be win–win situations in which a particular business decision will lead to manifest improvements across all, or most, of the dimensions of sustainability. In other cases, more complex trade-offs may be required.

From a business perspective, these trade-offs must ultimately be resolved in the boardroom. It would, however, be naïve to expect directors and corporate strategists to have unique insights on how the concept of sustainable development might be made operational. In pursuing sustainable development, the corporate sector is part of a broader social enterprise. To define it in ways that will be acceptable to society at large, business must work closely with its stakeholders – customers, suppliers, policy-makers, regulators and communities. Unless business works with its partners towards a shared vision of what sustainable development might imply, the concept will not be able to take into account the environmental and social consequences of real decisions. Without losing sight of the broad goals expressed in the Brundtland definition of sustainable development, and without retreating to the proposition that sustainable development is a process rather than an objective, it is clear that consultation and stakeholder involvement are essential ingredients.

Making Business Sustainable

Sustainability and the Market

Earlier in the chapter, we noted that part of the way forward for industry lies in searching out cost-effective opportunities to reduce waste and environmental releases. For many companies, especially in the chemicals sector, this objective has taken on a longer-term and more strategic flavour. A broader goal has been defined to reduce the flow of materials required to generate 'value-added'. On one level, this goal can be expressed in physical terms. Examples include Dow Chemical's eco-efficiency approach to environmental affairs.

This physical and material approach has been expressed in even more visionary terms by various writers and environmental advocates. At one end of the spectrum, it has been suggested that a factor-ten reduction in the production of materials will place developed economies on a sustainable development path over a period of 50 years or so.[11] This, however, is extraordinarily difficult for commercial organizations to accept. It appears incompatible, to a radical degree, with current and foreseeable patterns of activity. A similar proposal which is more modest has been made by Hawken.[12] He argues that a factor-*four* reduction in materials intensity over a period of 40 years is not only environmentally desirable but will also be economically necessary if companies are going to survive in the marketplace.

It is important to distinguish between Hawken's approach and those of the factor-ten advocates. Factor-ten is argued from an ecological imperative. Factor-four is based on the premise that the win–win opportunities associated with dematerialization are so large that commercial organizations which do not pursue them will become uncompetitive. The message is that companies which remain environmentally unsustainable do so at their peril. Hawken's message has struck a chord with some major companies. Both process investment and product design are now being undertaken, with reductions in materials flow and environmental impact in mind. A widespread uptake of the factor-four type of thinking espoused by Hawken is clearly a trend-busting development which will begin to shift industry onto a more sustainable path.

There are also important considerations about the *means* by which dematerialization and reduced environmental impacts might be promoted by companies. A striking new feature for some companies is a recognition that value-added is created not in the upstream manufacture of basic materials but in the shaping of products and services for the benefit of customers. This service approach is discussed a great deal in the energy sector, parts of which have traditionally operated on a monopolistic basis. The liberalization of industries such as electricity and gas generated an unprecedented interest in customer choice and the possibility of providing service packages which include energy efficiency as well as the supply of energy commodities.[13] The service approach has also been adopted by some chemical companies which lease chemicals to their customers, relieving them of the responsibility for disposal or recycling and closing the loop in terms of the flow of potentially toxic materials.[14] What is not yet clear is the degree to which service approaches will yield environmental benefits. The potential exists, but so do the risks. What if leasing and service approaches lead to product-churning; the more rapid turnover of products? If the most competent and innovative companies focus on services, will they contract upstream, low value-added activities to companies with short-time horizons which cannot afford to invest in environmental improvements?

Moves towards eco-efficiency, customer orientation and service approaches, patchy though they may be, show that there are at least drivers and opportunities in the marketplace which can lead companies towards sustainable approaches. These may not solve the problem of sustainable development by themselves. But they do illustrate the existence of concrete mechanisms, embedded in the market itself, which can be used to promote sustainability.

Citizens and Consumers

Public concern about environmental issues remains one of the most important latent forces which can induce a switch to more sustainable patterns of business behaviour. Consumers are beginning to flex their muscles. Shell's experience following its proposal to dispose of the *Brent Spar* oil rig at sea shows how vulnerable even major corporations are to a determined public which has its own perceptions of what constitutes sustainable behaviour.

A small group of consumers appears to be prepared to pay a premium for green products in the marketplace. Those who do so are acting altruistically, paying for environmental benefits which their free-riding fellow citizens will appropriate. Realistically, this form of environmentally conscious behaviour is unlikely to spread throughout the population. What is much more common is a readiness to punish what is seen as poor corporate behaviour, excluding 'bad' products from markets where adequate competition exists, at little or no cost to the individual consumer. This type of behaviour appears likely to be consolidated, sending important and compelling signals to companies. Consumer boycotts will inhibit incidences of unsustainable behaviour but will not necessarily promote more incremental moves towards sustainable development, especially when practices across an industry are relatively uniform.

Reflecting Environmental Costs

Setting all of the rhetoric about sustainable enterprise aside, the fact remains that business is not exposed to price signals which adequately reflect the true cost of pollution or the use of resources. Under these circumstances, companies which take decisions specifically intended to promote sustainability will be at a competitive disadvantage with those which overconsume environmental resources. In an ever more competitive global business environment, the current state of affairs appears to be inimical to the achievement of sustainable development.

The case for ecological tax reform, switching the burden of taxation away from public goods – such as employment – towards bads – such as environmental pollution – has been made by a wide range of commentators and is at least acknowledged in official policy at both the national and EU levels.[15] Business has often opposed specific proposals for environmental taxes; the notorious case of the EU carbon tax is discussed in Chapter 9. At least some opposition is based on the premise that all forms of taxation must be opposed because they are bad for business. However, a significant shift in the burden of taxation towards environmentally damaging activities would be one of the most potent means of reconciling industrial activity with sustainable development. Fiscal measures work with the grain of the market, sending economic signals that business is uniquely well placed to interpret. They would provide incentives for appropriate modifications of business behaviour. Reconciling the business community with the concept and practice of ecological tax reform would be a major and remarkable trend-busting step towards sustainable development.

Shocks and Anxieties

Recent history shows that crisis and anxiety have played a major role in driving forward the environmental agenda. Innovative work in Germany goes so far as to assert that risk and fear of the unknown have become endemic features of a modern society where the division between society and nature is blurred and technological advances, in fields such as biotechnology, are experiments with nature itself.[16]

Of course, the unpredictability and uncontrollability of environmental crises are the very features which companies try to diminish. But in case after case, a sense of crisis – heightened by dramatic media reporting – has triggered changes in public policy and company strategy. The discovery of the ozone hole, the identification of forest dieback in Germany, growing asthma rates in children and the apparently increased frequency of severe storms have led to urgent demands for policy action in relation to problems such as air pollution and climate change. Industry has all too often been a follower – a reluctant follower – rather than a leader in relation to these new challenges. It is inconceivable that the sustainable development agenda will not be propelled forward by further crises which, by their very nature, are unpredictable. Companies cannot hope to avoid these pressures but must focus on strategies and procedures for accommodating and negotiating unexpected social demands. Those companies that do not will be forced back into the reactive hole out of which the corporate sector has been steadily pulling itself during the 1990s.

By definition, the unpredictable cannot be predicted. But there are some indications of where public anxieties may be leading after two decades during which environmental issues have grown in importance. An increasing concern with the potential health impacts and risks of products and processes, as well as concern about ecological damage, is becoming ever more evident. Genetic manipulation, for example, is an area where business aspirations which might appear sustainable from one point of view, may come into conflict with quite different public perceptions. Different corporate approaches in this are exemplified by Monsanto and Unilever. Monsanto argues straightforwardly that genetically modified potatoes and cotton are sustainable products because they help to reduce pesticide use.[17] Unilever, on the other hand, a company which operates closer to the final consumer – and has recently decided to dispose of some of its upstream chemicals production – has approached genetically modified organisms a great deal more cautiously. It has sponsored respected independent academics to review and publish a report on public attitudes to genetically modified organisms in order to promote a more open public debate.[18]

Sustainable Values and Inclusive Approaches

In the first paragraph of this book, we noted how employees can help to permeate a company with attitudes and values which reflect broader social change. This is never more true than when the senior managers in a company are the messengers of change. They uniquely have the authority and resources to institutionalize value changes and turn aspirations into practice. Business and environment literature is replete with case studies showing how personally committed managers have turned around company strategy with respect to environmental affairs. There is a strong consensus that change must be driven from the top and that turning around values and behaviour is just as important as rules and procedures. Moving business towards sustainability therefore requires that all major companies – and preferably small- and medium-sized companies as well – make high-level commitments towards environmental goals and build internal company cultures which emphasize the importance of sustainable development and the assumption of social responsibilities.

Good intentions and sincere commitment may be necessary for the promotion of sustainable development, but they will surely not be sufficient in themselves. Positive attitudes will flourish when sustainable behaviour brings tangible rewards created through appropriate systems of incentives. It is essential that sustainable development practices do not become a burden which employees bear at their own cost. When attitudes and forced patterns of behaviour come into conflict, it is all too often the positive attitude which is abandoned. Employees, as well as other stakeholders, must be included when sustainability goals are defined and the means for pursuing them are adopted.

To build a consensus within and around a company concerning sustainable development will require what the Royal Society for the Encouragement of Arts, Manufacture and Commerce (RSA) *Tomorrow's Company* report described as an inclusive approach to stakeholder groups.[19] Employees, consumers, investors and local communities will need to be involved if a shared and stable vision of what sustainable development might mean is to be achieved. This is a challenging goal, but one which is satisfying and, ultimately, perhaps profitable.

Challenges

If we can be satisfied with movement in the direction of sustainability, then this book has revealed patchy successes. Even within the framework of profit-motivated companies and fallible political institutions, progress is being made. Within larger companies, strategies and procedures are being put in place which will allow more sustainable practices to be adopted. Companies are acting not only in direct response to regulation, but as a result of more sophisticated views of relationships with stakeholder groups. There is a real belief that the capacity to earn sustained profits is intimately interrelated with the achievement of high levels of environmental performance.

Much remains to be done. Changed conduct among large companies is not matched by changes in SMEs, which lack the managerial and financial capacity to lift performance. Both governments and larger companies have a role to play in transferring good practice. At the same time, larger companies will continue to face wider social demands for changes in environmental practice which may threaten profits and competitiveness. In a more global economy, competitive pressures are becoming ever harder to ignore. Major systemic environmental challenges at the global level, such as climate change, have, however, scarcely been addressed. This book paints a picture of much constructive activity over the last decade. But much more is needed to put society and industry itself on a path of sustainable development.

Endnotes

Chapter 1

1   RSA Inquiry (June 1995) *Tomorrow's Company: The Role of Business in a Changing World* Royal Society for the Encouragement of Arts, Manufacture and Commerce, London

2   Regulation is only one type of external pressure on companies to modify the environmental impacts of their activities. Others, discussed in Chapter 2, include customer pressure, investor requirements and links with local communities.

3   A recent book has documented conclusively the role of business in influencing European environmental policy. See F Lévêque (ed) (1996) *Environmental Policy in Europe: Industry, Competition and the Policy Process* Edward Elgar, Cheltenham

4   See, for example, S Baker et al (1997) *The Politics of Sustainable Development* Routledge, London

5   These seven problems have been selected from the thirteen which were addressed by CEST in its original strategic overview report: B Good (January 1991) *Industry and the Environment: A Strategic Overview* Centre for the Exploitation of Science and Technology, London

6   Department of the Environment (1990) *This Common Inheritance: Britain's Environmental Strategy* Cm 1200, HMSO, London

Chapter 2

1   See, for example, K Fischer and J Schot (1993) *Environmental Strategies for Industry, International Perspectives on Research Needs and Policy Implications* Island Press, US; S Schmidheiny (1992) *Changing Course: A global business perspective on development and the environment* The MIT Press, Cambridge, MA

2   T Burke (1996) 'The Earth now needs smarter friends' *The Independent*, 6 May

3   *Cleaner Production*, UNEP, quarterly

4   M Porter and C van der Linde (1995) 'Green and Competitive, Ending the Stalemate' *Harvard Business Review*, **73** (5) September–October, pp 120–134

5   M Porter (1991) 'America's Green Strategy' *Scientific American*, April, p 96

6   N Walley and B Whitehead (1994) 'It's Not Easy Being Green' *Harvard Business Review*, **72** (3) May–June, p 46

7   B Good (1991) *Industry and the Environment: A Strategic Overview* Centre for the Exploitation of Science and Technology, London

8   K D Mason (1993) *The UK Environmental Foresight Project: Preparing for the Future* HMSO, London. This presented the results of the first phase of the project. Transport-related environmental problems were dealt with in more detail in a second phase.

9   For example, F Lévêque (ed) (1996) *Environmental Policy in Europe: Industry, Competition and the Policy Process* Edward Elgar, Cheltenham; K Green, A McMeekin and A Irwin (1994) 'Technological Trajectories and R&D for Environmental Innovation in UK Firms' *Futures*, **26** (10) pp 1047–1059

10 Following the adoption of the EU's Directive on Integrated Pollution Prevention and Control (IPPC), the number of companies who will require authorization for carrying on prescribed processes is set to double.

11 See Advisory Committee on Business and the Environment *Environmental Reporting and the Financial Sector: Draft Guidelines on Good Practice* ACBE, Room C11/13, Department of the Environment, London

12 K Fischer and J Schot (1993) *Environmental Strategies for Industry, International Perspectives on Research Needs and Policy Implications* Island Press, US

13 See J Hass (1996) 'Environmental ('Green') Management Typologies: An Evaluation, Operationalization and Empirical Development' *Business Strategy and the Environment*, **5** (2) pp 59–68, for a review of various models

14 The EC is currently trying to bridge the gap between ISO 14001 and EMAS. Substantial differences still exist. The main differences consist of greater details under EMAS on what issues must be addressed by companies' environmental policies, programmes and environmental audits and also greater details under EMAS on how audits should be carried out.

15 See, for example, Chapter 9 of the EU White Paper (1993) *Growth, Competitiveness and Employment* Commission of the European Communities, Brussels

16 M Porter and C van der Linde (1995) 'Green and Competitive, Ending the Stalemate' *Harvard Business Review*, **73** (5) September–October, pp 120–134

17 In the foreword to A Gore (1992) *Earth in the Balance: Forging a New Common Purpose* Earthscan, London

18 A B Jaffe, S R Peterson, P R Portney and R N Stavins (1995) 'Environmental Regulation and the Competitiveness of United States Manufacturing: What Does the Evidence Tell Us' *Journal of Economic Literature*, **33** (1) pp 132–163

Chapter 3

1   Depletion of stratospheric ozone, by allowing a greater amount of UV to reach the lower atmosphere, actually increases the rate of tropospheric ozone formation and can extend ground-level ozone episodes.

2   Other ozone-depleting chemicals include: methyl chloroform (CH_3CCl_3), carbon tetrachloride (CCl_4), methylene chloride (CH_2Cl_2), methyl bromide (CH_3Br), oxides of nitrogen (NO_X) and hydrochloric acid (HCl). With the exception of NO_X and HCl, these chemicals are known as halogenated hydrocarbons – that is, molecules of carbon and hydrogen in which one or more of the hydrogen atoms have been replaced by atoms of chlorine, fluorine, bromine or iodine.

3   R Benedick (1991) *Ozone Diplomacy, New Directions in Safeguarding the Planet* Harvard University Press, Cambridge, MA

4   Benedick, *ibid*

5   Benedick, *ibid*

6   'Ozone layer left at risk as talks stumble over funding' *ENDS Report* 251, December 1995, pp 35–37

7   'Ozone layer left at risk by new global agreement' *ENDS Report* 214, November 1992, pp 13–15.

8   H Landis Gabel (1995) 'Environmental Management as a Competitive Strategy: The Case of CFCs' in: H Folmer , H Landis Gabel and H Opschoor H (eds) *Principles of Environmental and Resource Economics: A Guide For Students And Decisions-Makers* Edward Elgar Publishing Ltd, Cheltenham, pp 328–346

9   In 1974, Du Pont's chief executive officer publicly stated that "should reputable scientific evidence show that some fluorocarbons cause a health hazard through depletion of the ozone layer, we are prepared to stop production of those compounds".

10 For example, the electronics industry replaced CFC-113 cleanser with soap and warm water, with extracts of orange rinds. Other process changes made cleanser unnecessary.

11 ICI has been producing HFCs at its Runcorn plant since 1991. The company actively promotes the use of KLEA 66, a mixture of three hydrofluorocarbon (HFC) refrigerants, as "an ozone-benign alternative" refrigerant to both CFCs and HCFCs. The industry also promotes HFCs on the basis of the industry developed measure of *total equivalent warming potential* – that is, their potential to reduce overall warming because of energy-saving benefits associated with their use. Cadburys, among others, have commenced a programme of retrofitting refrigeration equipment, including Europe's largest cold store, at Minworth near Birmingham, using 3.5 megawatt refrigeration capacity with HFCs.

12 In 1994 Electrolux announced that all models marketed in Europe will use isobutane refrigerant. Ironically, partly due to delays in obtaining safety approval, models currently being manufactured in the UK using propane or butane technology are not available for sale in the UK. Electrolux originally went down the HFC route in response to the phase-out of CFCs.

13 The IPCC, in its 1995 report, concludes that the evidence now suggests that there is a discernable human influence on global climate.

14 J T Houghton et al (1996) *Climate Change 1995: The Science of Climate Change* Contribution of Working Group I to the Second Assessment Report of the Intergovernmental Panel on Climate Change, Cambridge University Press, Cambridge

15 Based on current trends and projections, emission levels for most developed countries (or Annex I Parties to the Convention) are actually forecast to exceed their 1990 levels in the year 2000.

16 J Williams (1992) *Environmental Opportunities: Building Advantage out of Uncertainty* CEST, London

17 To restore the long-term equilibrium, this increased warming, or positive radiative forcing, leads to an increase in outgoing radiation (net incoming solar radiation at the top of the atmosphere, averaged over the globe and over long periods of time, must be balanced by net outgoing radiation). Intergovernmental Panel on Climate Change (1994) *Radiative Forcing of Climate Change: The 1994 Report of the Scientific Assessment Working Group of the IPCC* Cambridge University Press

18 The direct radiative forcing due to CFCs and HCFCs combined has been estimated at about 10 per cent.

19 J T Houghton et al (1996) *Climate Change 1995: The Science of Climate Change* Contribution of Working Group I to the Second Assessment Report of the Intergovernmental Panel on Climate Change, Cambridge University Press, Cambridge; Intergovernmental Panel on Climate Change (1994) *Radiative Forcing of Climate Change: The 1994 Report of the Scientific Assessment Working Group of the IPCC* Cambridge University Press, Cambridge

20 This, in turn, could lead to a dramatic increase in migration and conflicts as people try to move away from those areas worst affected to more fertile and productive regions.

21 One GtC (gigatonne of carbon) equals one billion (one thousand million (10^9)) tonnes of carbon.

22 For example, an estimated 2190 GtC are stored in vegetation and soil detritus and the atmosphere is estimated to store in the order of 750 GtC.

23 One Tg = one million million grammes or 1 million tonnes.

24 J T Houghton, B A Callander and S K Varney (1992) *Climate Change 1992: The Supplementary Report to the IPCC Scientific Assessment* Cambridge University Press, Cambridge

25 Since CFCs are controlled by the Montreal Protocol, and are consequently not covered under the UNFCCC, they are not dealt with in this section.

26 Department of the Environment (1994) *Climate Change: The UK Programme* HMSO, London

27 Based on the direct global warming potentials. More recently, GWPs have been revised upwards significantly. For example, the 100 year-year GWP for N_2O has been increased from 270 to 320 times that of CO_2 and, allowing for both direct and indirect effects, the GWP of methane has been increased from 11 to 24.5 times that of CO_2.

28 Department of the Environment (1994) *Climate Change: The UK Programme* HMSO, London

29 Department of the Environment (1995) *Climate Change: The UK Programme – Progress report on Carbon Dioxide Emissions* HMSO, London

30 According to the Department of Trade and Industry, gas prices fell by 1.1 per cent and electricity by 1.3 per cent, in real terms and including VAT, between 1992 and 1994. Over the past ten years, the real-term prices have fallen by 20 per cent and 4 per cent respectively.

31 The disclosure and classification of expected savings in the Progress Report is not consistent with the Climate Programme. For example, savings in the electricity generating sector (including 'encouragement of renewables and CHP') were allocated to final users in the Climate Programme, whereas the revised programme discloses a separate 'renewables' figure and includes savings of one MtC from CHP under 'Industry, Commerce and the Public Sector'.

32 Department of the Environment (1995) *Climate Change: The UK Programme – Progress report on Carbon Dioxide Emissions* HMSO, London

33 Department of Trade and Industry (1995) *Energy Projections for the UK: Energy Use and Energy-Related Emission of Carbon Dioxide in the UK* Energy Paper 65, HMSO, London

34 Department of the Environment (1995) *Climate Change: The UK Programme – Progress report on Carbon Dioxide Emissions* HMSO, London

35 Based on revised assumptions, the electricity supply industry alone is expected to reduce its CO_2 emissions by 18 MtC by 2000, compared to just two MtC in earlier predictions. Key assumptions include: 16 to 18GW of new CCGTs are expected to be running by 2000; postponement of the closure of the ageing Magnox reactors beyond 2000 is anticipated to increase nuclear capacity to 12GW rather than the 11GW assumed in earlier projections; and the nuclear sector is now expected to contribute 34 per cent of the UK's power while coal's market share is expected to fall to just 20 per cent in 2000.

36 United Nations Environment Programme *Press Release* 19 July 1996

37 Timothy Wirth, US Under-Secretary for Global Affairs, Geneva 1996

38 'Battle joined over energy efficiency standards for fridges' *ENDS Report* 223, August 1993, pp 39–40

39 For a fuller discussion of this Directive, please see Boardman, B et al (1997) *Transforming the UK Cold Market: Third Report from the DECADE. Team (Domestic Equipment and Carbon Dioxide Emissions)* Energy and Environment Programme, Environmental Change Unit, University of Oxford

40 'Appliance industry obstructs EC drive on energy efficiency' *ENDS Report* 244, May 1995, pp 40–41

41 'Battle joined over energy efficiency standards for fridges' *ENDS Report* 223, August 1993, pp 39–40

42 'Ministers agree weak standards for fridge energy efficiency' *ENDS Report* 252, January 1996, p 42

Chapter 4

1 By 1968 Swedish scientists had linked increased acidity of rain in Sweden to sulphur emissions in the UK. Evidence on the long-range transporation of pollutants and of the damage being caused to soils and lakes was later presented at the 1972 UN Conference on the Human Environment.

2 Acidity is measured on the pH (paper hydrion) scale which runs from zero (very acidic) to 14 (very alkaline). Pure rain is actually a mild carbonic acid (because of dissolved CO_2) and has a pH of about 5.6. Over much of industrial Europe the pH of rain has now decreased to between 4.0 and 4.5.

3 S Boehmer-Christiansen and J Skea (1991) *Acid Politics: Environmental and Energy Policies in Britain and Germany* Belhaven Press, London

4 National Society for Clean Air and Environmental Protection (1996) *1996 Pollution Handbook* NSCA, Brighton

5 Department of the Environment (1995) *Digest of Environmental Protection and Water Statistics* No. 17, HMSO, London

6 Department of the Environment, *ibid*

7 Under the UK's national plan, established under the EPA 1990, sectoral emission quotas were set for power stations, refineries and other industry. PowerGen and National Power each received annual emission totals. Consequently, the plan embodies, in a very limited sense, the concept of emissions trading since companies will be able to transfer emission rights from one site to another as long as their company total is not breached.

8 Despite failing to sign the original (Helsinki) Sulphur Protocol, the UK did achieve the required emission reductions of the Protocol (30 per cent by 1993 from 1980 levels).

9 'Commission throws SO_2 policy back in the melting pot' *ENDS Report* 246, July 1995, pp 33–34

10 According to the European Commission, the petroleum sector accounted for 46.6 per cent of the 12.2 million tonnes of SO_2 emitted in the EC in 1990.

11 S Boehmer-Christiansen and J Skea, *op cit*

12 K D Mason (1993) 'Road Transport and the Environment: The Future Agenda in the UK' vol 2 of *The UK Environmental Foresight Project* HMSO, London

13 Royal Commission on Environmental Pollution (1995) *Transport and the Environment* Eighteenth Report, Oxford University Press, Oxford

14 This is analysed in detail in D Maddison et al (1996) *Blueprint 5: The True Costs of Road Transport* Earthscan, London

15 Other air pollutants for consideration include carbon monoxide, cadmium, acid deposition, benzene, polyaromatic hydrocarbons, arsenic, fluoride and nickel.

16 The 14 areas include London, Cambridge, Hampshire, Cornwall, Avon, north-east Derbyshire, Ribble Valley, Merseyside, Tyne and Wear, Glasgow, Aberdeen and South Wales.

17 In the mid-1980s West Germany produced about three million new cars per year and exports were booming. In contrast, the UK manufactured under one million new cars per year and its exports had been in decline for over two decades.

18 By the end of June 1995, 4.85 million cars were equipped with three-way catalysts – 21.8 per cent of the total fleet of 22.2 million at the end of 1994. With current rates of vehicle replacement it may take until 2015 for all cars to be fitted.

19 Organic refers to compounds containing carbon and hydrogen. They may also contain oxygen, nitrogen, chlorine, fluorine, etc. Although they do not contain hydrogen, CFCs and other fully halogenated compounds are often described as VOCs. 'Volatile' describes compounds which have a high vapour pressure at normal temperatures and can therefore be present in significant amounts in the atmosphere.

20 Inflammation and changes in lung function have been observed in people exposed to 80 to 100 ppbv ozone over several hours. Under a new EC Directive, which came into effect in January 1995, the public must be informed when ozone concentrations of 90 ppbv are reached (one hour mean). A value of 180 ppbv (one hour mean) requires that the public are informed that high concentrations have been reached.

21 Background ozone concentrations are in the range of 10 to 30 ppbv, twice the level 100 years ago.

22 'DoE firms up on VOC target but blows cold on EC controls' *ENDS Report* 238, November 1994, pp 24–25

23 *The Financial Times*, 31 May 1995

24 'MPs hear industry attack on costs of solvent controls' *ENDS Report* 241, February 1995, pp 32–33

25 Both the British Rubber Manufacturers Association (BRMA) and the Film Coating Industry Group (FCIG) have stated that their members faced an average capital investment of just under £1 million in abatement technology. The FCIG informed the House of Commons Environment Committee that the suggestion that solvent-borne coatings can be replaced within four to five years with water-based or low-solvent systems was "technically naïve and impractical". *ENDS Report* 241, *op cit*

26 'Paint industry calls for legislation to back low-solvent products' *ENDS Report* 240, January 1995, pp 28–29

27 The sectors included printing and coating of metal packaging; textile and fabric coating and finishing; film coating; drum coating; paper coating; leather finishing; rubber processes and adhesive coating.

28 Despite the success of the programme to reduce ambient lead levels – by reformulating fuel – the possibility for reducing other pollutants via a fuel quality route has not been given much consideration in the UK, despite the success of such measures in the US under the Clean Air Act. The potential of reformulated and cleaner fuels (together with tougher vehicle emission standards) to reduce air pollution from transport also appears not to have been given much consideration by the RCEP. An obvious advantage of addressing air pollution by reformulating vehicle fuels is that pollution levels could be reduced immediately from the entire fleet – rather than just from new vehicles. However, as for auto catalysts, the resulting benefits could also be cancelled out by the ever-increasing fleet size and distances travelled.

29 'Royal Commission slams the brakes on 'unsustainable' transport policy' *ENDS Report* 237, October 1994, pp 14–18

Chapter 5

1   J Rees (1993) *Water for Life: Strategies for Sustainable Water Resource Management* Council for the Protection of Rural England, London

2   Water Services Association (1994) *Waterfacts* London

3   N Johnston (1994) *Water: Resource and Opportunity* CEST, London

4   J Rees, *op cit*

5   J Rees, *op cit*

6   The setting of minimum acceptable flows (MAFs) to provide adequate protection for riverine and fisheries environments, and to ensure adequate dilution and degradation of effluent discharges, could help to reduce the environmental impacts of abstraction and prevent the complete loss and disappearance of streams – for example, the Darent in Kent – from overabstraction in times of drought.

7   Rivers and canals are classified as good (1A and 1B), fair (2), poor (3) and bad (4). Waters classified as good should be suitable for potable supply abstractions, game and high-class fisheries and have high amenity value; waters classified as fair should be suitable for the same purposes although the quality is not so high. Poor-quality waters may not be able to support fish life and waters of bad quality are "grossly polluted and likely to cause a nuisance".

8   River Quality objectives, established before privatisation in the 1970s and 1980s, were due to be translated by Government into Statutory Water Quality Objectives (SWQO) for the private industry immediately after privatisation. The NRA had intended all waters to be covered by SWQOs by 1995. The Government now intends to use SWQOs "so as to at least restore or maintain the quality of waters concerned at levels achieved in 1990" – the year in which river quality had deteriorated to its lowest level since the 1970s.

9   'Pesticide in drinking water linked to breast cancer' *ENDS Report* 241, February 1995, p 8

10 The water and pesticide industries have long argued for the 0.1 microgram per litre to be replaced by "scientific limits" for individual compounds based on toxicological data.

11 National Society for Clean Air and Environmental Protection (1993) *1993 Pollution Handbook* NSCA, Brighton

12 National Society for Clean Air and Environmental Protection, *ibid*

13 'Lengthy negotiations ahead for Directive on water resources' *Ends Report* 266, March 1997, pp 41–44

14 Both the European Commission and the UK agreed that 28 water supply zones in England did not comply with the 50 micrograms per litre nitrate standard. The commission also claimed that the UK had failed to comply with the Directive in respect of the lead standard in 17 supply zones in Scotland. However, this was dismissed by the court.

15 Initially the UK identified only 27 bathing waters, which excluded well-known resorts such as Blackpool, under their interpretation of what constituted a 'bathing beach'. Under the Directive, bathing waters were defined as those where bathing is explicitly authorized – not applicable in the UK – or where it is "traditionally practised by a large number of bathers". The Government's methodology has since been revised, following pressure from the Commission and adverse public opinion at home. The number of bathing waters bought under the scope of the Directive now stands at 457.

16 The Government's compliance data are based on waters' compliance with EC standards for coliforms. However, the Directive also sets a zero standard for entroviruses which, according to the NRA, were present in 223 of the 377 samples checked for them in 1994.

17 'Best ever bathing water results boosted by bad weather' *ENDS Report* 250, November 1995, p 11

18 Under the existing Directive, there is a guide value only for faecal streptocci of 100 per 100 millitres. A recent report commissioned by the Department of the Environment suggests that an increased incidence of diarrhoea among bathers was correlated with mean streptocci levels exceeding 35 to 40 per 100 millitres. In the UK the 95 percentile of faecal streptocci levels is 412 per 100 millitres, suggesting that most waters would comply with the new standard.

19 'Strategy proposal for EC's growing sewage sludge mountain' *ENDS Report* 243, April 1995, p 13

20 'EC proposal on ecological quality of surface waters out at last' *ENDS Report* 235, August 1994, p 36

21 Conventionally, the distinction between contaminated and non-contaminated land was based on the presence of various contaminants in concentrations likely to cause concern. These include toxic heavy metals, combustible compounds, flammable gases, aggressive substances (sulphates, chlorides, acids), oils and tarry compounds and asbestos. The Environment Act 1995 defines contaminated land as any land appearing to a local authority to already be contaminated or likely to become contaminated as a result of substances in or under the land. The Act also defines contaminated land as land where water pollution is or is likely to be caused.

22 The availability of landfill space and the cost of disposal to landfill have a strong influence on approaches to contaminated land remediation. Following the introduction of the UK's landfill tax, in October 1996, landfill costs have risen by £2 per tonne for inert waste and £7 per tonne for active waste.

23 *The Financial Times*, 21 June 1995

24 *ibid*

25 'A rickety framework for contaminated land' *ENDS Report* 238, November 1994, pp 15–19

26 *The Financial Times*, 21 June 1995

Chapter 6

1 I Christie and H Rolfe (1995) *Cleaner Production in Industry: Integrating Business Goals and Environmental Management* Policy Studies Institute, London

2   A Smith (1997) *Integrated Pollution Control: Change and Continuity in the UK Industrial Pollution Policy Network* Aveburg, Aldershot

3   The EPA 1990 also specified a secondary level of regulation by local authorities for less-polluting processes releasing emissions to air, and covering a much wider range of businesses than IPC.

4   *Environmental Protection (Prescribed Processes and Substances) Regulations*, SI 1991/472 as amended. See Department of the Environment (1994) *The Environmental Protection (Prescribed Processes and Substances) Regulations: A Consolidated Version* HMSO, London

5   The selection of monitoring techniques is a complex matter. HMIP has no policy on monitoring other than to favour continuous emissions monitoring (CEM) in principle. However, CEM techniques may not always be accurate and the cost may be prohibitive. In some sectors which are perceived to have the financial resources and in which releases can be monitored reliably – for instance, power generation and cement manufacture – CEM has become almost the automatic choice.

6   Her Majesty's Inspectorate of Pollution (1992) *Integrated Pollution Control: A Practical Guide* Environment Agency, Bristol

7   Her Majesty's Inspectorate of Pollution (1994) *Environmental, Economic and BPEO Assessment Principles for Integrated Pollution Control: Consultation Document* London

8   Processes vary considerably in their complexity and charges are related to the number of *components* – discrete items of process equipment – which make up process.

9   For example, see K Allott (1994) *Integrated Pollution Control: The First Three Years* Environmental Data Services Ltd, London

10 The European Integrated Pollution Prevention and Control Directive, agreed by Environmental Ministers in September 1996, will require a further 5000 processes not subject to IPC, possibly more, to be controlled. These include intensive livestock units, parts of the food and drink industry and several hundred manufacturing processes currently under local authority control.

11   'HMIP's 3Es project points to big savings at Allied Colloids' *ENDS Report* 248, September 1995, pp 6–7

12 Allied Colloids and HM Inspectorate of Pollution, *3Es Project: Concluding Report*

13 'Big savings at Allied Colloids confirm 3Es success' *ENDS Report* 255, April 1996, p 7

14 A Smith (1995) 'Voluntary Schemes and the Necessity for Statutory Regulation: The Case of Integrated Pollution Control', paper presented at the Business Strategy and the Environment Conference, University of Leeds, September 20–21

15 'Agency chief wants less litigation, 'deal' with industry' *ENDS Report* 249, October 1995, p 5

16 *ibid*

17 The inclusion of these units was resisted by the UK, with the Ministry of Agriculture arguing that the 1991 Directive on nitrate pollution from agriculture already provided adequate control over their releases to the environment. Some 3000 units in the UK are likely to come within the Directive's definitions of qualifying units – based on livestock numbers.

18 Water companies may not be regarded as suitable candidates for deciding what constitutes BAT for discharges to sewer, since there may be a conflict with their commercial interests in treating industrial effluents. One option the Department of the Environment is considering is to refer such decisions to the Environment Agency.

19 'Labour favours EC harmonization of emission limits for IPPC' *ENDS Report* 251, December 1995, p 25

20 BAT is considered by the Department of the Environment to be broadly consistent with the UK's BATNEEC. However, in one or two areas the EC definition is wider. For example, IPPC broadens the scope of techniques to include decommissioning. Techniques, as with IPC, also cover technology used, installations design, construction, operation and maintenance.

21 A Smith, *op cit*

Chapter 7

1 N Johnston (1992) *Water Resource and Opportunity* CEST, London

2 'Yorkshire firms to demonstrate waste reduction benefits' *ENDS Report* 206, March 1993, p 12

3 'Waste minimization project succeeds on Merseyside' *ENDS Report* 233, June 1994, p 6

4 Sponsorship for these initiatives was originally agreed by the National Rivers Authority and HMIP before their functions were taken over by the Environment Agency in April 1996.

5 N Johnston (1995) *Waste Minimization: A Route to Profit and Cleaner Production: Final report on the Aire and Calder Project* CEST, London

6 N Johnston and A Stokes (1995) *Waste Minimization and Cleaner Technology: An Assessment of Motivation* CEST, London

Chapter 8

1 The 50 tonnes per year threshold cuts the number of businesses involved from 200,000 to some 11,500 but ensures that 94 per year of all packaging will be included under the regulations.

2 The following example illustrates how this shared responsibility would operate: a business performing the conversion activity to produce 10,000 tonnes of plastic packaging would have the converter's obligation to recover 550 tonnes (10,000t × 11 per cent × 50 per cent) and to recycle a minimum of 165 tonnes (10,000t × 11 per cent × 15 per cent). If, in addition, the business packs and sells the plastic packaging on, using 2000 tonnes of fibreboard, it would have to recover 830 tonnes of the fibreboard (2000 tonnes × 36 per cent – packer's obligation – × 50 per cent) plus (2000 tonnes × 47 per cent – retailer's obligation – × 50 per cent) and to recycle 249 tonnes (2000 tonnes × 36 per cent × 15 per cent) plus (2000 tonnes × 47 per cent × 15 per cent). Adapted from *The Producer Responsibility Obligations (Packaging Waste) Regulations*.

3 The original Producer Responsibility Group (PRG) plan envisaged that a single organization, VALPAK (which is a registered collective scheme), would meet the national recovery and recycling targets on behalf of industry. Businesses would pay a fee to become a member of such schemes. In return, VALPAK (or another registered scheme) would take over responsibilities for tonnage obligations of member companies, negotiate contracts for reprocessed material and purchase certificates of compliance from material reprocessors to demonstrate that obligations were being met.

4 'Electronic goods recycling hits funding obstacle' *ENDS Report* 235, August 1994, pp 16–17

5   R Ratul (1991) *End of Life Electronic Equipment Waste* CEST, London

6   ICER has over 40 members including Apple Computers UK, IBM, British Telecom, the Dixons Group, ICL, Hewlett Packard UK, Dow Chemicals, R Frazier, Mann Organisation and the Bird Group.

7   One of the main aims of the organization, according to Boots, one of ICER's initial members, is to develop a recycling infrastructure based on collections by local authorities, with manufacturers and retailers only involved in buying back the recycled materials. This contrasts with the German system and the European Commission's apparent thinking that responsibility should lie with producers and retailers.

8   R Ratul, *op cit*

9   'Venture to reclaim electronic waste' *ENDS Report* 243, April 1995, p 11

10 EMERG membership includes Panasonic, Hewlett Packard, IBM, Toshiba, Sony, Apple, Canon, Motorola and other major manufacturers. Under the initiative, EMERG members will not fund collection and recycling. This will be left to contracts between Mann and sources of EOL electronic equipment. In an attempt to make recycling more economical, the group is considering four projects: mechanical methods for decontaminating plastics, recycling of printed circuit boards, development of glass reprocessing and reuse for cathode ray tubes (CRTs), and the development of an incineration facility for non-recyclable materials.

11 German legislation is likely to resemble the well-known packaging Ordinance and is expected to come into force in 1996, while Denmark and The Netherlands have opted for 'voluntary' covenants backed by the threat of a levy at the point of sale. In Sweden legislation has made manufacturers financially responsible for the waste – but they have proposed that local authorities should pay through increased local taxes.

12 'Tough EC decisions ahead on electronic waste recovery' *ENDS Report* 245, June 1995, p 41

13 To put this figure in perspective, West Sussex County Council operates kerbside collection services for recyclable materials (plastics, papers, cards, and mixed cans and bottles) for 20,000 households in Worthing, and Adur District Council has a similar scheme covering some 19,000 households.

Chapter 9

1   S Schmidheiny (1992) *Changing Course: A Global Business Perspective on Development and the Environment* The MIT Press, Cambridge, MA

2   F Cairncross (1993) *Costing the Earth: The Challenge for Governments, The Opportunities for Business* Harvard Business School Press, Boston, MA

3   Cairncross, *ibid*

4   Organization for Economic Cooperation and Development (1991) *Recent Developments in the Use of Economic Instruments* Environment Monographs No. 41, Paris

5   There is nothing tremendously new about the idea of green taxes. They were first mooted in 1920 by the Cambridge University economist Arthur Pigou who proposed that such taxes could be used as a means of bridging the gap between social and private costs – the root cause of environmental damage.

6   Four EU countries – Sweden, Finland, The Netherlands and Denmark – already have CO_2-related energy taxes and Germany and Austria may soon also develop their own taxes.

7   T Ikwue and J Skea (1994) 'Business and the Genesis of the European Community Carbon Tax Proposal' *Business Strategy and the Environment*, 3 (2) Summer, pp 1–10

8   Clearly, the precise impacts of the tax would also depend upon the way the tax revenue was recycled – through reduced payroll taxes, income taxes or VAT – and the nature of other measures adopted outside the European Community.

9   Ikwue and Skea, *op cit*

10 Ikwue and Skea, *op cit*

11 Ikwue and Skea, *op cit*

12 T Ikwue and J Skea (1996) 'Atmospheric Emissions and the Energy Sector' in: F Lévêque (ed) *Environmental Policy In Europe: Industry Regulation and Policy Process* Edward Elgar, Cheltenham

13 Essentially plant covered by the EU's Large Combustion Plants Directive: 88/609/EEC.

14 The problem of air quality along the Thames Estuary was a particular difficulty.

15 Desulphurization plant has been fitted at Drax and Ratcliffe power systems. However, the plant does not need to operate to meet sulphur quotas and the 'clean' coal plant has occasionally been turned off in favour of 'dirtier' stations.

16 Although expected to raise £450 million in its first full year, the National Insurance offset will cost £500 million, and in 1997–98 the gap is projected to widen to £120 million and perhaps more; some analysts have suggested that the Government has overestimated the amount of taxable waste produced in the UK.

17 'Concessions on contaminated soil wastes to cut landfill tax yields' *ENDS Report* 254, March 1996, pp 30–32

18 Advisory Committee on the Business and the Environment (1995) *Fifth Progress Report*, Department of Trade and Industry/Department of the Environment, London

Chapter 10

1   T Burke (1996) 'The earth now needs smarter friends' *The Independent*, 6 May

2   B Good (1991) *Industry and the Environment: A Strategic Overview* Centre for the Exploitation of Science and Technology, London

3   Nevertheless, the overarching concept of industrial ecology embodies a global vision.

4   See, for example, N Roome (1992) 'Developing Environmental Management Strategies' *Business and the Environment*, 1(1) Spring

5   See, for example, N Walley and B Whitehead (1994) 'It's Not Easy Being Green' *Harvard Business Review*, 72 (3) May–June, 46

6   Walley and Whitehead, *ibid*

7   M Porter and C van der Linde (1995) 'Green and Competitive, Ending the Stalemate' *Harvard Business Review*, 73 (5) September–October, pp 120–134

8   Department of the Environment (1996) *This Common Inheritance: UK Annual Report 1996* Cm 3188, HMSO, London, paragraph 148

9   Department of the Environment (1996) *Indicators of Sustainable Development for the United Kingdom* HMSO, London

10 World Commission on Environment and Development (1987) *Our Common Future ('The Brundtland Report')* Oxford University Press, Oxford

11 F Hinterberger *et al* (1994) *Increasing Resource Productivity Through Eco-Efficient Services* Wuppertal Institute, Wuppertal, p 25

12 P Hawken (1995) *The Ecology of Commerce: A Declaration of Sustainability* Phoenix, London

13 S Guy and S Marvin (1996) 'Disconnected Policy: The Shaping of Local Energy Management' *Environment and Planning C: Government and Policy*, **14**, pp 145–158

14 'Putting Eco-efficiency on the map' *ENDS Report*, No 252, January 1996, p 17

15 Practical examples are discussed in European Environment Agency (1996) *Environmental Taxes: Implementation and Environmental Effectiveness* EEA Environmental Issues Series No 1, Copenhagen

16 U Beck (1992) *Risk Society: Towards a New Modernity* Sage, London

17 J Margetta (1997) 'Growth through Global Sustainability: An Interview with Monsanto's CEO Robert B Shapiro' *Harvard Business Review*, January–February, pp 79–88

18 R Grove-White, P Mcnaghten, S Mayer and B Wynne (1997) *Uncertain World: Genetically Modified Organisms, Food and Public Attitudes in Britain* Lancaster University

19 RSA Inquiry (1995) *Tomorrow's Company: The Role of Business in a Changing World* Royal Society for the Encouragement of Arts, Manufacture and Commerce, London

Selected Bibliography

The literature on business and the environment has expanded enormously during the 1990s. Several milestone books, such as Schmidheiny's *Changing Course: A Global Business Perspective on Development and the Environment*, have been published while there are now journals devoted exclusively to business and environment issues. Examples include *Business Strategy and the Environment* and the UN Environment Programme's *Cleaner Production and Industry*. The volume of material on clean technology, life-cycle assessment and industrial ecology has also expanded and is often closely linked to the business and environment theme. However, business-oriented material is still dwarfed by other types of environmental literature. Non-governmental organizations, journalists and academics alike have been drawn to specific high-profile environmental issues such as climate change. The growth of the sustainable development agenda since the late 1980s has drawn a much broader range of social scientists, including sociologists and political scientists, into the environmental debate. Previously, economists made the most prominent contributions. In practice, academics have been drawn primarily to the sustainable development theme and to the analysis of public policy options.

This selected bibliography aims to draw attention to some of the most important contributions relevant to the themes addressed in this book. The material covered is *relevant* to the business and environment and clean technology themes but does not focus on them exclusively. The bibliography is broken down into five areas: business and the environment; technological change and the environment; sustainable development; environmental policy and regulation; and the specific environmental issues covered in the case studies. There is a commentary on the material in the first three areas.

Compiling the bibliography has been much easier in some areas than others. The literature on sustainable development, for example, is vast and it has been necessary to select only a few key texts. There is also a huge literature on climate change but little, other than technical material, on most local and regional environmental problems. Environmental taxes have been advocated and analysed at great length while new and rapidly developing approaches, such as voluntary agreements, have received remarkably little attention. The selection of material is inevitably arbitrary. But we hope that it provides useful pointers to subsets of the literature which will illuminate the way in which business actors, in particular, identify and respond to environmental questions.

Business and the Environment

There is considerable debate in the business and environment literature about the relationship between environmental performance and competitiveness. This debate is far from resolved. Much business and environment literature has been quite normative in character, especially in the early 1990s. More analytical approaches have begun to develop.

Cairncross, F (1993) *Costing the Earth: The Challenge for Governments, The Opportunities for Business* Harvard Business School Press, Boston, MA

Cairncross, F (1995) *Green Inc.: Guide to Business and the Environment* Earthscan, London

Frances Cairncross, a writer for *The Economist*, provides a realistic yet hopeful account of the role which business can play in addressing environmental problems. She does not discount the need for some regulatory incentives and the need to make hard choices.

Christie, I and Rolfe, H (1995) *Cleaner Production in Industry: Integrating Business Goals and Environmental Management* Policy Studies Institute, London

Findings of a qualitative UK survey on the take-up and benefits arising from cleaner production systems. Also addresses employment and training issues, information availability and makes policy recommendations.

Fischer, K and Schot, J (1993) *Environmental Strategies for Industry: International Perspectives on Research Needs and Policy Implications* Island Press, London

A book of essays, written mainly by academics, from the earlier stages of the business-and-environment debate. Drawn from papers presented at the first conference of the *Greening of Industry* network.

Folmer, H, Landis, Gabel H and Opschoor, H (eds) (1995) *Principles of Environmental and Resource Economics: A Guide For Students And Decisions-Makers* Edward Elgar, Cheltenham

An edited text on environmental economics, a quarter of which addresses the firm and the environment.

Good, B (1991) *Industry and the Environment: A Strategic Overview* Centre for the Exploitation of Science and Technology, London

CEST's first foray into the business/environment arena, scoping out the agenda at the start of the 1990s.

Korten, D (1995) *When Corporations Rule the World* Earthscan, London

An articulate polemic against the globalization of markets, trade liberalization and international business activities which draws heavily on environmental examples to make its case.

Lévêque, F (ed) (1996) *Environmental Policy in Europe: Industry, Competition and the Policy Process* Edward Elgar, Cheltenham

A set of case studies demonstrating how firms interact with policymakers and regulators during the development of European environmental policies.

Mason, K D (1993) *The UK Environmental Foresight Project: Preparing for the Future* HMSO, London

A CEST study for the UK Department of the Environment identifying the perceived future development of the environmental agenda.

Organization for Economic Co-operation and Development (1993) *Environmental Policies and Industrial Competitiveness* OECD, Paris

An authoritative set of essays reviewing the various strands of the debate about the impact of environmental regulation on competitiveness.

Porter, M (1991) 'America's Green Strategy' *Scientific American*, April, p 96

Porter, M and van der Linde C (1995) 'Green and Competitive: Ending the Stalemate' *Harvard Business Review*, **73** (5) September–October, pp 120–134

These two papers present the 'Porter hypothesis' – that environmental regulation, far from damaging competitiveness, enhances it by stimulating innovation.

Roome, N (1992) 'Developing environmental management strategies' *Business and the Environment*, **1** (1) pp 11–24

An early contribution to the literature on 'stages' in corporate environmental management.

Schmidheiny, S (1992) *Changing Course: A Global Business Perspective on Development and the Environment* The MIT Press, Cambridge, MA

Schmidheiny, S and Zorraquin, F (1996) *Financing Change: The Financial Community, Eco-efficiency and Sustainable Development* The MIT Press, Cambridge, MA

Relatively optimistic accounts, from the World Business Council on Sustainable Development, of how business might contribute to sustainable development. The second book is more esoteric and less visionary but remains one of the few coherent accounts of the potential role of the financial sector.

Schot, J (1992) 'Credibility and markets as greening forces for the chemical industry' *Business Strategy and the Environment*, **1** (1)

An empirically based analysis of how the chemical industry identified the importance of environmental issues and began to address the problem.

Walley, N and Whitehead, B (1994) 'It's Not Easy Being Green' *Harvard Business Review*, **72** (3) March–June 46

Counter-arguments to the Porter hypothesis from two management consultants. Argues that environmental regulation inevitably costs money, thus destroying value.

Welford, R (1995) *Environmental Strategy and Sustainable Development: The Corporate Challenge for the 21st Century* Routledge, London

A mixture of chapters dealing with more radical changes to business practices (business ethics, culture change, bioregionalism) and nitty-gritty techniques such as environmental auditing and life-cycle assessment.

Welford, R (1996) *The Earthscan Reader in Business and the Environment* Earthscan, London

A compilation of some classic recent journal articles on the business-and-environment theme.

Williams, J (1992) *Environmental Opportunities: Building Advantage out of Uncertainty* Centre for the Exploitation of Science and Technology, London

CEST's second contribution to the industry-and-environment debate began to develop arguments about potential competitive advantage.

Technological Change and the Environment

The literature on technological change and the environment is very diverse. It ranges from detailed empirical studies of innovation in specific firms through to grander texts about industrial ecology and the transformation of material flows at the level of entire economies. Perhaps too much effort has been expended on defining and interpreting terms such as 'clean technology'.

Advisory Council on Science and Technology (1992) *Cleaner Technology* HMSO, London

ECOTEC (1992) 'The Development of Clean Technologies: A Strategic Overview' *Business Strategy and the Environment*, 1 (2) Summer, pp 51–58

Two formal characterizations of clean and cleaner technology from the early 1990s.

Green, K, McMeekin, A and Irwin, A (1994) 'Technological Trajectories and R&D for Environmental Innovation in UK Firms' *Futures*, 26 (10), pp 1047–1059

Groenewegen, P and Vergragt, P (1991) 'Environmental Issues as Threats and Opportunities for Technological Innovation' *Technology Analysis and Strategic Management*, 3 (1)

Irwin, A and Hooper, P (1992) 'Clean technology, successful innovation and the greening of industry: a case-study analysis' *Business Strategy and the Environment*, 1 (2) Summer, pp 1–12

Irwin, A and Vergragt, P (1989) 'Re-thinking the Relationship between Environmental Regulation and Industrial Innovation: The Social Negotiation of Technical Change' *Technology Analysis and Strategic Management*, 1 (1)

These four papers adopt a more sociological perspective of the innovation process in firms and the development of cleaner technologies. The thinking largely predates the current business-and-environment debate.

Jackson, T (1996) *Material Concerns: Pollution, Profit and the Quality of Life*
  Routledge, London

A very readable and visionary account of how industrial ecology principles could be applied to maintain quality of life while reducing consumption of materials.

Kemp, R (1994) 'Technology and the Transition to Environmental Sustainability:
  The Problem of Technological Regime Shifts' *Futures*, **26** (10) pp 1023–1046

Kemp, R and Soete, L (1992), 'The Greening of Technological Progress' *Futures*, **24**
  (5) pp 437–457

Two closely related papers which look at environmental pressures through the lens of evolutionary economics, viewing them as changing the 'selection environment' for innovative technologies.

Organization for Economic Cooperation and Development (1985) *Environmental
  Policy and Technical Change* OECD, Paris

Organization for Economic Cooperation and Development (1994) *Life-Cycle
  Management and Trade* OECD, Paris

Two authoritative accounts of various aspects of the environmental policy and technical change debate. The 1985 volume is essential reading for anyone wishing to avoid the reinvention of wheels.

Rothwell, R (1992) 'Industrial Innovation and Government Environmental
  Regulation: Some Lessons from the Past' *Technovation*, **12** (7) pp 447–458

A concise and authoritative account of what academics and policy-makers learned from the 1970s wave of environmental regulation.

Skea, J F (1995) 'Environmental Technology' in Folmer, H, Landis, Gabel H and
  Opschoor, H (eds) *Principles of Environmental and Resource Economics: A Guide For
  Students And Decisions-Makers* Edward Elgar, Cheltenham

A brief review of the role which technology can play in reducing the environmental impacts of industrial activity.

Socolow, R *et al* (ed) (1994) *Industrial Ecology and Global Change* Cambridge
  University Press, Cambridge

Industrial ecology is the organizing theme, but this is an ambitious volume covering human vulnerability and adaptation, material cycles and industrial ecology from the business perspective.

Uman, M F (ed) (1993) *Keeping Pace with Science and Engineering: Case Studies in
  Environmental Regulation* National Academy Press, Washington, DC

A set of case studies about environmental regulation and induced technological change. In practice, the emphasis is often on public policy and the focus tends to be on science rather than engineering.

Wallace, D (1995) *Environmental Policy and Industrial Innovation: Strategies in Europe, the US and Japan* Royal Institute of International Affairs/Earthscan, London

International comparisons of government and industry links in six OECD countries. Less about the policy and innovation link than one might expect but good on the impacts of different regulatory styles.

Sustainable Development

Baker, S et al (ed) (1997) *The Politics of Sustainable Development: Theory, Policy and Practice within the European Union* Routledge, London

A political analysis of sustainable development which explores theoretical and philosophical issues and examines evolving practices within Europe from both top-down and bottom-up perspectives.

Department of the Environment (1990) *This Common Inheritance* Cm 1200, HMSO, London

Department of the Environment (1996) *Indicators of Sustainable Development for the UK* HMSO, London

Department of the Environment (1997) *This Common Inheritance: UK Annual Report 1997* Cm 3556, HMSO, London, February

The development of official UK government thinking and practice in relation to sustainable development. Progress reports have been appearing annually since 1991.

European Commission (1994) *Growth, Competitiveness and Employment: The Challenges and Way Forward into the 21st Century* White Paper, European Commission, Brussels

Chapter 9 of the 'Delors White Paper' attempts to square the circle in terms of employment creation, growth and sustainability.

Meadows, D H et al (1972) *The Limits to Growth* Island Press, London

The classic text on unsustainable development. Very influential at the time but the pessimistic predictions were not borne out by subsequent events.

Pearce, D W et al (1989) *Blueprint for a Green Economy* Earthscan, London

Others in the Blueprint series are: *Blueprint 2: Greening the World Economy* (1991); *Blueprint 3: Measuring Sustainable Development* (1993); *Blueprint 4: Capturing Global Environmental Value* (1995); and *Blueprint 5: The True Costs of Road Transport* (1996).

A set of classic texts looking at sustainable development from an environmental–economics perspective. The 1989 *Blueprint* was based largely on a report for the UK Department of the Environment. It became the textbook for the greening of Government in the early 1990s. Subsequent volumes have inevitably become more specialized.

Redclift, M and Benton, T (ed) (1994) *Social Theory and the Global Environment* Routledge, London

A series of papers which looks in a fundamental way at how the social sciences – not including economics – can contribute to thinking about sustainable development.

United Nations Conference on Environment and Development (1993) *Agenda 21: Programme of Action for Sustainable Development* United Nations, New York, NY

The authorized version of the sustainable development bible.

World Commission on Environment and Development (1987) *Our Common Future* Oxford University Press, Oxford

The 'Brundtland Report' which firmly placed the concept of sustainable development on the political agenda.

Environmental Policy and Regulation

Traditional Regulation

A very large literature on traditional – 'command and control' – environmental regulation has developed since the 1970s. The following represents a few more recent and practical contributions to the literature. The *Journal of Environmental Economics and Management* is a crucial resource for those interested in more theoretical perspectives on key issues such as regulatory design.

Allott, K (1994) *Integrated Pollution Control: The First Three Years* Environmental Data Services Ltd, London

Jaffe, A B *et al* (1995) 'Environmental Regulation and the Competitiveness of United States Manufacturing: What Does the Evidence Tell Us' *Journal of Economic Literature* 33 (1) pp 132–163

Gray, T (ed) (1995) *UK Environmental Policy in the 1990s* Macmillan, Basingstoke

Her Majesty's Inspectorate of Pollution (1992) *Integrated Pollution Control: A Practical Guide* Environment Agency, Bristol

Organization for Economic Cooperation and Development (1985) *Environmental Policy and Technical Change* OECD, Paris

Porter, M and van der Linde, C (1995) 'Green and Competitive: Ending the Stalemate' *Harvard Business Review*, **73** (5) September–October, pp 120–134

Smith, A P (1997) *Integrated Pollution Control: Change and Continuity in UK Industrial Pollution Regulation* Avebury Press, Aldershot

Walley, N and Whitehead, B (1994) 'It's Not Easy Being Green' *Harvard Business Review*, **72** (3) May–June, p 46

Market-Based Instruments

The literature on environmental taxes and related instruments, such as tradable permits, has exploded since the mid-1980s. The following is a very small selection of some relevant books and papers. A steadily increasing proportion of the available material deals with practice as opposed to theory. The EEA document and the O'Riordan book both grapple with the key elements of the debate on environmental taxation.

European Environment Agency (1996) *Environmental Taxes: Implementation and Environmental Effectiveness* EEA Environmental Issues Series No 1, Copenhagen

Ikwue, T and Skea, J (1994) 'Business and the Genesis of the European Community Carbon Tax Proposal' *Business Strategy and the Environment,* **3** (2) Summer, pp 1–10

O'Riordan, T (ed) (1997) *Ecotaxation* Earthscan, London

Organization for Economic Cooperation and Development (1991) *Recent Developments in the Use of Economic Instruments* Environment Monograph No 41, Paris

Raufer, R K and Feldman, S L (1987) *Acid Rain and Emissions Trading: Implementing a Market Approach to Pollution Control* Rowman and Littlefield, Totowa, NJ

Sorrell, S (1995) *Pollution on the Market: The US Experience with Emissions Trading for the Control of Air Pollution* STEEP Special Report No 1, Science Policy Research Unit, Brighton

Tietenberg, T (1985) *Emissions Trading* Resources for the Future Inc, Washington DC

Voluntary and Partnership Approaches

Very little academic material on the role of voluntary agreements in environmental policy has yet been published. There is much larger practical literature giving specific examples, of which a small proportion is listed here.

Carraro, C and Lévêque, F (ed) (1996) Proceedings of the International Workshop: *The Economics and Law of Voluntary Approaches in Environmental Policy* 18–19 November, Fondazione ENI Enrico Mattei, Venice CERNA–École des Mines de Paris

A so-far unique collection of papers examining voluntary approaches from both theoretical and practical policy perspectives.

Department of the Environment (1995) *Making Waste Work: A Strategy for Sustainable Waste Management in England and Wales* Cm 3040, HMSO, London

Johnston, N (1995) *Waste Minimization: A Route to Profit and Cleaner Production* Final report on the Aire and Calder Project, Centre for the Exploitation of Science and Technology, London

Johnston, N and Stokes, A (1995) *Waste Minimization and Cleaner Technology: An Assessment of Motivation* Centre for the Exploitation of Science and Technology, London

Ratul, R (1991) *End of Life Electronic Equipment Waste* Centre for the Exploitation of Science and Technology, London

Solesbury, L and Wiederkehr, P (1995) 'Voluntary Approaches for Energy-related CO_2 Abatement' *The OECD Observer*, No 196, October–November, pp 41–45

Environmental Issues

There is a wealth of material focusing specifically on several of the environmental issues examined in this book, particularly climate change, air quality and road transport and water quality. There is far less available on lower-profile topics such as the control of volatile organic compounds (VOCs) and contaminated land. Much of the available literature is in the form of specialist reports, scientific papers, official documentation and 'grey' literature. Policy-relevant material is mainly to be found on high-profile environmental issues such as ozone depletion, climate change and acid rain.

Global Issues

Ozone Depletion

These contributions look at international diplomacy and firm responses respectively.

Benedick, R E (1991) *Ozone Diplomacy, New Directions in Safeguarding the Planet* Harvard University Press, Cambridge, MA

Landis, Gabel H (1995) 'Environmental Management as a Competitive Strategy: The Case of CFCs' in Folmer, H, Landis, Gabel H and Opschoor, H (eds) *Principles of Environmental and Resource Economics: A Guide For Students And Decision-Makers* Edward Elgar, Cheltenham, pp 328–346

Climate Change

A mixture of official reports and policy analysis. Bruce *et al* provide a comprehensive account of the key controversies in climate control policy, albeit from a perspective somewhat too academic for its intended audience in the policy-making world.

Bruce, J P *et al* (1996) *Climate Change 1995: Economic and Social Dimensions of Climate Change* Contribution of Working Group III to the Second Assessment Report of the Intergovernmental Panel on Climate Change, Cambridge University Press, Cambridge

Department of the Environment (1997) *Climate Change: The UK Programme* The Stationery Office, London

Department of Trade and Industry (1995) *Energy Projections for the UK: Energy Use and Energy-Related Emission of Carbon Dioxide in the UK* Energy Paper 65, HMSO, London

Houghton, J T *et al* (1996) *Climate Change 1995: The Science of Climate Change* Contribution of Working Group I to the Second Assessment Report of the Intergovernmental Panel on Climate Change, Cambridge University Press, Cambridge

Ikwue, T and Skea, J (1996) 'Atmospheric Emissions and the Energy Sector' in Lévêque, F (ed) *Environmental Policy In Europe: Industry Regulation and Policy Process* Edward Elgar, Cheltenham

O'Riordan, T and Jäger, J (ed) (1996) *Politics of Climate Change: A European Perspective* Routledge, London

Watson, R T *et al* (1996) *Climate Change 1995: Impacts, Adaptation and Mitigation of Climate Change: Scientific-Technical Analyses* Contribution of Working Group II to the Second Assessment Report of the Intergovernmental Panel on Climate Change, Cambridge University Press, Cambridge

National Issues

Acid Rain

Acid rain policy development in Europe and North America respectively.

Boehmer-Christiansen, S and Skea, J (1991) *Acid Politics: Environmental and Energy Policies in Britain and Germany* Belhaven Press, London

Cohen, R E (1992) *Washington at Work: Back Rooms and Clean Air* Macmillan, New York

Air Quality and Road Transport

Mason, K D (1993) *The UK Environmental Foresight Project: Volume 2* Road Transport and the Environment: The Future Agenda in the UK, HMSO, London

National Society for Clean Air (1997) *1997 Pollution Handbook* NSCA, Brighton, UK

Royal Commission on Environmental Pollution (1995) *Transport and the Environment* Eighteenth Report, Oxford University Press, Oxford

Volatile Organic Compounds

Air Pollution Abatement Review Group (1996) *Report on the Abatement of Volatile Organic Compounds (VOCs) from Stationary Sources 1995* Department of the Environment, London

Department of the Environment (1993) *Reducing Emissions of Volatile Organic Compounds (VOCs) and Levels of Ground Level Ozone* HMSO, London

Regional and Local Issues

Water Quality

All but the last of these documents deals with policy dimensions.

Johnston, N (1992) *Water: Resource and Opportunity* Centre of the Exploitation of Science and Technology, London

Rees, J (1993) *Water for Life: Strategies for Sustainable Water Resource Management* Council for the Protection of Rural England, London

Royal Commission on Environmental Pollution (1992) *Freshwater Quality* Sixteenth Report, Cm 1966, HMSO, London

Water Services Association (1994) *Waterfacts 1994* London

Contaminated Land
A uniformly technical perspective, apart from Tromans and Turrall-Clarke which is a legal text.

Cairney, T (1995) *The Reuse of Contaminated Land: A Handbook of Risk Assessment* Wiley, Chichester

Gibb Environmental Sciences (1991) *Contaminated Land* Report for CEST's Industry and the Environment Project, Centre for the Exploitation of Science and Technology, London

House of Commons Environment Committee (1990) *Contaminated Land* First Report Session 1989–90, HMSO, London

Parliamentary Office of Science and Technology (1993) *Contaminated Land* POST, London

Tromans, S and Turrall-Clarke, S (1994) *Contaminated Land* Sweet and Maxwell, London

Index